PRAISE FOR *BEIN*

Being Lutheran by Rev. Trevor Sutton is a
dig deeper. It is a great resource for pastor.
"new" Christians and "old." It is good for anyone who seeks a better under-
ing of what it means to be a follower of Christ, one who desires even more to get
to know Jesus and the power of His Word in his or her life. This book would be
excellent for any individual, but it is especially useful for small groups because of
Sutton's use of today's relevant concerns and apathies as the context into which
to speak the things of Jesus and the Good News of God's grace. Complete with
vignettes and discussion questions, this is a resource that is sure to bless.

—*The Rev. Dr. Gregory P. Seltz*
"The Voice of the Lutheran Hour"

With a crisp and vivid style, Trevor Sutton's *Being Lutheran* is a well-structured,
easily digested overview of a faith that is uniquely spiritual and earthly, Christ-
centered, and creation-aware. This is a great book for a small-group book study;
patiently thumbing through each chapter week after week will challenge readers
to think *and* act in ways that fit with Scripture and the lavish grace of God in
Christ. This is a hopeful book that sees faith in Jesus as more than just a ticket
to heaven. Every page invites us to join many others (by name!) in the faithful
discipleship that marks one who is truly Lutheran. In short, *Being Lutheran* helps
faith work right.

—*Rev. Scott Seidler, DMin*
Senior Pastor, Concordia Lutheran Church, Kirkwood, MO

A far cry from "blatant Lutheran grandstanding," Sutton's provocative text re-
claims the Lutheran narrative with exceptional style and substance, extending to
the lifelong congregant and the uninitiated alike a fresh invitation to live boldly
under God's open and expansive grace—grace that animates our thinking and
doing. Every Lutheran should read this book and dive headlong into being what
and who they are, in Christ.

—*Gretchen M. Jameson*
Senior Vice President—University Affairs
Concordia University Wisconsin and Ann Arbor

Not religious bravado! Not highbrow stuffiness! Rather, Pastor Sutton refreshingly shows us how God uses the ordinary to do the extraordinary: humankind created from earth, sinners saved with water, everyday believers motivated by ordinary words in God's Word, doing a world of good.

Sutton's accessible style weaves references to hipsters, marital love, digital content, Sacraments, quantum physics, ennui, the workplace, texting, bloodletting, and the problem of evil. With a global and multiethnic scope, Sutton remains insistently confessional, never oversimplifying Lutheran identity, focused unapologetically on the mystery and the clarity of the Good News in the cross of Jesus Christ.

—Rev. John Nunes, PhD
President, Concordia College—New York

A. Trevor Sutton's work, *Being Lutheran*, is both a delightful and a truly helpful look at the depth and the richness of the biblical faith. He undergirds this important writing in the sharing of brief stories (vignettes) about individuals whose heartfelt faith made a difference. In fact, the brief story of Ben's life and faith moved me to tears of joy and thankfulness. As I read the book, I was at different times encouraged, challenged, comforted, affirmed, and motivated in the truth of God's love for me. Readers, be blessed!

—Rev. Luke R. Schnake, DMin
Director of Ministries, Christ Lutheran Church, Lincoln, NE

In an increasingly multiethnic America and global landscape, being Lutheran has to be more than being German. What, at the essential core, is a Lutheran? In a fresh way, Sutton insists being Lutheran is more about a "who" than a "what." First, it is an unhindered focus on Jesus Christ. From there, being Lutheran is a life of beliefs and actions that flow from the Gospel center. This is a useful tool for new generations exploring Lutheran thinking and practice.

—Rev. Jeff Cloeter
Senior Pastor, Christ Memorial Lutheran Church, St. Louis, MO

BEING LUTHERAN

BEING LUTHERAN

Living in the Faith
You Have Received

A. Trevor Sutton

DEDICATED TO

Mom and Dad
My firm foundation

Elizabeth
My loving bride

Grace and Hannah
My unending joy

Published by Concordia Publishing House
3558 S. Jefferson Ave., St. Louis, MO 63118-3968
1-800-325-3040 • www.cph.org

Manufactured in the United States of America

Library of Congress Cataloging-in-Publication Data

Names: Sutton, A. Trevor, author.
Title: Being Lutheran : living in the faith you have received / A. Trevor Sutton.
Description: St. Louis : Concordia Publishing House, 2016. | Includes bibliographical references and index.
Identifiers: LCCN 2016008214 (print) | LCCN 2016009013 (ebook) | ISBN 9780758651785 (alk. paper) | ISBN 9780758651792 ()
Subjects: LCSH: Lutheran Church--Doctrines. | Lutheran Church--Customs and practices. | Lutheran Church--Missouri Synod.
Classification: LCC BX8065.3 .S88 2016 (print) | LCC BX8065.3 (ebook) | DDC 248.4/841--dc23
LC record available at http://lccn.loc.gov/2016008214

1   2   3   4   5   6   7   8   9   10   25   24   23   22   21   20   19   18   17   16

Contents

FOREWORD

We are told that if the Church is to be relevant to our contemporary generations, it needs to proclaim a Christianity that is not legalistic, moralistic, or political. The twenty-first-century Church needs a theology that is grace-filled, inclusive, and down-to-earth. Rather than being a philosophical exposition of abstractions that aims at intellectual understanding, twenty-first-century theology needs to affirm mystery. For all of its spiritual mystery, this theology somehow should also relate to everyday life. Worship in the twenty-first-century-Church should resemble neither a lecture hall nor an entertainment venue; rather, it should manifest that mystery and that practicality in a shared experience of a community of faith. As "emergent Christians," postmodern theologians, and church-growth experts try to devise such a church and such a theology, Trevor Sutton shows that such a church and such a theology already exist: it's called Lutheranism.

Whereas the various attempts to reform Christianity along those lines are devolving into cultural conformity, religious relativism, and new variations on the failed liberal theology, this book shows how the original Reformation still has the same effect; the way forward for the Church is to recover its confessional legacy and to apply it in a new cultural context. Lutherans themselves, as the book shows, have often forgotten and drifted away from Lutheranism, to the diminishment of their church and their witness. This book can help Lutherans understand what it means to be Lutheran, even as it points those of other traditions and those of no traditions—including those who are "spiritual but not religious"—to a place where they will find Jesus.

Although this book is about being Lutheran, above all it is about Jesus. This book mentions Jesus far more than it does Luther, which is, of course, the main point of being Lutheran. Every Lutheran doctrine comes back to Jesus—the incarnation of God, His cross, His resurrection, His saving work, His love, His Word, His Sacraments, His presence, faith in Him—and this book makes that clear on virtually every page.

The theology—Christology, justification, the Word of God, Baptism, Holy Communion, vocation—is all here. Trevor Sutton expresses it and explains it in utterly fresh ways, in terms that never existed in previous centuries. He draws analogies and examples from the world of open-source software, contemporary science, and today's social scenes. He does not fawn over contemporary culture as do so many Christians who try too hard. In fact, he criticizes contemporary culture, but he is also communicating with it.

> **Every Lutheran doctrine comes back to Jesus**

Members of contemporary culture do have their good qualities. Raised in a world that often seems artificial and as though it's trying to sell them something, they crave authenticity. Ironically, many churches try to reach these people by using the same techniques that they are sick of. These churches try to use modern marketing techniques to sell Christianity, try to change themselves artificially in a mostly vain attempt to make the Church more attractive, and thus come across as fake. This book, by contrast, is authentic. It presents Lutheranism warts and all. It is honest, realistic, and open to correction. It admits that Lutheranism does not have all of the answers, that Lutherans make mistakes and have a history of not living up to their own ideals. But such transparency makes Lutheranism—and what Lutherans say about the radical effects of sin and our constant need of God's grace—seem more believable.

As an example of how the author uses a contemporary cultural movement to drive home important Lutheran teachings, consider what he does with localism. Reacting against today's uprootedness, mass consumerism, and cultural homogenization, many people today are rediscovering the value of a sense of place. They are cultivating an appreciation for the "local." They want to eat food that was grown by nearby farmers, drink beer that was brewed where they live, and live in unique local communities. Sometimes, of course, the impulse to eat locally, drink locally, and act locally devolves into just another kind of consumerism, but it arguably comes out of a healthy reaction against today's impersonal mass society. Pastor Sutton shows how Lutheranism emphasizes the local: God localized Himself by becoming incarnate as a specific human being in a specific locale at a specific time in history. This incarnate God, Jesus Christ, is locally present in the bread and wine of Holy Communion. He is thus present and active in the local congregation, however humble it may seem.

Also unique in this treatment is that Pastor Sutton treats not only Lutheran beliefs, but he also treats the attitudes and mind-sets that those beliefs inform. Thus, he divides his book into two parts: what Lutherans challenge (being closed, lukewarm, confused, lazy, and "pastel"), followed by what Lutherans cherish (the new, the ordinary, the unresolved, purpose, and the local). This helps explain the quirks of Lutherans—why they are so doctrinally rigorous, yet so fond of paradoxes and unresolved doctrinal tensions; why they seem both conservative and radical; how their theological strictness manifests itself in a spirit of freedom; how they can make such strong supernatural claims, while also focusing on the much-neglected spiritual significance of what is ordinary—while also accounting for what we could describe as the Lutheran theological culture.

To further ground this theology, this spirituality, in real life, Pastor Sutton includes in each chapter a vignette of an actual person who has lived out the issues he has been writing about. All of this in a style that is original, stimulating, and often (significantly) humorous.

For the already Lutheran, this treatment takes beliefs and practices that have become so familiar they are taken for granted and defamiliarizes them, presenting them in a new way so that they can be experienced as if for the first time with full astonishment. For Christians in other traditions, this treatment shows what a Christ-centered theology built wholly around the Gospel looks like. For non-Christians, this treatment presents a compelling proclamation of Christ, one that points to His saving work and where He can be found.

Gene Edward Veith

ACKNOWLEDGMENTS

*Trust in the LORD with all your heart, and do not lean
on your own understanding. (Proverbs 3:5)*

I am thankful for the many influential people in my life. God has blessed me with a family—Mark and Jane, Bill and Gwen, Ashleigh, Connor, and Steven—to be my firm foundation filled with love and trust in the Lord. My wife, Elizabeth, is my endlessly patient and supportive bride. My daughters, Grace and Hannah, are my unending joy. Without their love and prayers, this book would not have been written.

God has used many to shape my faith: I would like to thank Paul Moldenhauer, Mark Bushuiakovish, Jeremy Schultz, Dave Davis, as well as the people of St. Matthew Lutheran Church (Walled Lake, Michigan), St. Paul Lutheran Church (Royal Oak, Michigan), and St. Luke Lutheran Church (Haslett, Michigan).

God has used many to shape my understanding: I am indebted to the faculties of Concordia University in Ann Arbor and Concordia Seminary in St. Louis for forming me as a thinker. I would particularly like to thank Dr. Neal Migan for teaching me how to write and Dr. Charles Arand for teaching me how to think theologically. I am also thankful to my colleagues in the Writing and Rhetoric Department at Michigan State University.

God has also used many people to turn this project into a book: I would like to thank Scot Kinnaman and the rest of the team at Concordia Publishing House for their guidance and editorial wisdom. I also appreciate the careful work of Joshua Miller in reviewing the manuscript.

And God has used many others not listed here. I am grateful for everyone who has taught me to trust in the Lord.

INTRODUCTION

Being Lutheran

Being Lutheran. Not thinking Lutheran. Not acting Lutheran. Being Lutheran. Being is where thinking and acting collide. It is more than going through the motions. It is more than simply considering an idea or pondering a subject. Being is thinking *and* acting.

We can think yet never act. We can know all about a subject yet never do anything about it. Intellectually grasping God's desire for neighborly love can fail to get us off the front porch. Knowing that hungry people live just beyond our front porch can barely rouse our compassion. Understanding that entire communities are in despair without the Gospel can lead to nothing more than a shrug of the shoulders. It is possible to think as Lutherans, yet never act as Lutherans.

Or we can act without thinking. We could rise to action before a single synapse fires in our brain. Caring for others can be fueled by a misguided hope to earn salvation. Prayer can be as thoughtless as dropping coins in a slot machine. Worship can become nothing more than a spectacle. It is possible for us to act as Lutherans, yet never think as Lutherans.

Perhaps you are reading this right now and thinking, Not me. My thinking informs my actions, and my actions reflect my thinking. I always think as a Lutheran, and I always act as a Lutheran. Congratulations! You are among the five people in human history who can make that claim.

For the rest of us, me included, we constantly need to merge our thinking and acting. There are days when we think Lutheran thoughts and fail to act accordingly. And there are other days when we act as Lutherans yet are completely misguided in our thinking. If you struggle to put it all together, then this book is for you. If you need help in living out your Lutheran theology in daily life, then this book is for you. If you need a better understanding of Lutheran theology and heritage, then this book is for you. I hope that this book helps you to grow closer to Jesus.

Perhaps you are reading this book and you are not Lutheran. Maybe you are of the Reformed tradition. Maybe you are Roman Catholic, Methodist, nondenominational, or some other tradition. Welcome! You will bring good thoughts to these pages. Your tradition undoubtedly has a rich heritage of theologically informed thinking and acting. By reading this book, you will gain a better context by which to examine your own tradition. If you are reading this book from a non-Lutheran perspective, then it will certainly raise questions that you can bring back to your own heritage. Ask these questions of your own tradition. Find answers. I hope this book helps you to grow closer to Jesus.

I suspect that there are still other readers of this book as well. Perhaps you are reading this and you are not a Christian. Welcome! You also bring a beneficial perspective to these pages. Reading this book will allow you to be well-informed and have thoughtful discussions with your Christian friends. The world needs more well-informed people. And the world needs more thoughtful discussions. I hope this book helps you to grow closer to Jesus.

This book is about being Lutheran. It is about theologically informed practice, biblically based behavior, and godly action. It is about living in the faith you have received. Being Lutheran is to know what Lutherans believe and to act on those beliefs.

WHAT TO EXPECT

It will be helpful to have some guidance about what to expect from this book. Questions will arise as you read. Certain topics may initially seem out of reach. Contradictions will create a tension. Objections will undoubtedly cause you to consider putting it down. Fight the urge. Keep reading. Chapters will push against other chapters. Objections will come up in one chapter, and answers will appear in another chapter. Balance comes from all the counterweights working together. Read this book in its entirety. And then you can tell your friends that you entirely disagree with it. Here is what you can expect from this book:

> **Expect Jesus.** He makes all things new. He is victorious over death. He has the power to forgive sins. He is the Good Shepherd. You may be thinking to yourself, I thought this book was about being Lutheran! It is. Being Lutheran is about following Jesus. A Lutheran's primary identity is in Jesus, who has claimed you as His own, given you new life through the waters of Baptism, and invited you to come follow Him.

Being Lutheran is about following Jesus

And as you follow Jesus, you will find that you keep on bumping into other people. Certain people have followed Jesus in such a profound way that it is hard not to notice them. If you follow Jesus long enough, you will inevitably bump into Martin Luther. If you follow Jesus long enough, you will eventually bump into Philip Melanchthon, Martin Chemnitz, C. F. W. Walther, Dietrich Bonhoeffer, and many others. If you follow Jesus long enough, you will find yourself repeatedly bumping into

Lutheran theology and practice. Being Lutheran is about following Jesus. Lutheran theology aims only at faithfully following the teachings of Jesus Christ. This book is ultimately about Jesus.

Expect honesty. This book is not Lutheran hagiography. Authors writing about the saints—a genre known as hagiography—will write volumes of praise about an individual. These sorts of texts depict an impossibly perfect image of a person or group of people. Hagiography tends to go something like this: "St. so-and-so could do no wrong. Everybody loved him. He invented sliced bread. He won 'Most Likely to Succeed' in high school."

This is not that sort of book. This book will claim Lutheran theology is the fullest articulation of the Gospel of Jesus Christ. This book will explore various attributes of our belief. This book will tell the story of various Lutherans living out their faith in tremendous ways. This book will point out errors in other denominations. It will occasionally sound like blatant Lutheran grandstanding. However, this book will be painfully honest in recognizing that Lutherans seldom live up to their own theology. We talk the talk but often miss walking the walk. Being Lutheran has become pretty vanilla. This book will not be a chest-thumping, back-patting, self-aggrandizing depiction of Lutheranism.

We do not always embody the attributes that we claim as our own. Perhaps there was a time in our history when we embodied more of these traits. However, we have long since forgotten their importance. We do not always live out the practices of Lutheranism. We have distorted our practices into an unrecognizable condition. We forego their value and pretend to be like other denominations. We have cashed in our beliefs on numerous occasions for any shiny new trend that comes our way. This book is going to be brutally honest.

Expect theology. Most people assume that theology is as exciting as reading tax law or the phone book. Theology brings to mind dead guys with epic beards. Many folks would rather tailgate at *Antiques Roadshow* than read a book about theology. People assume theology is boring. They are mistaken. Theology is not some sort of esoteric, quasi-philosophical muttering. Theology is about daily life. It situates God's eternal truths in the present. It takes Scripture and applies it to your challenges as student, spouse, employee, friend, and parent. Theological reflection tries to make sense out of life and death, suffering and violence, love and marriage, work and rest.

> **Theological reflection tries to make sense out of life and death, suffering and violence, love and marriage, work and rest**

Theology has gained a bad name for a couple of reasons. It is a complicated discipline occupied by theological scholars. As happens with many disciplines, scholars engage in conversations with one another. Scientists discuss science with other scientists. Historians debate history with other historians. Theologians talk theology with other theologians. A problem arises when theology becomes inwardly focused. God came to His people and spoke to them in their own language. Theology gets a bad name when it fails to speak to average people in their own language.

Another grievance cited against theology is irrelevancy. Medieval theologians used to postulate how many angels could dance on the head of a pin. This was relevant to them because it fit into broader questions they were asking at that time. The average farmer in that day was far more concerned with how many cows he could fit in his barn. Theology can fixate on discussions that are relevant only to a small group of specialists. Instead of that, expect that in this book we will discuss theology using accessible language and will make it relevant to daily life—make it relevant to you.

Expect history. Theology often draws on history. Certain figures from the past come up frequently. This book will reference various times in Church history. Ancient Christianity and the Reformation will provide context for our present beliefs. You will hear certain names come up repeatedly: Augustine of Hippo, Martin Luther, and C. F. W. Walther. It may seem as though theology is just stuck in the past and overly fixated on dead people. While this may be partially true, there is a reason for referencing different times and people.

We are not the smartest people to ever live. Science, medicine, literature, and art have advanced since the time of the Early Church. We know much more now than people did in the past. Bloodletting is out, and antibiotics are in. Our geocentric universe is now a heliocentric universe. Curly mustaches came and went. And then they inexplicably came back again. Tweets, posts, and snaps are the new scrolls. Still, we are not nearly as smart as we think we are.

The ancients had an incredible knowledge of astronomy, architecture, language, and philosophy. Memorizing whole works of literature was standard practice. Martin Luther would read through the entire Bible twice a year. We can barely read through our in-box. Theology unabashedly draws on other times and people. God does not change. Sin and salvation do not change. Scripture is already written. This book uses the past to illuminate the present.

Expect people—real people. People matter to God. He fearfully and wonderfully made every person who has ever lived. God knows His people by name. God loves people so much that He is willing to die for them. God stays up at night and counts the hairs on your head (Luke 12:7). Lutheranism is not about institutional survival or perpetuating a brand. People are not just a nameless statistic or demographic. Being Lutheran is sharing in God's love for people.

Each chapter concludes with a vignette depicting a real person. Some of the people in the vignettes are exceptional individuals from history. Most of the people are just average folks: recovering alcoholics, mothers, teachers, doctors, and immigrants. These are composites of real people who have really grappled with being Lutheran. These individuals embody some aspect of being Lutheran. These vignettes will help you translate theology into daily life. Their stories will show you what it looks like to be Lutheran.

Expect Lutheranism. This book will explore the core characteristics of Lutheran thinking and practice. It will give you a better understanding of how Lutheran theology is unique. It will explain how we are like other denominations. It will point out the ways in which the Lutheran Church differs from other church bodies. Central figures and events in the history of the Lutheran Church will give you context for present-day Lutheranism. There will not be any recipes for German potato salad, lutefisk, or casseroles. It will give you what you need to develop a thoughtful explanation for being Lutheran.

BOOK OVERVIEW

This book is divided into two parts. In the first section, we look at the human tendencies Lutherans challenge. We push against the broken inclinations of sin. Lutherans challenge a closed culture with a radical openness to sharing God's grace. We loathe apathy and actually defend our faith. We refuse to be ignorant by actually knowing what we believe. We resist the urge to work for God's love and instead work for our neighbor's well-being. We detest being pastel like every other church body. Being Lutheran is challenging broken human tendencies.

In the second section, we look at those things that are distinctive about being Lutheran. Lutherans cling to the peculiarities of the Gospel and believe that Scripture is the Word of God. We embrace the fact that salvation comes from beyond ourselves; Christ makes all things new without sinners contributing anything. We marvel at the mystery of how God uses ordinary material to deliver Christ's extraordinary grace; God takes ordinary stuff and makes it extraordinary. We recognize that certain tensions in Scripture are better left unresolved; every theological dilemma does not have to be untangled. We celebrate Christ working in and through us; our identity and purpose in life come from God. We look to the worship of the local congregation to see Christ coming to us; worship is where God dwells in the midst of the community. Being Lutheran is cherishing the peculiarities of the Gospel.

The book concludes with a chapter about following Jesus. Although we call ourselves Lutheran, our primary identity is in Jesus Christ. Lutherans do not follow Martin Luther because he is among the greatest theologians in history. We do not follow Luther because he liberated the Church from false teaching. We do not follow Luther because he brewed his own beer. Rather, we are Lutheran because it enables us to faithfully follow Jesus. Being Lutheran is faithfully following Jesus.

By the end of this book, you will be able to better articulate what it is to be Lutheran. You will be able to stop googling all of your questions about Lutheranism. You can stop explaining Lutheranism as being somewhere between Baptist and Catholic. You will know what Lutherans believe. Your answer can go beyond explaining the differences between Martin Luther and Martin Luther King Jr. You can stop being boring. And you can start being Lutheran.

Part 1

Being Lutheran:
What We Challenge

Chapter 1

CLOSED

Through Him we have also obtained
access by faith into this grace in
which we stand, and we rejoice in
hope of the glory of God.
(Romans 5:2)

Hipsters know how to be cool. Plastic-frame glasses have a sophisticated vibe with just a hint of nerdy. Moustaches and flannel shirts pair well with single-speed bicycles and scooters. Fanny packs offer an ironic twist. And skinny jeans make a statement to the entire world: "I am a brave man for cramming myself into these pants!"

Hipsters also talk about cool topics: indie music, sustainability, farm-to-table, biofuels, and third spaces. Hang around a coffee shop long enough and you will also hear someone talking about open source. The term *open source* emerged from computer programming. Starting in the 1980s, computer programmers began openly sharing the recipes for software. The code was free and open for anyone to use. Other programmers would then take the code and remix it for some other use. This remixed software code was again openly shared with others.

Open-source practices have since spread beyond computer programming. Open-source architects make blueprints available to others for collaboration. Universities embrace open source by freely sharing lectures and course material via the Internet. Pharmaceutical scientists share the recipes for various drugs to promote global accessibility to medicine. Open source is showing up everywhere. Wikipedia is an example of open source. Anybody can contribute to the collective knowledge on a topic. Suppose you are an expert in your field. Your field just so happens to be designer dog clothing. You can contribute your substantial knowledge of pooch handbags on the wiki page. Suppose you were to make an outlandish claim about the topic: you wrote an entry stating that dogs do not appreciate dressing up like humans. Other experts could then come and correct your falsity. Likewise, you can correct the false claims of other contributors. Knowledge is openly shared. Collaboration is crowdsourced.

Linux, Firefox, Creative Commons, and Khan Academy are all open-source projects. Code, photos, and knowledge are all openly shared via the Internet. Users are welcome to remix, redux, and revamp. Users do not have to pay for software, code, or content. Open source is pretty awesome.

Hidden behind all the awesomeness, however, are some serious problems. Open source is not nearly as open as it appears. Massive barriers keep many people from accessing these resources. Obstacles have closed open source. Without Internet access or a computer, these tools are useless. No Internet access means zero access to digital encyclopedias, video learning, and educational material. No computer access means no sharing in open collaboration. This excludes billions of people from open-source access. In 2013, more than 45 million people, or 14.5 percent of all Americans, lived at or below the poverty line.[1] Globally, over 1.3 billion, 18 percent of all people, do not have access to electricity.[2] Open-source access is irrelevant

---

1 Mark Gongloff, "45 Million Americans Still Stuck Below Poverty Line: Census," *The Huffington Post*, September 16, 2014, www.huffingtonpost.com/2014/09/16/poverty-household-income_n_5828974.html

2 International Energy Agency, www.iea.org/topics/energypoverty/ (accessed January 5, 2016).

when you warm your hut by burning dried cow dung. Correcting a falsehood about designer dog clothing takes a backseat when you have had no fresh water in two days. There are also social barriers to open-source access. Literacy is a requirement for the majority of Internet usage. Users must be able to do more than just read; most open-source access relies on being computer literate and adept at coding. Racial barriers keep minority voices quiet. Finances build walls around who can and cannot participate since open source is not entirely free. Computer programmers sell tech support and add-ons for their free software. Architects sell their expertise when customizing free blueprints. Pharmaceutical companies use free recipes to help develop products for profit. Universities offer open access to some content so that you will pay tuition for all the content. Open source is closed to many.

CLOSED IS OUR DEFAULT POSITION

Open source is not the only thing closed. The urge to be closed dwells deep in our bones. We are closed to others. We are closed to different ethnicities, ideologies, and cultures. We are closed to different opinions, strange foods, and rival sports teams. Put a Yankees fan in the same room with a Red Sox fan and you will see what I mean. A Cardinals fan would rather scale the side of a building than ride an elevator with a Cubs fan. On a serious level, racism divides entire communities. Genocide destroys whole tribes. Members Only® is not just a late '80s clothing company; many social circles are for members only. Disparity of wealth is real. Closed is our default position.

Sin demolished our relationship with God

We are closed to one another. And this comes from being closed to God. Sin demolished our relationship with God. Rebellion destroyed our openness to Him. Sin closes us to God's goodness and love. Sin slams the door on His mercy and justice. We are closed to God. It is our default position.

It was not supposed to be like this. God created you to be open to Him. He made His entire creation to be open to Him. God openly delighted in His work (Genesis 1:31). Adam and Eve had open access to God and to each other in the beginning (Genesis 2:25). God openly walked in the garden of His creation (Genesis 3:8). Creation had open access to the source of all good things.

And sin closed it all. Sin bent our relationship with God. It mangled and destroyed our ability to reflect the image of God. Rather than being open to Him, sin has bent us in on ourselves. We bend God to fit into our own puny purposes. We bend our desires away from God's perfect desires. We bend our eyes away from Him and onto ourselves. Sin makes us self-concerned, rebellious, insolent, and closed to God. Closure began with original sin. And closure persists in us today.

Martin Luther wrote plenty about the closure that comes from sin. He drew upon the theology of St. Augustine and described sin as a bent relationship closed to God. Luther used other images to help explain the destructive power of sin. He explained the inclination to sin, perhaps talking to the bearded hipsters of Wittenberg, by saying:

> The original sin in a man is like his beard, which, though shaved off today so that a man is very smooth around his mouth, yet grows again by tomorrow morning. . . . Just so original sin remains in us and bestirs itself as long as we live, but we must resist it and always cut off its hair.[3]

Our default position is closed to God. Just as facial hair silently grows, sin silently closes our relationship with God. Closure to God

---

3   *WLS* § 4176.

brings closure to others. Sin closed Adam off to God. He literally concealed himself from the presence of God (Genesis 3:10). Sin closed Paradise to Adam and Eve (Genesis 3:23–24). It is no coincidence that Cain killed Abel (Genesis 4:8) after sin had closed humanity to God. Self-worship replaced true worship (Genesis 11:4). Separate languages led to separate clans, communities, and cities (Genesis 11:9).

> **Closure to God brings closure to others**

Violence then filled the earth (Genesis 6:11). And the rest is the painful history of a people closed to God and one another.

OPEN IN CHRIST JESUS

Enter Jesus. He is God's response to the closure of sin. Jesus opened what sin had closed. God opened the heavens to take on human flesh. The heavens were literally opened at the Baptism of Jesus (Matthew 3:16). Jesus opened eyes that were once closed (Matthew 9:27–31; Mark 8:22–26; John 9:1–7). Jesus opened lives closed by sin (Luke 19:1–10). Jesus opened ears and minds previously closed to truth (John 18:20; Luke 24:45). Jesus opened the tomb of Lazarus, closed for four days, and restored life to his rotting corpse (John 11).

And Jesus opens our relationship to the Father. God in human flesh, Jesus restores our connection to the Father:

> Jesus said to him, "I am the way, and the truth, and the life. No one comes to the Father except through Me. If you had known Me, you would have known My Father also. From now on you do know Him and have seen Him." (John 14:6–7)

Opened and unbent, Jesus makes you new. Faith in Christ Jesus replaces your mangled heart with a new one. He replaces your inwardly curved heart with one that is aimed straight at God. He opens your relationship with God and restores the image of God within you. Eyes opened by Jesus. Ears open to hear God's Word. Heart open to God's will. Hands open to receive His mercy. Mind open to care for others. Mouth open to proclaim the Gospel of Jesus Christ. Christ Jesus opens you back up to God.

Jesus also opens you to proclaim the Gospel. Scripture makes it clear that faith in Christ opens us to God and one another. We see a vivid depiction of this in the Early Church. The Holy Spirit opened sinners to believe and share the name of Jesus.

Saul was closed. Sin closed him to God's grace. He breathed threats and murder against Christ's Church. He terrorized Christians. God came to a closed Saul and opened him to be a follower of Jesus (Acts 9). This was not at all Saul's doing; the Holy Spirit took a closed sinner and made him an open believer. He then went by the name of Paul and openly shared the Gospel throughout the Roman Empire. God opened Paul to share the Gospel with non-Jewish people.

Lydia was closed. Sin closed her to God's grace in Christ Jesus. She heard the Gospel proclaimed by Paul. God transformed her closed heart: "The Lord opened her heart to pay attention to what was said by Paul" (Acts 16:14). Baptized into Christ Jesus, she then opened her house to others. This was not simply a polite invitation. She did not open her house to them while secretly hoping they would not accept. Scripture makes it clear that she insisted on opening her house to others: "And she prevailed upon us" (Acts 16:15). A mother offering dinner with a wooden spoon aimed at your head can be very persuasive.

Peter was closed. Sin closed him to sharing God's grace with other nationalities. Peter excluded anyone outside the Jewish people. Peter excluded Gentiles. He thought they smelled funny and ate strange food. God then opened him to proclaim the Gospel to all people, all nations, and all ethnicities. God gave Peter a vision that opened him to share God's Word with all people. Opened by God, Peter preached to other nationalities: "So Peter opened his mouth and said: 'Truly I understand that God shows no partiality, but in every nation anyone who fears Him and does what is right is acceptable to Him' " (Acts 10:34–35).

Gentiles were closed. Sin closed them to the Gospel of Jesus. Instead, they were open to misguided beliefs in Epicurean and Stoic philosophy. They chased after the religion of the week and worshiped any god but God. Although they were spiritually closed, God opened the door of faith to them: "And when they arrived and gathered the church together, they declared all that God had done with them, and how He had opened a door of faith to the Gentiles" (Acts 14:27).

Jesus opened lives closed by sin

Opened to God in Christ Jesus, the Church is open to sharing the Gospel with all people. We are open to share about Christ Jesus, "in whom we have boldness and access with confidence through our faith in Him" (Ephesians 3:12). Jesus opens His people to proclaim the Gospel.

OPEN ACCESS TO THE GOSPEL

Better than open-source access, the Gospel is truly open to all. The Gospel does not exclude on account of race, literacy, or socio-economic standing. The Good News of Jesus offers open access to God for all people.

Open access to God's grace is at the heart of being Lutheran. This was a central issue leading up to the Reformation. At various points throughout Church history, people have tried to close access to the Gospel. But Lutherans have always resisted the urge to close the Gospel.

Martin Luther was born into a time of closed access to the Gospel. Before the time of the Reformation, the majority of worship was in Latin. The Latin used in the Church of the day was little more than gibberish to the average German worshiper. This caused people to come in and tune out. The Bible was equally inaccessible to people, since it was not written in the common language. A small group of literate clergy held a disproportionate amount of biblical knowledge. For most people, hymns, stained glass, hearsay, and a few recognizable Latin phrases were the closest they could come to accessing God's Word.

Lack of access to worship and Scripture was not the only limitation on the Gospel. The laity were not allowed to receive Communion in both kinds. This means that although priests could receive both the body and blood of Christ in Holy Communion, the laity could receive only the body of Christ. The thought behind this practice was that the average layperson was not holy enough to receive the Eucharist in both kinds. Priests had prayed the prayers, fasted the fasts, and confessed the confessions, so they could have all of Jesus. Joe the pauper could have only half.

This lack of access to the Gospel left people very confused about their faith. The modern phrase "hocus-pocus" likely came out of this period of Church history. When speaking

Lack of access to the Gospel left people very confused about their faith

the Words of Institution for the Eucharist, the priest would turn his back to the congregation and speak in Latin: "*Hoc est corpus meum.*" This translates into English as "This is My body." The average person assumed this was an incantation of sorts. The magic of *hoc est something-or-other* turned bread and wine into Jesus. The Gospel was closed to many people.

Exploitation thrived in this environment. Before the Reformation, Church hierarchy had more authority than Scripture. Pardons for sin were bought and sold in order to finance cathedrals and build Our Lady of Revenue. Selling indulgences became a big business for the Church. An indulgence was like purchasing a "get out of jail free" card. Fear of purgatory drove people to cash in their savings for indulgences. Individuals put their trust in pieces of paper. Faith in receipts replaced faith in Christ.

Uncertainty fueled the selling of indulgences. The Church during that time in history taught that God's grace was a spiritual steroid for doing good works. Grace empowered believers to reach salvation. Forgiveness was earned by doing good works as repayment for sin. This period of theological history, known as Scholasticism, left believers questioning their salvation. People were uncertain whether their good works could ever outweigh their sins. There was also uncertainty about how often one needed to buy indulgences: Should I buy a new indulgence every time I empty my chamber pot on my neighbor's lawn? Should I buy extra indulgences if my child is a brat? Does Uncle Jim need extra indulgences because he is crabby all the time? Believers purchased indulgences to tip the scale in their favor. Fear drove the market.

Worship of the saints became a primary focus for many Christians during this time in Church history. Uncertain salvation had people relying on the help of saints. Believers would call on saints as advocates before God. Rather than addressing God directly, Christians would ask St. Anne to put in a good word with Jesus. As with indulgences, daily Christian life focused on everything but the Gospel of Jesus Christ.

Luther pushed against this closed Gospel. Silence was not an option for him. He publicly posted his Ninety-Five Theses on the door of All Saints' Church in Wittenberg on October 31, 1517. This document waged war on a Gospel closed by indulgences. He railed against many false practices in the Church:

> Thus those indulgence preachers are in error who say that a man is absolved from every penalty and saved by papal indulgences. (Thesis 21)

They preach only human doctrines who say that as soon as the money clinks into the money chest, the soul flies out of purgatory. (Thesis 27)

Any true Christian, whether living or dead, participates in all the blessings of Christ and the church; and this is granted him by God, even without indulgence letters. (Thesis 37)[4]

Indulgences were just the beginning for Luther. He openly opposed the pope and church councils when they contradicted Scripture. He opened access to God's Word by translating the Bible into German. The Reformation sparked by Luther opened worship to the masses by conducting services and singing hymns in their language, opened Communion in both kinds to the laity, and opened marriage to clergy. All these reforms shared a common purpose: open access to the Gospel of Jesus Christ.

Luther led the Church back to the source of salvation, God's grace in Jesus Christ

Lutheranism grew by going back to the sources. *Ad fontes* was a popular Latin phrase during the time of the Reformation. This phrase translates as "back to the sources." It was a call to return to the sources of Christian belief and practice. Luther opened the Bible. He yielded his beliefs to God's Word. He led the Church back to the source of salvation, God's grace in Jesus Christ. He directed people to rely on the source of eternal comfort, God's gift of faith. He led believers back to the source of their beliefs, God's Word in Scripture. Being Lutheran is having open access to the Gospel.

---

4   LW 31:27–29.

OPEN GOSPEL HERITAGE

The Gospel loops and swirls in a heavenly helix through every strand of Lutheran DNA. It is in the blood. The word *evangelical* originated with the Lutheran Church. Lutherans claimed it first. In Germany, the Lutheran Church was historically called the *Evangelische Kirche*, the Evangelical (that is, Lutheran) Church. Lutherans were evangelical before it was cool. The word comes from the Greek word (*evangelion*) for "good news" or "Gospel." Although it is now an evangellyfish buzzword, evangelical originally meant proclamation of the Gospel. An evangelical church confesses the Gospel of Jesus Christ.

> **An evangelical church confesses the Gospel of Jesus Christ**

Lutherans are evangelical in the historical sense of the term. Lutherans openly confess and proclaim the Gospel. Not just to some people. Not just to white people. Not just to Germans, Norwegians, and Swedes. Not just to rich suburbanites. And not only from nine to eleven on Sunday mornings. Lutherans share the good news of Christ's life, death, and resurrection with all people all the time. Open access to God through Jesus Christ is for all people. Generations of Lutherans have openly shared the Gospel with all people.

Being Lutheran in Europe: Following the death of Martin Luther in 1546, Lutheran theology continued to spread throughout Europe. Princes and rulers became Lutheran. Whole regions shifted away from Roman Catholicism and adopted Lutheran beliefs and practices. This caused massive strife within the Holy Roman Empire. Wars ensued. Blood was shed. People died to be Lutheran. Proclaiming the pure Gospel was worth more than life.

Peace eventually prevailed. The Peace of Augsburg came in 1555. This allowed rulers to decide the religion of their territory. The Lutherans wrote a central confession of their faith—the Book of Concord—articulating their beliefs on the basis of Scripture. This religious freedom allowed Lutherans to openly proclaim the Gospel for generations. They shared the Gospel. They ate bratwurst with their neighbors. They brewed beer and wrote theology books just for fun. Life was good.

However, this heritage of open proclamation ended. Open access to the Gospel came under attack. A movement called Rationalism became popular throughout Europe. In the eighteenth century, a philosopher named Immanuel Kant (1724–1804) argued that God must fit within the limits of human reason. Kant argued that it is through reason that one comprehends what is real. Human reason tried to close faith in Jesus Christ. Scripture was closed. Scholars regarded the Bible as a myth since it was hard to reason a complex creation made in six days. Jesus Christ was closed. Preachers called Him a great moral teacher because the resurrection could not fit into a test tube. The Gospel was closed. The Church preached morality instead.

Ecumenism also constricted the open proclamation of the Gospel. This movement attempted to unite all Christian churches around one tepid confession. Political pressure forced Lutheran congregations to adopt state-sanctioned beliefs. The Prussian Union of 1817 forcibly merged the Lutherans and Calvinists to join one state-sanctioned church. This required believers to cede their convictions on Scripture, Baptism, and Holy Communion.

Being Lutheran in America: Open proclamation of the Gospel quickly spread to the American colonies. Lutherans began immigrating to North America in the early part of the seventeenth century. The first Lutheran settlement, New Sweden, was established in 1638 along the Delaware River. Swedes, Finns, and a number of Dutch settlers built a thriving colony in this region. The Lutherans living in the Delaware Valley planted a church, Gloria Dei Church, in 1677. The construction of the church building was completed in 1700, five years before the founding of the city of Philadelphia. It is the oldest church in Pennsylvania. Another Lutheran congregation, Holy Trinity Church, began worshiping thirty miles away in Wilmington, Delaware. These immigrant Lutherans also brought with them their passion for education; they refused to let illiteracy close the Bible. The first Lutheran schools were opened in the 1600s.

Religious freedom in Pennsylvania was a catalyst for Lutheran immigration. A growing number of Lutherans in the American colonies led to the formation of the Pennsylvania Ministerium. This was the first Lutheran church body in North America. Formed in 1748, the Pennsylvania Ministerium supported open proclamation of the Gospel by creating an informal network of Lutheran congregations as well as a common liturgy. Henry Muhlenberg (1711–87) emerged as a leader of the colonial Lutherans, traveling from New York to Georgia to support the open proclamation of the Gospel.

Furthering the efforts to organize, Lutheran church bodies in America gathered together to form the General Synod in 1820. Ministeriums from New York, Virginia, Maryland, Pennsylvania, and other states formed this synod. The term *synod* derives from the Greek language and means "walking together." These believers wanted to walk together in their Lutheran theology. Samuel Schmucker (1799–1873) led the Synod during its formative early years. Schmucker also worked to open a Lutheran seminary and college in Gettysburg, Pennsylvania. Open proclamation of the Gospel continued through the formation of future pastors and missionaries.

Meanwhile, open proclamation was closed in Europe. Being Lutheran became illegal. This caused a group of Lutherans to leave Saxony in search of religious freedom. A group of roughly seven hundred Lutheran immigrants packed up their lederhosen and moved. They left the old sod behind them on September 4, 1838. They landed in New Orleans, Louisiana. After a brief stay there, they continued northward to St. Louis, Missouri. This entire voyage centered on a common purpose: open access to the Gospel of Jesus Christ.

Like the Lutherans before them, they were foreigners in a foreign land. The language was unfamiliar. The culture was strange. Their funds were gone. Yet the Gospel was openly proclaimed. As the Saxon Lutherans established a new congregation, they also established and supported a parochial school. In addition, on April 26, 1847, twelve pastors from fourteen congregations formed a new church body called the German Evangelical Lutheran Synod of Missouri, Ohio, and Other States. One of the stated purposes of organizing the Synod was the spreading of the Gospel of Jesus Christ. Here again we see that the Gospel is in every DNA strand of Lutheran theology.

C. F. W. Walther (1811–87) was the leader of this newly formed synod. He encouraged open access to the Gospel for all people. In 1842, Walther preached to his congregation, encouraging them to openly proclaim the Gospel:

> Dear friends, through faith a Christian receives not only the holy desire to bring souls to Christ. He receives this task as a sacred duty. No one should say, "I am not a pastor, a teacher, or a preacher; let them teach, instruct, comfort, and lead souls to Christ! I wish to remain in my own vocation." No. Christian, you are baptized and through holy baptism you have already been called and anointed to be a priest of God. Through holy baptism each Christian has been consecrated, ordained and installed into the ministry to teach, admonish, and comfort his neighbor. Through holy baptism each Christian has obtained not only the authority, power, and right but also the high, holy obligation—under pain of losing the divine grace—of rousing himself to care and to help so that others may be brought to Christ.[5]

5   C. F. W. Walther, "Bringing Souls to Christ: Every Christian's Desire and Duty," Sermon for the Twelfth Sunday after Trinity, 1842, in *Gnadenjahr: Predigten über die Evangelien des Kirchenjahres* (St. Louis: Concordia, 1891), 439–45, translated by Bruce

Roused by Walther's preaching, the Synod began sending missionaries to the American frontier. These missionaries (*Reiseprediger*) shared open access to the Gospel with local settlers. Other missionaries proclaimed the Gospel to American Indian communities. Missionaries to tribal communities included E. J. Meier (b. 1828), E. G. H. Miessler (1826–1916), and E. R. Baierlein (1819–1901). These tribal communities were not Lutheran because of their parents; they were Lutherans because all people have access to the Good News of Jesus Christ.

The Gospel crossed other racial boundaries as well. Following the Civil War, reconstruction began in the American South. Lutherans openly shared the Gospel with newly emancipated slaves. A Lutheran publication known as *The Pioneer* circulated news about mission work among "the freedman of the South." Black Lutheran congregations formed throughout America. Two generations after the Civil War ended, there were black Lutheran congregations in Alabama, Arkansas, Georgia, Illinois, Missouri, New York, South Carolina, Virginia, and Washington DC. In addition, a passionate teacher named Rosa Young worked tirelessly to start Lutheran schools throughout the American South; these Lutheran schools ensured that the Gospel would never be closed on account of illiteracy. Like many others, the people in these congregations and schools were not Lutheran because of their parents; they were Lutherans because of open access to the Gospel.

The rural South was not the only place open to the Gospel. Urban congregations soon followed. Between 1920 and 1950, thirty-four black Lutheran congregations opened in cities throughout the United States. Being Lutheran involved more than German immigrants. Being Lutheran meant open access to the Gospel for *all* people.

Cameron in *Missio Apostolica: Journal of the Lutheran Society for Missiology* 6 (1998): 6–16.

Being Lutheran around the Globe: Access to the Gospel spread beyond Europe and America. The seventeenth century saw Lutheranism spreading to Africa and South America through European traders. A Lutheran missionary, Bartholomäus Ziegenbalg (1682–1719), began sharing the Gospel throughout India in 1706. Meanwhile, other Lutherans engaged in global mission by leaving Germany and coming to America. F. C. D. Wyneken (1810–76) and Wilhelm Löhe (1808–72) trained, financed, and sent Lutheran missionaries to America. Wyneken raised awareness for global missions through his publication *Notruf.* He called on people to support the struggles of the German Lutherans in North America. At that time in European history, the American frontier was not far from the ends of the earth.

Lutherans in America then began sending their own missionaries to foreign countries. Theodore Naether and his family traveled to India in 1895. Henry Mizuno Shigetaro, a Japanese Lutheran, left America in the same year to be a missionary in Japan. These early missionaries started a windfall of other global Lutheran missionaries. Following Luther's pattern, global missionaries focused on translating the Bible for individuals to read in their own language. Indigenous worship and hymnody grew. Congregations formed in other countries. Lutheran potlucks added tofu and naan to the menu. The Lutheran Church's anthem "A Mighty Fortress" was set to drums in Africa. Lutherans have since spread the Gospel to the ends of the earth.

IMPERFECTIONS

I would be a liar if I told you that Lutherans have perfectly maintained open access to the Gospel. We have not. Although we hate to hear it, Lutherans are sinful folks prone to closing the Gospel. At times, we have defied our own heritage. On occasion, we have willingly closed the Gospel to groups of people.

Luther found this happening early in the Reformation. As he was opening access to the Gospel, people were closing their hearts to God's will. Influenced by Luther's theology, people used grace as permission to sin. Salvation freely given was reason to freely neglect worship. Complete forgiveness in Jesus led people to completely disregard the needs of their neighbors. Elector John the Steadfast (1468–1532) wrote to Luther suggesting that he learn about these problems firsthand. Luther agreed, and he traveled throughout the surrounding villages on a visitation of local congregations. He found that Lutherans knew little about their beliefs. And they had distorted the few beliefs that they did know.

These visitations were frustrating for Luther. He witnessed whole communities willfully closing the Gospel. Since they were abusing the Good News of Jesus, Luther stopped preaching the Gospel for a time. He focused only on preaching and teaching the Law. He wrote a handbook about basic Christian beliefs— Luther's Small Catechism—to help parents teach their children.

There were theological struggles to keep Lutheran theology about the Gospel

Lutherans in America also had problems maintaining open access to the Gospel. There were theological struggles to keep Lutheran theology about the Gospel. For instance, in the eighteenth century, there was a movement called Pietism that emphasized personal piety over the Gospel. The Civil War divided Lutheran church bodies and congregations. Lutheran church leaders fell to sexual misconduct, embezzlement, and bad theology.

Racism, ethnocentrism, and xenophobia have occasionally enticed Lutherans to close access to the Gospel. White Lutherans excluded black congregations. Tribal mission work shared European culture more than it shared the Gospel. The desire to perpetuate their tradition caused some Lutherans to close the Gospel to others. It is true. We are sinners indeed.

OPEN GOSPEL TODAY

Despite our imperfections, being Lutheran is still about open access to the Gospel. It will always be about access to God in Christ Jesus. It gets us more hyped than ten cups of coffee. It puts a thump in our chests and a charge in our bones. We love the Gospel. And we love to share the Gospel.

Despite our imperfections, being Lutheran is still about open access to the Gospel

Yet open access to the Gospel is threatened. Closed mouths cannot proclaim the Gospel. Closed churches cannot confess the forgiveness of sins in Christ Jesus. Closed Bibles cannot impart the Word of God. Closed Lutheran schools cannot equip believers to defend their faith. Assaulted on every side, the open Gospel of Jesus Christ is under attack from many different directions.

Political Correctness: The golden calf of our culture is political correctness. Openly sharing the Gospel may offend somebody. Praying before a meal at a restaurant could make the waitress uncomfortable. The shine of your cross necklace might blind some poor, unsuspecting chap. We stand down to political correctness. We let political correctness close open access to the Gospel. Our culture says that loving your neighbor requires closing your mouth. Jesus says that loving your neighbor requires opening your mouth with the Gospel: "What I tell you in the dark, say in the light, and what you hear whispered, proclaim on the housetops" (Matthew 10:27).

Fighting: Congregational squabbling closes the Gospel. Fighting about how the Lenten suppers have too much sodium stops proclamation. Debating the length of the shag carpet on the chancel ensures that others will not know Jesus. A monthly subcommittee to review the committee proceedings from the mission committee will do a fine job in closing the Gospel. Open access to the Gospel thrives when we stop fighting about petty issues: "Complete my joy by being of the same mind, having the same love, being in full accord and of one mind" (Philippians 2:2).

Forgetting to Fight: Sometimes we fight too much. And sometimes we forget to fight. Guarding the Gospel from error is worth a fight. Stand up and say something when Scripture is treated like a mythological fairy tale. Say something when the Gospel is depicted as mere do-goodery. Ask for further explanation when you hear someone say that all religions are essentially about being a good person. Resist bad preaching that confuses human responsibility with Christ's righteousness. Straighten crooked interpretations of the Bible: "But Jesus answered them, 'You are wrong, because you know neither the Scriptures nor the power of God'" (Matthew 22:29).

False Openness: Watch out for false openness claiming to be true open access to the Gospel. Many denominations raise the banner of open and affirming inclusivity. This means that they openly affirm all lifestyles. This is wrong dressed up as right. The Holy Spirit is open to all sinners turning from sin. God openly invites all people to turn from sin. Yet nowhere in Scripture does God affirm ungodly behavior. Whether it is speeding in a school zone or sleeping with your girlfriend, God calls sin by name. We close the Gospel when we brush sins aside. Open access to Christ's forgiveness ceases when sins are withheld from His mercy. Open Communion is also a false openness. Dressed up as a nice way to welcome outsiders, open Communion says that anyone can commune regardless of belief or confession. Atheist, agnostic, and any other confession are welcomed. This dilutes the Gospel into an unrecognizable soupy mess. Open proclamation of the Gospel closes by trying to make everyone happy. Rather than stopping to explain the gift of forgiveness given in the Lord's Supper, it is easier to just welcome anyone with a pulse. Opening a sham gospel closes the true Gospel: "For am I now seeking the approval of man, or of God? Or am I trying to please man? If I were still trying to please man, I would not be a servant of Christ" (Galatians 1:10).

CONCLUSION

Being Lutheran challenges our natural inclination to be closed and clings to the open proclamation of the Gospel. The Good News of Jesus Christ is the only open source of salvation for all people. God alone offers open access to a better life in Christ Jesus. Jesus opens a creation closed by sin. God opens access through Christ. Jesus opens lives to healing. The Holy Spirit opens hearts to the Gospel. All people have access to the Gospel regardless of race, money, or power. Being Lutheran is resisting a closed Gospel.

Luther refused to let indulgences and language barriers close the Gospel. Nearly a century later, Lutherans in Germany refused to let the government or false philosophy close the Gospel by closing their churches. Black Lutherans refused to confine the name of Jesus to the rural South. Lutheran schools refused to let illiteracy close the Bible.

And still today we refuse to let anything close the Gospel of Jesus Christ. Openly pray for your co-workers when they are struggling. Openly read your Bible at the gym. Openly tell your friends about the hope that you have in Christ Jesus. Openly stand up for truth in Scripture. Being Lutheran is being opened by the Gospel.

Vignette: Seliman

They had one of the nicer churches in Sudan. Rather than roasting in the sun through the long sermon, the congregation met in a long mud hut. Even with the luxury of a roof overhead, the building was dark, hot, and sweaty. They fanned themselves throughout the service. They sat on metal stools and benches. On particularly crowded Sundays, people had to sit on temporary benches made of stray tree branches tied together.

Every Sunday was crowded.

Seliman's father was a leader in the congregation. A shortage of pastors meant that many congregations had to rely on lay leaders to assist with worship. Occasionally, the congregation would travel to the capital for a large worship service with many other people. More often, they gathered together to hear the Gospel openly proclaimed in their local congregation. The Holy Spirit moved in that place. The presence of the Lord was with them.

The government was increasingly suspicious about the open proclamation of the Gospel happening in the congregation. Pressure grew against Seliman's father and the church: "Keep your mouth shut." "Stop preaching the Gospel." "We are watching you."

Threats grew more frequent. Violence became more imminent. This forced Seliman's family to flee Sudan in the middle of the night. His father woke him at 2 a.m. and told him they were leaving. They had sold the house and everything in it.

Cash in hand and shoes on their feet, Seliman and his family left Sudan to find somewhere else to openly proclaim the Gospel.

Egypt was a temporary home after leaving Sudan. Seliman was about ten years old when they traveled there by train. People were immediately suspicious of him and his family: *Who are these people coming from Sudan? Why do they have so much cash on them? What are they carrying in those bags? Where are they going? Are they Christian?*

Every car on the train was filled with greedy eyes looking at Seliman. He prayed for God's protection. He always kept one eye on his father. He ran fast when his father told him to go. He ran too fast; he lost a shoe running through the train station. Seliman entered Egypt with only one shoe.

Open proclamation of the Gospel was no easier in Egypt. They could not worship in a congregation. Instead, the family met together with a few others in their studio apartment. The doors were locked. The shades were closed. The tension was high. And the Gospel was proclaimed. Relying wholly on the Lord, Seliman craved God's Word. He had a fire in his bones that was kindled by prayer. He longed for the day when the Gospel could be openly shared with all people. Doors open. Windows open. And mouths open, proclaiming the Gospel.

His father worked a construction job in Egypt. He had the job until they found out he was a Christian. He did not shout it from the top of the building they were constructing; he simply prayed a blessing over his meal before he ate. Even that was too much. He was fired on the spot: "Turn in your hard hat and tools. Do not plan to return tomorrow. We will not have any Christians working for us."

Seliman and his family were not comfortable in Egypt. He was constantly running from discrimination. Fear followed him every-where. Persecution was a daily reality. Although violence was always close, God was always closer. Jesus had opened Seliman's heart to God. Only ten years old, Seliman trusted God for his eternal salvation and his daily protection. The Holy Spirit worked a spiritual maturity in him through daily hardship.

God provided an opportunity for Seliman and his family to move to America. February in Ohio is much colder than it is in Africa. In a little over a day, he went from sweltering ninety-degree heat to frosty sub-zero winds. Nevertheless, his family was warmed by the opportunity to worship without persecution. Proclaiming the Gospel was not punishable by death. Preaching the Good News of

Jesus would not get you fired. For the first time in his life, Seliman could pray with both eyes closed.

Some friends in America invited Seliman and his family to attend a church. The church was a Lutheran church. Many other refugees had found their way to this Lutheran congregation. This is what they had craved for so long. The Gospel of Jesus Christ was openly preached from the pulpit. There was no veil of good works covering the grace of Jesus. The Good News was not obscured by rationalism, political correctness, or fear. All people had open access to God's salvation in Christ Jesus.

Seliman has no desire to return to a land of persecution. He does not long for the days when his family had to worship with closed doors, closed windows, and hushed voices. He rejoices in the open access to the Gospel that he and his family now enjoy.

Nevertheless, there is something missing. Persecution kept his faith sharp. Threats of violence honed his prayers. Rumors of people suffering for the Gospel drove him closer to the Lord. Experiencing the open proclamation of the Gospel—even if it was in hushed worship behind closed doors—was precious. Hearing the Gospel whispered made it speak even louder in his heart.

In a land of persecution, Seliman was keenly aware that he had to rely wholly on God. In a land of plenty, he still has a fire for the Gospel of Jesus Christ. However, that fire feels a bit more temperate now. Zeal is oddly harder to maintain in a land where there is free and open access to the Gospel. He certainly does not want to go back to those days of struggle. He does, however, want to go back and experience the power of God at work in the midst of persecution.

To be certain, Seliman counts it a blessing to finally pray with both of his eyes closed. Still, as great as it is, praying with both eyes closed makes it that much easier to fall asleep.

Chapter 1
Discussion Questions

1. What is the appeal to open source?

2. How have you witnessed sin close you off to other people in your own life? Read Acts 28:17–31.

3. Jesus opens our relationship to God. How has Jesus opened your eyes, ears, heart, mind, and hands to God?

4. This chapter looks at Saul, Lydia, and Peter. Are there other individuals in Scripture who were opened up to God by Jesus Christ? Read Acts 8:9–25 for one example.

5. Luther fought to make worship and Scripture accessible to all people. What are some ways that these gifts are neglected today? How might we reverse this practice?

6. Since the Reformation, open access to the Gospel has been threatened. What are some ways that open access to the Gospel is threatened today? Are these new threats or ancient threats? Read 1 Peter 5:8–9.

7. The Good News of Jesus Christ is the only open source of salvation for all people. How does your congregation share the Gospel? How do you personally share the Gospel?

8. The vignette about Seliman discusses how open access to the Gospel is closed throughout many parts of the world. Can persecution benefit the proclamation of the Gospel? How do you see God at work through persecution? Read Daniel 3:8–30 and Acts 12:6–19.

9. How might you more openly live out your faith in Jesus Christ? What part of your daily life needs to be opened by the Holy Spirit?

Chapter 2

LUKEWARM

*Why do you call Me "Lord, Lord," and
not do what I tell you? (Luke 6:46)*

Meh. This word is often accompanied by a shrug of the shoulders
or a sleepy yawn. It is an expression of apathy or boredom. Our
culture loves to describe everything as meh. It is our new favorite
word. Everything from riding the bus to swimming with the sharks
fits into one beautifully blasé word: meh.

What did you do last night? Meh. Are you having a good day?
Meh. Do you want regular or diet? Meh. Have you tried the new
social media site that posts all your internal dialogue? Meh. What
do you think of the new smartphone that turns into a hoverboard?
Meh. Did you hear about that guy named Jesus who came back from
the dead? Meh.

Nothing impresses us anymore. Fascinating innovations may
catch our attention, but they will not get us off the couch. Global
tragedy will cause us to stop for thirty seconds between snapping
selfies. Six-figure student loans are cause for only moderate concern. Straight-faced and unimpressed, we hear about the cure for
horrific diseases.

Cat memes might be the only thing our culture truly finds exciting anymore.

Lukewarm is the wave of the future. We are lukewarm about new
technology, global strife, and advancements in medicine. There will

always be some new invention with a little more shine and sheen. Tomorrow's headlines will tell of a greater sadness and sorrow. There is no point in getting excited about today when there is something new coming tomorrow.

Christians have developed a meh mentality. Apathy and boredom have extinguished the fire in our bones for Jesus. Your neighbor does not know Christ and His forgiveness. Meh. Jesus, Buddha, and Steve Jobs were really good teachers. Meh. I call myself a Christian, but I do not know what is in the Bible. Meh. I call myself a Lutheran, but I think that just means my family came from Northern Europe. Meh. Jesus Christ died to forgive your sins. Meh.

JESUS ≠ MEH

Jesus delivered mankind from meh. Jesus nailed boredom and apathy to the cross. Lukewarm beliefs died in the tomb after the resurrection. Jesus turned tepid tax collectors and fearful fishermen into martyrs. Shy shepherds and misguided Magi became evangelists. Worried widows and confused centurions were led to confess the name of Jesus.

And even before He was born, Jesus was already saving the world from apathy. Mary met Jesus through the angel Gabriel. She was greatly troubled by his visit. She stopped texting her friends and listened intently to Gabriel. He told her that God had found favor with her and that she would give birth to a child. She was to give Him the name Jesus.

Gabriel proclaimed to her the mighty deeds He would accomplish: "He will be great and will be called the Son of the Most High. And the Lord God will give to Him the throne of His father David, and He will reign over the house of Jacob forever, and of His kingdom there will be no end" (Luke 1:32–33). A timid young teenager became a tenacious believer in Jesus. She spoke strong words depicting this child disrupting kingdoms and dismantling evil (Luke 1:46–56). Jesus lit a fire in Mary's bones.

John the Baptist met Jesus while still in utero. It happened one day when Elizabeth was pregnant with John and Mary was pregnant with Jesus. These women were relatives, and Mary had come to visit Elizabeth. A pregnant Mary walked into the house, "and when Elizabeth heard the greeting of Mary, the baby leaped in her womb" (Luke 1:41). Twiddling his thumbs in his mother's womb, John leapt for joy in the presence of Jesus. Mere proximity to Jesus moved John to worship. Two babies in the womb; one would prepare the way for the other. Jesus lit a fire in John's bones.

Shepherds met Jesus at His birth. They were counting sheep in the field—or perhaps in their dreams—one evening. Angels greeted them sweetly singing over the plains: "Fear not, for behold, I bring you good news of great joy that will be for all the people. For unto you is born this day in the city of David a Savior, who is Christ the Lord" (Luke 2:10–11). These shepherds found Jesus and worshiped Him. Exhilarated from meeting Jesus, they went and shared the Gospel: "And when they saw it, they made known the saying that had been told them concerning this child. And all who heard it wondered at what the shepherds told them" (Luke 2:17–18). Jesus lit a fire in the shepherds' bones.

Simeon and Anna met Jesus when He was just a few months old. Joseph and Mary took Him to the temple for a Jewish ritual. This event involved presenting Jesus at the temple and making a sacrifice on His behalf. While at the temple, Simeon approached Jesus and His parents. He looked at Jesus and declared that he had seen God's salvation (Luke 2:29–30). Then an elderly woman named Anna approached Jesus. She looked at Him, gave thanks to God, and began to sing the name of Jesus to everyone around her (Luke 2:38). Jesus lit a fire in Simeon's and Anna's bones.

All this was before Jesus' first birthday. You spent your first year of life filling diapers and sucking your thumb; Jesus spent His first year of life bringing a lukewarm world to a boil.

Throughout His ministry, Jesus disrupted kings and kingdoms, hearts and humanity. He drove demons away, lifted lowly lives, and filled empty bellies. He raised the dead from their graves and the blood pressure of the Pharisees. He restored heat to lifeless hearts. Jesus turns up the temperature on a lukewarm world.

Just ask Cleopas. He did not know his heart was frozen until Jesus turned up the heat. Cleopas was walking with a companion on the road to Emmaus. Jesus met them along the way, but they did not recognize Him. He walked with them and asked about their conversation. They gasped when this stranger was ignorant about the man named Jesus of Nazareth.

Cleopas went on to instruct Jesus about Jesus. He told Jesus all about the crucifixion and resurrection. He told Him about the startling news of the empty tomb. When he finished sharing the news, Jesus pointed out that it was necessary for the Christ to suffer before entering into glory. Jesus led them through Scripture to see all the prophecies about His death and resurrection. Jesus must have fascinated Cleopas with His teaching; he asked Jesus to join him for dinner. As they ate, Jesus took bread and blessed it. He then vanished from their sight. Upon realizing that he had just met Jesus, Cleopas asked, "Did not our hearts burn within us while He talked to us on the road, while He opened to us the Scriptures?" (Luke 24:32).

Cleopas did not know his heart was frozen until Jesus turned up the heat. Jesus' speaking restored heat to his chest. Jesus' presence returned warmth to his bones. Jesus' power over the grave ferried Cleopas from death to life. A lukewarm heart boiled in the presence of Jesus. Jesus ≠ Meh.

FOLLOWING JESUS

Follow Me. It is a simple invitation. It is hard to misunderstand the meaning of this invitation: stop what you are doing, rise, and follow Me. Jesus offered this invitation to His disciples (Matthew 4:19; 9:9; John 1:43). He extended this offer to a rich man and others (Matthew 19:21; Luke 9:57–62). And Jesus has invited all people to stop what they are doing, rise, and follow Him (Luke 9:23). Apathy ends **Jesus puts a nail through your lukewarm heart** with this invitation. Jesus awakens drowsy disciples and disrupts daily life. Jesus puts a nail through your lukewarm heart.

We see this happen in the lives of Christ's disciples. Peter stopped what he was doing to follow Jesus: "While walking by the Sea of Galilee, He saw two brothers, Simon (who is called Peter) and Andrew his brother, casting a net into the sea, for they were fishermen. And He said to them, 'Follow Me, and I will make you fishers of men.' Immediately they left their nets and followed Him" (Matthew 4:18–20). Jesus extended an invitation. And Peter followed.

With fish flopping around on the deck, Peter dropped the nets and followed Jesus. He tossed his comfortable life into the sea and embraced Jesus. He might as well have burned the boat, because he would not need it anymore; his life was now aimed at fishing for souls rather than sardines. This simple fisherman plunged into a life of adventure with Jesus. He witnessed the miracles of Jesus. He saw the empty tomb and Christ's resurrected body. Peter slept in jail, healed in the name of Jesus, met angels, and died a martyr's death. Jesus did pyrotechnics on the life of a lukewarm fisherman.

And Jesus had a similar impact on Martin Luther. He followed Jesus. He did not merely wave at Jesus from afar. Luther followed Jesus so closely that he was stepping on the backs of His sandals. He was not a lukewarm follower of Jesus. Martin Luther was a bold and brazen bombardier of the Gospel.

Luther was not always this way. Fear drove the early part of Luther's life. Medieval theologians emphasized Christ's righteous indignation. It was commonly taught that Jesus died on the cross for your sins and is really mad about it. This led people to approach Mary and other saints rather than Jesus. The mother of Jesus was far kinder than her Son. Luther, like other Christians in that day, was raised believing that Mary was the first line of support. Go to her instead of Him.

Theologians also taught that Christ's righteousness revealed the need for our own righteousness: Jesus is perfect and you should be too. Luther struggled with this concept. Comparing his righteousness to Christ's righteousness drove Luther to despair. Despite his best efforts to follow Jesus, he would never be good enough. Despite his many good works, he could always do more. Fear led Luther to pray harder to St. Anne. Terror made him punish himself with ever-sharper penalties. Dreading God's judgment made Luther gaze a little longer at the relics. Luther grew up following fear instead of following Jesus.

Fearing Jesus eventually turned into following Jesus. Nevertheless, before he could truly follow Jesus, Luther had to discover the true meaning of the Gospel. The Book of Romans was particularly troubling for Luther. He struggled to understand what Scripture meant by "Christ's righteousness." He described the basis of his struggle: "All the while I was aglow with the desire to understand Paul in his Letter to the Romans. But . . . the one expression in chapter one (v. 17) concerning the 'righteousness of God' blocked the way for me."[6]

Burning desire propelled Luther to study God's Word. His teachers trained him to understand the righteousness of God to mean the standard by which God would judge sinners. God had set the

---

6   *WLS* § 3905.

standard pretty high in Jesus. Luther could not overcome the fear that perfect righteousness was impossible for sinners:

> For I hated the expression "righteousness of God," since I had been instructed by the usage and custom of all teachers to understand it according to scholastic philosophy as the "formal or active righteousness" in which God proves Himself righteous by punishing sinners and the unjust.[7]

The righteousness of God is a gift freely given through faith in Christ Jesus

Anger and fear subsided when Luther finally understood that Christ's perfect righteousness was a gift of faith. He came to realize that the righteousness of God is not an impossibly perfect standard believers had to obtain. Instead, the righteousness of God is a gift freely given through faith in Christ Jesus:

> Finally, after days and nights of wrestling with the difficulty, God had mercy on me, and then I was able to note the connection of the words "the righteousness of God is revealed in the Gospel" and "the just shall live by faith." Then I began to understand that the "righteousness of God" is that through which the righteous lives by the gift (*dono*) of God, that is, through faith.[8]

Faith delivers Christ's righteousness. The Holy Spirit gives us faith to receive Christ Jesus. His perfect life and resurrection become our perfect life and resurrection. Faith gives sins to Jesus and receives perfect holiness in return. Luther realized that God's righteousness

---

7   *WLS* § 3905.

8   *WLS* § 3905.

was the joyous gift of faith. Faith produces devotion, not dread. Following Jesus comes through faith, not fear. Luther called this gift of faith passive righteousness. Our standing before God is not earned or merited by any human effort. Rather, our standing before God (*coram deo*) depends on Christ's righteousness gifted to us through the Holy Spirit. We do nothing to deserve it. It is purely by the grace of God.

Luther, however, saw another type of righteousness taught in Scripture. He called this active righteousness. It is our standing before fellow humans (*coram mundo*). Unlike passive righteousness, our standing before one another depends on our own efforts and work. We earn trust from others by keeping our word. We gain favor with our neighbors through hard work. We have an obligation to meet our earthly responsibilities. Unlike God's grace freely given in Jesus, our earthly righteousness must be earned.

Distinguishing these different kinds of righteousness shaped much of Luther's theology. It allowed him to separate God's work from human work. He could proclaim that human work does nothing to earn God's favor. He could also rail against spiritual apathy within the active life of faith.

CHALLENGE APATHY

Following Jesus does not lead *to* salvation. Following Jesus comes *from* salvation. New life in the Spirit calls us to follow Jesus. He restores our true nature and empowers us to follow Him. Discovering this Gospel truth changed Luther. He realized that fear and self-preservation do not motivate the Christian life. Faith in Christ propels us to new life in Him: "I have been crucified with Christ. It is no longer I who live, but Christ who lives in me. And the life I now live in the flesh I live by faith in the Son of God, who loved me and gave Himself for me" (Galatians 2:20).

Apathy is incompatible with being Lutheran. Martin Luther openly challenged apathetic believers. He pushed people on their Bible reading. He encouraged serious practices of prayer and worship. He called on God's people to love their neighbors and be servants to all. Lukewarm faith is without a home in Lutheran theology. Bible reading is an example of Luther's passionate practices. He made a habit of reading the entire Bible twice a year. He did not pick up the Bible five minutes before he fell asleep at night. He refused to simply read a few verses on occasion when the mood was right. Luther was a lifelong student of God's Word. He knew the Bible well. He had translated every word of it from Hebrew and Greek into German. And even after reading it multiple times, Luther read the Bible again. And again. And again.

Luther challenged an apathetic practice of reading Scripture. He wrote about how many Christians neglect the Bible:

> It is certainly one of the greatest calamities on earth that Holy Scripture is so lightly regarded. . . . All other matters, arts, and books one uses and practices day and night, and there is no end to working and laboring. Holy Scripture alone lies there as if one had no need of it. Moreover, those who honor it enough to read it occasionally quickly know it all; nor has any art or any book ever appeared on earth that everybody has mastered so soon as Holy Scripture. And yet Scripture certainly does not contain words that are merely to be read (*Leseworte*), as they think, but it is full of words that are to be lived (*Lebeworte*) that are put down there, not to speculate and philosophize about (*hoch zu dichten*) but to turn into life and action.[9]

---

9   *WLS* § 256.

Bible reading is only one of many practices Luther championed. He believed that worship is indispensable to the Christ follower. Christ comes to His people through Word and Sacrament. Worship is where Jesus meets His people. Luther emphasized that Christ is really present in worship. God is not present on

Christ comes to His people through Word and Sacrament

the golf course in the same way that He is present in, with, and under the bread and wine of Holy Communion. A liver quiver, racing heart, or sense of peace are not divinely appointed indicators of God's presence. Rather, God tells His people where He is located. God speaks through Scripture. God visits His people through the preaching of His Word, the forgiveness of sins, and the Sacraments.

Lukewarm worship was impossible for Luther. He had a keen awareness of God's presence in worship. Luther also had a keen sense of Satan's hatred for Christian worship. He encouraged believers in the Large Catechism by writing, "If you could see how many knives, darts, and arrows are every moment aimed at you [Ephesians 6:16], you would be glad to come to the Sacrament as often as possible."[10] Lukewarm liturgy, calm Collects, and a sedate Sanctus vanish when you realize Satan has a knife to your throat.

Prayer was another bulwark for Luther. He constantly complained of demonic oppression. While he translated the Bible into German, Luther spent sleepless nights battling Satan's attacks. Legend has it that Luther threw an inkwell at the devil. Historians question the veracity of this story and suspect it may not have happened. Either way, Luther experienced many periods of spiritual attack (*Anfechtung*). He was deeply serious about the power of prayer over Satan:

---

10   Large Catechism, Part V, paragraph 82.

We need to know this: all our shelter and protection rest in prayer alone. For we are far too weak to deal with the devil and all his power and followers who set themselves against us. They might easily crush us under their feet. Therefore, we must consider and take up those weapons with which Christians must be armed in order to stand against the devil.[11]

God commands prayer. Luther connected the Second Commandment to prayer: God commands His people to call upon Him in every need. Prayer is actively calling on God in times of need. Sometimes our need is God's forgiveness or healing. Other times, our need is to offer God praise or thanksgiving. Luther also recognized God's promise in prayer. Believers can pray with full confidence that God hears prayer. Not just eloquent prayers. Not just well-worded pastor prayers. God hears the prayers of all His people. Placid prayers vanish when you realize the God of the universe is listening.

> **Prayer is actively calling on God in times of need**

Lukewarm love was another practice dismantled by Luther. Prior to Luther's reforms, the Church taught that caring for others was a good work meriting forgiveness of sins. Give some money to a beggar, and you would reduce your time in purgatory. Help an old lady cross the street, and God would look the other way on those extra pints you had at the pub. This obviously went against the clear teaching of Scripture. Furthermore, it turned neighborly love into selfishness. A neighbor in need was an opportunity to earn God's favor through good works. Luther's discovery of the Gospel dismantled this practice; rather than good works, it was God's grace in Jesus Christ that delivered the forgiveness of sins.

---

11   Large Catechism, Part III, paragraph 30.

Yet neighborly love does not end as a result of the Gospel. It thrives. Heaven has more than enough good works in Christ Jesus. Our neighborhoods, on the other hand, suffer from a shortage of good works. Luther's understanding of active righteousness allowed him to confront lukewarm Christians. God made us to love and serve others. We have hands and feet, eyes and ears, mind and heart to serve the people around us. Made new and given our true nature in Christ Jesus, we actively work for one another. Serving others is not a path to our salvation. Loving your neighbor is simply doing that for which you were created.

LUTHERAN ≠ MEH

Being Lutheran opposes meh. We oppose meh in both thought and action.

We are not lukewarm about our neighbors. Our actions show that we are serious about putting our hands and feet, eyes and ears, mind and heart in service to the people around us. Luther explained our desire to serve others:

> Therefore serving and helping others is a specifically Christian way of life. Although a man occupies a higher and greater position than others, his life and activities should nonetheless be directed to the one goal of being useful to others thereby. The higher the position is, the more it should be directed to the profit and benefit of others.[12]

And Lutherans are not lukewarm in their beliefs. Others may prefer a lukewarm confession. Many denominations have cooled their confession of faith into a gelatinous goop: "We believe whatever

---

12   *WLS* § 4097.

makes you happy . . . " Not Lutherans. The core of Lutheranism radiates bold proclamation. We do not cool our confession to appease others. We do not stick our beliefs in the fridge so that sensitive palates are not burned. Lutherans speak their beliefs. And then they defend their beliefs. This has been done by Lutherans throughout history:

> **Lutherans speak their beliefs. And then they defend their beliefs.**

The Reformation: Luther was told that if he recanted, then it would all be over. Church officials gave this plea bargain to Luther at the Diet of Worms in 1521. This was a public request for Luther to cool his beliefs to a more palatable temperature. The Holy Roman Empire demanded that he renounce his beliefs and writings. They put all of his writings on a table and asked Luther to essentially say "meh." He refused. Instead, Luther spoke a bold confession of his beliefs:

> Unless I am convinced by the testimony of the Scriptures or by clear reason (for I do not trust either in the pope or in councils alone, since it is well known that they have often erred and contradicted themselves), I am bound by the Scriptures I have quoted and my conscience is captive to the Word of God. I cannot and I will not retract anything, since it is neither safe nor right to go against conscience.

> I cannot do otherwise, here I stand, may God help me, Amen.[13]

Dull left the room when he spoke those words. Boring was over. Emperor Charles V issued the Edict of Worms declaring that Luther was a heretic. Bounty hunters pursued him as a wanted man. The weight of the empire tried to squash Lutheran theology.

---

13   LW 32:112–13.

Lutheranism persisted. A professor at the University of Wittenberg named Philip Melanchthon worked with Luther to carefully craft the Augsburg Confession. This confession of faith was publicly presented in 1530. It is a detailed proclamation of Lutheran theology. With the core Lutheran beliefs clearly articulated in the Augsburg Confession, this was not a lukewarm statement of faith. When the empire told them to be quiet, Lutherans loudly spoke the Gospel. When Emperor Charles V requested that a lukewarm faith return to his land, Lutherans challenged apathy.

Defending our beliefs is absolutely central to Lutherans. Being Lutheran is following Jesus, resisting apathy, and challenging a lukewarm culture. This began in 1517 in Germany. And this has continued with every subsequent generation of Lutherans.

The Enlightenment: Deconstructing Christian beliefs is a favorite pastime of many modern scholars and philosophers. This attempt to deconstruct Christian beliefs swelled in the eighteenth century. This period of history was an age of cultural and intellectual upheaval in Europe and America. Philosophers and revolutionaries called this the Age of Enlightenment. Their core belief was that reason is the greatest good for humanity.

The French Revolution took this to an extreme. Revolutionaries during that time literally enshrined reason in the Cult of Reason (*Culte de la Raison*) by turning the cathedral of Notre Dame in Paris into a Temple of Reason. Atheistic zeal led people to physically dismantle the altar and replace it with a memorial to Liberty. Reason dismantled Scripture as an impossible myth. The miracles of Jesus were deemed religious constructions. Influenced by Enlightenment thinking, Thomas Jefferson took a pair of scissors to the Bible and cut out every supernatural event in the life of Jesus. Jefferson called it the *Life and Morals of Jesus of Nazareth* (1819).

While the Age of Enlightenment was cutting the Bible into unrecognizable pieces, Lutherans were busy keeping it together. A movement known as Lutheran Orthodoxy began near the end of the sixteenth century and persisted into the Age of Enlightenment. A Lutheran theologian named Johann Gerhard (1582–1637) helped his fellow Lutherans defend the truth of Scripture with a book entitled *Loci Theologici* (Topics of Theology). This extensive work helped many generations of Lutherans by clearly defending orthodox beliefs on the basis of Scripture. Another Lutheran theologian named David Hollatz (1648–1713) helped pastors and laypeople confront the mounting pressure to reject orthodox Lutheranism in exchange for a watered-down form of moralistic piety.

Modernity: The nineteenth century carried on the work of deconstructing Christianity. This was the age of Classical Modernity. Freeing the world from the tyranny of Christianity became the goal of many different thinkers. Charles Darwin published his highly influential book *On the Origin of Species* (1859). This book claimed that the diversity of species is the result of natural selection. Survival of the fittest accounts for the difference between whales, walruses, and wasps. Friedrich Nietzsche was also an influential thinker during this period in history. Nietzsche was a German philosopher remembered for two things: his moustache and nihilism. The philosophical concept of nihilism claims that life is without objective meaning, purpose, or value. Nihilism rejects God and absolute truth. It claims that right and wrong are simply human constructs. Nietzsche boldly proclaimed, "God is dead."

During this period in history, Lutherans did what they have always done: they boldly proclaimed that God is not dead. Lutheran theologians such as Adolf Hoenecke (1835–1908), George Stoeckhardt (1842–1913), Francis Pieper (1852–1931), and August Pieper (1867–1947) fiercely resisted modernity's claims. They pushed against the widespread deconstruction of Christianity through evolution, nihilism, and atheism. These Lutherans rolled up their sleeves, opened up their Bibles, and spoke the bold truth of the Gospel.

Today: Being Lutheran is actively confronting new challenges. We do not roll over and play dead when people say God is dead. We take a stand. We lean in and defend our faith. We rely on the strength of the Holy Spirit to help us speak. We follow in the path of previous Lutherans and clearly confess our hope in Christ Jesus.

We resist turning Jesus into nothing more than a really good teacher. Jesus is not dead like Joseph Smith, Buddha, or Muhammad. Jesus is God in human flesh raised from the dead. Scared disciples hiding in an upper room had their hearts boil with excitement when they met the resurrected Jesus. Countless Christians have since died for their faith in Jesus. And from the very beginning, Lutherans have been willing to die rather than renounce Jesus.

Jesus is God in human flesh raised from the dead

We will not stand for the Bible to be turned into a lukewarm book of fairy tales. Jesus treated Scripture as the Word of God. Jesus did not depict Adam and Eve as though they rode in on unicorns. Jesus spoke of Adam and Eve as real, historical people (Mark 10:6–7). Jesus confirmed that Jonah was actually swallowed by a giant fish (Matthew 12:39–41). Jesus opened the Scriptures and used the Word of God as proof of God's work (Luke 24:27). Lutherans do not waver on Scripture. We believe it is the inerrant Word of God.

Talk is cheap. Actions are costly. We do more than just say that Jesus is Lord. We do not quietly believe that Scripture is the Word of God. Lutherans act on their convictions. We learn about Jesus. We study the Bible. We learn the reasons why Jesus is a historically verifiable person. We examine the arguments for His existence and resurrection. We know the history of how the biblical canon came together. We have at least a basic understanding of how translators turn ancient Hebrew and Greek into modern languages. We can explain how fragments of texts are put together to form a complete biblical text.

Lutherans refuse to sit comfortably while a neighbor is in need. And Lutherans refuse to sit comfortably while atheists deconstruct Christianity. We will not be blasé about the Bible. We will not be numb to the needs of our neighbor. Luther acted when he saw the Christian faith dismantled by greed and empty superstition. Lutherans acted when they saw the Christian faith gutted by secularist thinking. What are you doing to defend your faith? Are you lukewarm? Do you have a meh mind-set about Jesus?

CONCLUSION

Jesus has called you to follow Him. Calling yourself a Christian means that you have been called by Jesus to live out your faith.

Let me ask you a gut-check question: how closely are you following Jesus? Perhaps you are so far away that you have to squint to see Him. Would a hybrid car run out of gas before you could catch up to Jesus? Do you wave at Jesus rather than actually follow Him? Or do you follow Jesus so closely that you are stepping on the heels of His sandals?

The Lutheran theologian Dietrich Bonhoeffer claimed that anyone not stepping on the heels of Jesus was not following Him closely enough. Bonhoeffer was critical of how many Lutherans in his day followed Jesus. He called his fellow Lutherans to task for imperfectly following Jesus.

Bonhoeffer, particularly in his book *The Cost of Discipleship*, wrote about how Lutherans had begun to misunderstand grace. He called it cheap grace. He thought that his own denomination had taken the grace of Jesus Christ as an invitation to be lukewarm. Cheap grace says that since salvation does not depend on obedience to Jesus, then there is no need to worry about being obedient at all. Cheap grace says that I can follow Jesus from ten miles away and still have forgiveness. This completely misunderstands what it means to follow Jesus.

Bonhoeffer went as far as to claim that Lutherans had become like birds gathered around the carcass of cheap grace. He argued that cheap grace was poisonous and had the power to kill the life of following Christ. Bonhoeffer described his fellow Lutherans as fearful that following Jesus was somehow a legalistic endeavor. Rather than accepting this clearly biblical invitation from Jesus, Lutherans were on the verge of abandoning discipleship and ceasing to follow Jesus.

Ouch. These are cutting words.

Thankfully, Bonhoeffer clarified what it means to follow Jesus. He did not leave Lutherans wallowing in the despair of cheap grace. Instead, he argued that when Christ calls a person to follow Him, He bids that person to come and die. The death that comes with following Jesus might be like that of the disciples, who had to leave home and work to follow Him. Following Jesus might lead to a death like Luther's when he had to leave the monastery and go out into the world. Following Jesus may even lead to physical death through martyrdom. Either way, following Jesus means being called by God to die to our old self and being made alive in Christ.

Jesus invites you to come and die

Jesus invites you to come and die. Jesus calls you to die to yourself and be alive in Him. Faith replaces your old heart with the heart of Jesus. You have new life in Christ. Lukewarm is over in Jesus. His heart thumps with eternal life. His life burns to do the Father's will. His actions burst with love for neighbors.

And His heart is your heart. His life is your life. His actions are your actions. Jesus never uses the word *meh*. And, in Christ Jesus, neither do you.

Vignette: Dietrich

Meh was not a word in Dietrich Bonhoeffer's vocabulary. Nothing about his life or his faith can be described as meh. Bonhoeffer was not a lukewarm kind of guy.

Born in 1906, Dietrich Bonhoeffer was raised in a family that consistently challenged apathy. The Bonhoeffer family was particularly opposed to intellectual apathy. His father was among the most brilliant psychiatrists in Germany. His mother was trained as a teacher and homeschooled all the children. One of his brothers worked with Albert Einstein to split the atom. Another brother was a prominent lawyer in Germany. The entire family was brilliant.

Knowledge was a burning passion in the Bonhoeffer household. The family read literature together, memorized poetry, and attended operas. Saturday evenings in the Bonhoeffer household were spent with the family performing musical instruments together. Dietrich could play multiple instruments before he was a teenager.

Despite the intellectual fervor of the Bonhoeffer family, their Christian faith tended toward lukewarm. The family worshiped infrequently in the German Lutheran Church. Bonhoeffer's father was likely agnostic in his faith. His mother, on the other hand, was a bit more confident in her faith. She raised the children on Bible stories and hymns.

At age 13, Dietrich decided that he would study theology. His father had reservations about his son's career choice. His siblings used his theological studies to heckle him. Nevertheless, these barriers did not impede Dietrich's faith. He enrolled in theological studies at Tübingen University and later Berlin University. While other kids were busy studying parlor tricks, Bonhoeffer became a Doctor of Philosophy, earning his PhD when he was only twenty-one years old.

Theological education in Germany during that time placed almost a singular emphasis on intellectual prowess. Aspiring pastors had to be smart, highly trained, and steeped in philosophy. Spiritual disciplines such as prayer and Bible reading were dismissed as unintellectual. Being a pastor meant being a passionate intellectual and a lukewarm Christ follower.

Although he was trained in this culture of lukewarm Christianity, Bonhoeffer refused to be a tepid follower of Jesus. Following his studies at Berlin University, he spent a period of nine months in New York City studying at Union Theological Seminary. While living in New York, Bonhoeffer attended Abyssinian Baptist Church and experienced something rarely seen in Germany during that time: people actually following Jesus.

Prayer. Worship. Actions. Service. Love. Witnessing a Christian community putting faith in action had a profound impact on Bonhoeffer. The experience in New York City set Bonhoeffer on a lifelong vendetta against lukewarm faith. In the summer of 1931, he returned to teach theology at Berlin University. Unlike the other faculty members in the theology department, Bonhoeffer referred to the Bible as the Word of God. He taught his students how to pray. He encouraged them in their love for Jesus.

While Bonhoeffer taught about the power of prayer, the Nazi party was busy growing in political power. The German Evangelical (Lutheran) Church (*Reichskirche*) endorsed the Nazis in 1933. A resistance movement, known as the Confessing Church (*Bekennende Kirche*), formed as a way to oppose the Nazis. The Confessing Church asked Bonhoeffer to be the director of a newly formed seminary in Finkenwalde. Bonhoeffer accepted the position and became *Herr Direktor* of the seminary.

Under Bonhoeffer's leadership, students at the seminary were immersed in Scripture. Bible reading was central to pastoral formation in Finkenwalde. Seminarians had to read large sections of Scripture as part of their core curriculum. The entire seminary community also engaged in a weekly reflection on a smaller portion of Scripture.

Another spiritual discipline emphasized by Bonhoeffer was prayer. He ensured that students were trained in Luther's Small Catechism on the Lord's Prayer. They studied Jesus in class. And they encountered Jesus outside of class in prayer and Bible reading. The Gestapo did not approve. Finkenwalde was shut down because it was an illegal seminary opposed to the Third Reich. Nazi pressure increased against the Confessing Church and Bonhoeffer. A famous American theologian named Reinhold Niebuhr procured a teaching position for Bonhoeffer at Union Theological Seminary. War was looming in Germany. Bonhoeffer decided to leave Nazi Germany and escape to America in 1939. He left the Nazis to inflect unthinkable violence on hundreds of thousands of people. He boarded a ship and went to New York City.

He was in America for only twenty-six days.

He knew he had made a mistake. He realized that he had run from persecution. Bonhoeffer quickly determined that he had to go back to Germany and resist the Nazi movement. He knew that this likely meant death. Nevertheless, his faith compelled him to return. Bonhoeffer felt God was leading him back to Germany.

War was raging throughout Europe. Bonhoeffer used family ties to secure a position with a German military intelligence group known as Abwehr. The Abwehr was at the center of a conspiracy movement against Hitler. As an Abwehr agent, Bonhoeffer was authorized to travel to neutral countries such as Sweden and Switzerland. He used these occasions to share information about Hitler with opposition forces. Bonhoeffer went from confession to conspiracy. He went from theology professor to double agent resisting the Nazis.

Smuggling information was only the beginning for Bonhoeffer. He worked with others to smuggle a group of Jews out of Germany. This illegal activity was discovered, and Bonhoeffer was arrested. He was taken to Tegel military prison in Berlin. He spent fifteen months in Tegel writing, praying, and waiting for the Allies to come save him.

They never came.

An assassination attempt, known as Operation Valkyrie, failed to kill Hitler. This resulted in the torture and death of numerous conspirators. Bonhoeffer was among the conspirators killed for resisting Hitler; he was hanged on April 9, 1945.

Soldiers liberated the camp just fourteen days later. However, it would not have mattered if they had come fourteen days sooner. Even if Bonhoeffer had been saved, his faith would have still burned with a willingness to die for Jesus.

Chapter 2
Discussion Questions

1. Nothing impresses us anymore. Agree or disagree?

2. Jesus challenged apathy long before His birth. Where do you see the promise of Jesus challenging apathy in the Old Testament? What were the prophets trying to do through their prophetic words? Read Isaiah 53.

3. Read Luke 9:23 and verses 57–62. What is the difference between these two invitations from Jesus? Why does it matter that one invitation is given to the crowd while the other is given to a specific person?

4. Read Romans 3:21–26. According to these verses, who performs the work of salvation? What comfort comes from knowing that God alone is the source of salvation?

5. Passive righteousness deals with our standing before God. Active righteousness deals with our standing before others. Why is it so important to rightly distinguish these two kinds of righteousness?

6. Luther read the Bible cover-to-cover twice a year. Why would someone so familiar with the Bible reread it each year? What is your practice of daily Bible reading?

7. Read Acts 17:10-12. Like the believers in Berea, Lutherans carefully examine the Scriptures. What more do you need to learn in order to better defend your faith in Jesus Christ?

8. Jesus invites you to die to yourself and be made alive in Him. What part of you has died as a result of following Jesus? What part of you has new life as a result of following Jesus? Read Romans 6:4.

9. Dietrich Bonhoeffer chose to die living out his faith rather than to live with a lukewarm faith. What role did prayer and Bible reading play in his daily life? How might these spiritual disciplines have compelled him to return to Germany and defend innocent lives?

Chapter 3

CONFUSED

*For God is not a God of confusion but
of peace. (1 Corinthians 14:33)*

Bloodletting was basic medicine for generations. Barbers, surgeons, and doctors routinely treated ailments by opening a patient's vein and releasing some liters of blood. They believed that bleeding a patient cured a patient. Do you have headaches, heartburn, or hematoma? Try bloodletting. Are you chronically depressed and lethargic? Try bloodletting. Do you laugh at bad jokes? Try bloodletting.

The reason for bloodletting was based on the concept of humors. Beginning with Hippocrates, doctors theorized that the human body consisted of four basic humors: blood, yellow bile, black bile, and phlegm. Ailments occur when the body's humors are unbalanced. If your spleen produces an excess of black bile, then you will be melancholy. If your liver floods your body with yellow bile, then you will be easily angered. Doctors thought that bloodletting put the body's humors back in balance.

They were wrong. Dead wrong.

There is nothing humorous about humoral medicine. Historians agree that bloodletting hastened the death of George Washington. America's first president had a throat infection. His doctor treated his infection by removing nearly four liters of blood. This left Washington anemic and weak. His symptoms worsened until he eventually died.

Modern medicine has since determined the cause of sicknesses. Germ theory replaced humoral medicine. Medication made blood-letting obsolete. However, this was not the only mistake of the past. History is littered with other tattered theories, erroneous experiments, and false facts: Miasma theory said that bad air spread the bubonic plague. Anatomical diagrams showed the liver circulating blood through the body. Cartographers flattened the globe. Astronomers put the earth in the center of the universe. Chemists believed atoms were the smallest of all particles. Newtonian physics claimed that light travels only in waves. Cigarettes were once doctor recommended. I could go on, if you'd like . . .

History is teeming with intellectual errors. These past mistakes make us suspicious of the present. We have been wrong before, and we are fearful that we will be wrong again. The inaccurate maps of the past make us question the accuracy of our maps today. A history of bad medicine leaves us wondering about the future of good medicine. Past errors have us doubting our present scientific knowledge. Encyclopedias once taught that certain races were genetically inferior to others. This was slavery. One man persuaded a nation that eugenics was a good idea. This was the Holocaust. We are convinced that we should not be convinced of anything. We are certain of our uncertainty. We are confidently unconfident.

Welcome to postmodernity. The blood has been let from our brains. Our trust in truth is anemic. We have opened the veins of certainty and poured everything out. Deconstructed truths leave us intellectually weak and unable to speak with conviction. Fear of error causes us to speak only in postmodern gibberish. Walk into any university classroom and you will experience this firsthand. Students do not learn in class; they engage in constructivist meaning making. There is no such thing as history; there are just intertextual multivocalities of the past. There is no right interpretation of Romeo and Juliet; there are simply differing and equally valid readings. Truth is out. Relativism is king.

TEACHING WITH AUTHORITY

Contrary to relativism, Jesus taught with authority. Every other rabbi in town just offered opinions. Rabbinical teaching during the time of Jesus was nothing more than hesitation, vacillation, and speculation. Walk into any first-century synagogue and you would experience this firsthand. Religious teachers would perpetually noodle around an idea. Every statement would begin with a caveat: "It has been said by others . . . " "My opinion on the Sabbath is . . . " "Some say that the Messiah will . . . "

Not Jesus. He was unlike any other teacher the Jewish people had known. He spoke with the authority of God. Crowds of people noticed that Jesus was unlike their other religious teachers: "And when Jesus finished these sayings, the crowds were astonished at His teaching, for He was teaching them as one who had authority, and not as their scribes" (Matthew 7:28–29). "And they were astonished at His teaching, for His word possessed authority" (Luke 4:32). "They were all amazed, so that they questioned among themselves, saying, 'What is this? A new teaching with authority! He commands even the unclean spirits, and they obey Him'" (Mark 1:27).

The authority of Jesus was foreign not only to the Jewish people. The entire civilized world was unaccustomed to authoritative religious teaching. The Roman Empire was an intellectually confused place. Rome began expanding in the sixth century BC. It continued to expand power and territory for the next several hundred years. New territories coming under Roman control were given a significant amount of independence. Greek and Latin were officially sanctioned languages, while various local languages were used by large parts of the population.

Different religions and ideologies also coexisted within the Roman Empire. Deities from conquered territories were absorbed into Roman religious beliefs. This led to thousands of different gods, shrines, and practices. Philosophical schools competed for students and followers. Rome was a patchwork of different languages, beliefs, and opinions.

Authoritative teaching came to this confused culture. Christ taught with certainty. He did not shirk away from teaching with authority. He did not hide behind plural opinions and speculations. Instead, Jesus taught by saying, "You have heard that it was said . . . but I say to you" (Matthew 5). He clarified the mistakes of the past. He straightened the crooked teaching of others. He did not cite His sources because He was the source of all truth. Rabbinical teaching was weak and anemic. Roman teaching was waffled and confused. Jesus' teaching was clear, strong, and authoritative.

Jesus taught with authority. And Jesus spoke with authority. His words evicted demons (Matthew 8:32). His words healed broken legs (John 5:8–9). His words delivered forgiveness of sins (Luke 7:48). His words calmed storms (Luke 8:24). Jesus spoke with the same authority that spoke creation into being. Word made flesh, Jesus spoke truth in the beginning. His Word made heaven and earth. And Jesus carried that same authoritative speaking into broken lives.

And then Jesus did something incredible. He gave that authority to others. Jesus commissioned the twelve disciples with His authority: "And He called the twelve together and gave them power and authority over all demons and to cure diseases, and He sent them out to proclaim the kingdom of God and to heal" (Luke 9:1–2).

Then He did it again by commissioning seventy-two others with His authority and sending them out into surrounding cities (Luke 10:1–12). And then He did it again by sending His disciples to the ends of the earth armed with His authority (Matthew 28:16–20). He commissioned them to go down from the mountain with His authority to baptize and teach all people. All authority in heaven and on earth was given to Jesus. And He sent His disciples out with authority to clarify confused thinking.

CONFUSION AND CONFESSION

First-century rabbis were not the only confused thinkers. Confusion has been a perennial problem for humanity. Certainly all people have struggled to overcome confused thinking. Some, however, struggle more than others . . .

Teenage boys often struggle with confusion. Even highly intelligent young men can be confused by very basic human tasks: Orchestrating a matching outfit can confuse the pubescent brain. Ironing wrinkled clothing is like driving a lunar rover across the surface of the moon. Cooking a can of soup requires a support team and great amounts of concentration. Conversing with cute girls is nearly impossible.

Mischief is different. Teenage boys are seldom confused about mischief. An empty paper bag can provide countless opportunities for troublemaking. While sitting still can be difficult, building a semi-automatic potato launcher out of plastic pipe and a piezo igniter is simple. It is a gift.

Modern teenage boys are not the only ones adept at mischief. Human history is strewn with ancient spitballs and "Kick Me" signs. One of the many ancient troublemakers was Augustine of Hippo (AD 354–430). He did not earn his title of St. Augustine during his teenage years. Although Augustine became one of the greatest writers and theologians in Christendom, he spent his adolescence in constant confusion.

Nevertheless, like most teenage boys, Augustine was not confused about troublemaking. Augustine had numerous stories of mischief in North Africa. One evening of knavery involved pears and pigs:

A pear tree there was near our vineyard, laden with fruit, tempting neither for colour nor taste. To shake and rob this, some lewd young fellows of us went, late one night (having according to our pestilent custom prolonged our sports in the streets till then), and took huge loads, not for our eating, but to fling to the very hogs, having only tasted them.[14]

Did he fling the pears *to* the pigs or *at* the pigs? The difference is one minor preposition. (My guess is that they threw the pears *at* the pigs but remembered it as throwing pears *to* the pigs. Teenage boys also have a penchant for selective memory.)

Regardless, Augustine admitted that his actions confused right and wrong. Wasting pears on pigs was only the beginning of Augustine's adolescent confusion. He fabricated stories about hooking up with the young women of Carthage so that his peers would respect him. He was confused about what he wanted from God. He prayed, "Give me chastity and continency, only not yet."[15] He dabbled in different religions and even had a mistress.

Augustine was an intelligent young man. He attended the best schools and studied under the best teachers of rhetoric. Nevertheless, Augustine was spiritually confused. He was raised Christian but did not understand his faith. His mother often prayed for him to have spiritual and intellectual clarity, yet he was profoundly confused.

He eventually joined the Manichaeans, a cult founded in Persia around the middle of the third century. Manichaeism was a confusing blend of various religions. Its basic teaching was a dualistic struggle between good and evil. Mani, the founder of the religion, claimed that evil existed because God lacked the power needed to overcome evil. Good and bad coexisted in a cosmic stalemate.

---

14   Augustine, *Confessions* 2.4.
15   Augustine, *Confessions* 8.7.

Augustine slopped up what Mani was serving. He filled his plate from a smorgasbord of confused teachings. He drank deeply of their spirits and called himself a Manichaean. He sat at their feet as they deconstructed Scripture. The end result was constant confusion for Augustine. Although he believed much of Mani's teachings, Augustine had reservations. Reflecting back on his time of confusion, Augustine wrote: "Furthermore, what the Manichees had criticized in Thy Scriptures, I thought could not be defended; yet at times verily I had a wish to confer upon these several points with some one very well skilled in those books."[16]

God granted Augustine's wish. He studied under a bishop in Milan named Ambrose. Captivated by Christian theology, Augustine regularly met with Ambrose to discuss his theological concerns. Ambrose captivated Augustine with his vast knowledge of Scripture. Truth soon replaced his confusion. During this period of clarity, the Holy Spirit moved Augustine to faith so that all the shadows of doubt were dispelled. The authoritative teaching of Jesus Christ came to this confused young man. His confusion was replaced with truth.

Freed from confusion, Augustine became a Christ follower. He stopped throwing pears at pigs. He stopped chasing after false teachers. He believed in Jesus with certainty and clarity. And he wrote a book called *Confessions*. As the title suggests, this book contained the confessions of a formerly confused young man. He confessed his mischief as a teenager stealing fruit from a vineyard. He confessed to having a mistress. He confessed to all of his false beliefs. He confessed his sins for all to read.

Yet, confessing sins was only a minor point of Augustine's book. Confessing truth was Augustine's primary aim. He wanted to clearly articulate God's truth for all to know. He wanted to help lift others

---

16 Augustine, *Confessions* 5.11.

from their confused thinking. He confessed that salvation comes through Jesus Christ. He confessed God's goodness and rule over evil. He confessed right and wrong, truth and falsehood. Freed by Jesus from his confusion, Augustine confessed belief in God with clarity.

Like He did for Augustine, moved by the Holy Spirit to faith, Jesus also frees you from a life of constant confusion. Jesus replaces your confusion with truth. Jesus puts you right side up in an upside-down world. And, because of Jesus, you now speak with authority. You are able to make a clear confession of your beliefs. You live with certainty. You think with clarity. This is not of your own doing. It is the gift of Jesus Christ. God's people do not live with anemic knowledge.

Jesus replaces your confusion with truth

You do not suffer from temporary truths, falsifiable facts, and ignorant illusions. You live by God's eternal truth. Jesus frees you from confusion.

OPPOSING CONFUSION

Being Lutheran is to oppose confusion. Being Lutheran is to know what you believe and why you believe it. Know where a teaching, doctrine, or passage is in Scripture. Know how to explain it to others. Know how to defend your faith. Know what atheists believe. Spiritual confusion is unacceptable now that truth has come through Jesus (John 1:17).

Lutherans formed as a reaction against theological ignorance. Through the Middle Ages and into the Renaissance, the Church developed a hierarchical structure. Average laypeople were on the bottom tier of believers. They had very limited knowledge of the Christian faith. This was not their fault; it was a result of the hierarchical church structure. Average Christians knew they worshiped Jesus. Some may have memorized the Lord's Prayer. Above-average

Christians would know the Apostles' Creed and perhaps a few selections from Scripture. Limited education and Church hierarchy left the vast majority of Christians ignorant of basic Christian teachings. Above the uneducated laypeople was a stratum of very committed Christians. These were nuns, monks, and friars. Within this group, there was great disparity in religious knowledge. Some friars had no formal training and knew little of Scripture. They would travel from town to town and preach a basic sermon that they knew by memory. Monks and nuns, on the other hand, lived an ascetic life of solitude, prayer, and fasting. Even among these committed Christians, however, basic biblical knowledge was often sparse.

The top of the Church hierarchy consisted of priests, bishops, archbishops, cardinals, and the pope. These individuals were almost exclusively of noble birth. Priests were ordained clergy who performed the Mass and consecrated the elements for Holy Communion. Bishops controlled a region of churches, and archbishops controlled an even larger region. Finally, cardinals were senior leaders responsible for selecting the pope. This very small group of Christians often had access to quality education and substantial libraries of information.

Lutheranism reacted against this culture of theological ignorance. Martin Luther, a student of Augustine's theology, encouraged all believers to know what they believed. He wanted every believer to know the Bible and the basics of the Christian faith. He made it clear that Christian ignorance was unacceptable for both clergy and laity. He emphasized daily Bible reading and training for children and adults.

Luther did not just tell others to do this. He did it himself:

> But for myself I say this: I am also a doctor and preacher; yes, as learned and experienced as all the people who have such assumptions and contentment. Yet I act as a child who is being taught the catechism. Every morning—and whenever I have time—I read and say, word for word, the Ten

Commandments, the Creed, the Lord's Prayer, the Psalms, and such.[17]

Luther understood learning the basics of the Christian faith as a lifelong endeavor. Although he was a college professor lecturing on the Psalms at the University of Wittenberg, Luther recited them every day like a child. Confirmation was not graduation for Luther. He believed that the Christian never completely arrives at full biblical knowledge. Luther described the Christian as being a perpetual student: "I must still read and study them daily. Yet I cannot master the catechism as I wish. But I must remain a child and pupil of the catechism, and am glad to remain so."[18]

Even on his deathbed, Luther described the Christian life as perpetual learning. He spoke of the importance of lived experience. Merely reading the Bible does not lead to complete understanding. Rather, the crucible of life completes our understanding:

Nobody can understand Vergil in his *Bucolics* and *Georgics* unless he has first been a shepherd or a farmer for five years.

Nobody understands Cicero in his letters unless he has been engaged in public affairs of some consequence for twenty years.

Let nobody suppose that he has tasted the Holy Scriptures sufficiently unless he has ruled over the churches with the prophets for a hundred years. Therefore there is something wonderful, first, about John the Baptist; second, about Christ; third, about the apostles. "Lay not your hand on this divine Aeneid, but bow before it, adore its every trace."

17   Large Catechism, Longer Preface, paragraph 7.
18   Large Catechism, Longer Preface, paragraphs 7–8.

We are beggars. That is true.[19]

Using classic works of literature to help explain Scripture, Luther emphasized the deep reading that comes with experience. Windowsill gardeners cannot fully understand a book about agriculture; lifelong farmers with chapped hands and dirty fingernails can. A third-grade class president cannot fully understand a book about governing nations; an elderly senator can. In the same way, distracted commuters whizzing by a "John 3:16" highway sign cannot fully understand Scripture; lifelong students of Scripture enlightened by the Holy Spirit can experience a far deeper reading of God's Word.

As Luther understood it, one hundred years of faith is not long enough to probe the depths of Holy Scripture. Luther died wanting to know more about his faith in Jesus Christ. He devoted his entire life to understanding what he believed. Luther wanted to know what he believed and why he believed it. Yet he died, wise doctor and preacher, admitting his ignorance and wanting greater knowledge.

THEOLOGICAL PEZ® DISPENSERS

"What do we believe about this?" Pastors receive this question at all hours of the day. Greeting parishioners after service is prime time for this question. Before, during, or after Bible study is another option. Occasionally, this question will come in the form of an evening text message: "What do we believe about evolution?" "What do we believe about cloning?" "Do we have an official position on the zombie apocalypse?"

Pastors frequently receive these questions. And they know what they are expected to do: tip their head back, open up their throat like a PEZ® Candy dispenser, and offer a compact theological treat.

---

19   LW 54:476.

People often want complex theological questions to be reduced to a simple one-word answer. If the answer takes more than ten words, then folks get impatient. If a pastor says that the question will require an extended conversation, then the question strangely becomes less urgent. To be certain, not all people want their theology in sugary pill form. Still, many people just want their pastor to tell them what to believe so they can get back to the regularly scheduled program.

It is unacceptable to ask your pastor, "What do I believe about this?" Pastors are not theological candy dispensers. They can guide you in Scripture. Their extensive training in biblical languages and history make them a great resource for Bible reading. And pastors can tell you where Lutheran theology stands on an issue. They can help you read and understand the Lutheran Confessions. Pastors will even tell you what they believe; they will gladly share personal beliefs.

A good pastor, however, will not tell you what *you* believe. He will tell you what is in Scripture. He will tell you what the congregation believes. He may even tell you what you *should* believe. Yet, he will not tell you what you believe.

That is your job.

God gave you a brain for a reason. Use it. Grapple with God like Jacob (Genesis 32:22–32). Wrestle with the Word of God like the believers in Berea (Acts 17:10–13). Pray for the Holy Spirit to guide you in godly wisdom (1 John 2:27). Chip away at your theological ignorance with urgency (Philippians 2:12).

God gave you a church for a reason. Use it. Discuss your questions among the community of believers. Join a Bible study and learn how to read the Bible better. Sit in on a new-member class and refresh your knowledge of the Small Catechism. Ask someone to keep you accountable in your daily Bible reading. Borrow a commentary from your church library. Grow in wisdom through the work of the Holy Spirit.

Luther refused to be a theological candy dispenser for his church members in Wittenberg. Early in the year 1535, Martin Luther was getting his hair cut by a barber named Peter Beskendorf. Luther's barber was also known as Master Peter the Barber. He cut hair (and likely performed bloodletting) for the people of Wittenberg. He was also a personal friend and parishioner of the church in Wittenberg.

Master Peter asked Luther a basic theological question: how do I pray? Rather than simply telling Peter what to believe, Luther wrote *A Simple Way to Pray* in which he explained his personal prayer habits: "I will tell you as best I can what I do personally when I pray. May our dear Lord grant to you and to everybody to do it better than I!"[20]

Peter wanted to know how to pray. Luther helped him overcome his confusion by giving him a valuable resource. The guide explained how Luther used the Lord's Prayer, Ten Commandments, and Creed to help guide his prayers. As a pastor, Luther explained his prayer habits. However, he encouraged Peter to develop his own personal habits. Luther did not want him merely regurgitating prayers:

> I repeat here what I previously said in reference to the Lord's Prayer: if in the midst of such thoughts the Holy Spirit begins to preach in your heart with rich, enlightening thoughts, honor him by letting go of this written scheme; be still and listen to him who can do better than you can.[21]

Luther helped his barber to develop his own articulation of prayer. Peter's articulation of prayer was based in Scripture and guided by the Holy Spirit. Peter was not taught to parrot back the words of his pastor. He did not merely copy someone else's beliefs. Instead, he was trained and equipped to overcome his confusion on prayer.

20　LW 43:193.

21　LW 43:201.

After this exchange with Luther, Peter knew how to pray, what to pray, and why to pray.

THEOLOGICAL BLOODLETTING

As previously mentioned, medical bloodletting died out in the early twentieth century. Theological bloodletting, however, is alive and well. Many Christian communities have willingly opened a vein and drained their beliefs. Supposing that discharging doctrine might restore them to health, many congregations have bled themselves to death. Anemic and emaciated, these Christian communities are deeply confused. Theological bloodletting has resulted in many confused Christians. Here are some symptoms of theological bloodletting:

Pluralism: The belief that all faiths lead to salvation. Pluralism claims that genuine and earnest people receive God's mercy regardless of the content of their religious beliefs. It does not matter if you are Mormon, Muslim, or Methodist; all that matters is that you have a good heart. This confuses Jesus with Joseph Smith, Buddha, and Krishna. This also confuses the words of Jesus: "I am the way, and the truth, and the life. No one comes to the Father except through Me" (John 14:6).

Skepticism: Favoring human reason over faith leads to skepticism. Theological skepticism leads to believing only parts of the Gospel. Confusion abounds with skepticism. Skeptics claim that Jesus merely passed out on the cross and woke up hours later (swoon hypothesis). Cynics say that the body of Jesus was stolen from the tomb by the disciples (stolen body hypothesis). Doubters think it is more plausible that Christ's followers had visions of the resurrection (vision hypothesis) than that they actually witnessed the risen Jesus. Lutherans believe and confess that Jesus is alive: "He is not here, but has risen" (Luke 24:6).

Moralism: Many have argued that Christianity is just about being a good person. Try your best, and you will win God's favor. Do good to others, and God will do good to you. Murky moralism confuses the Good News of Jesus Christ. Our hope is not in saccharine platitudes and tepid do-goodery. Our hope is in Jesus: "For we hold that one is justified by faith apart from works of the law" (Romans 3:28).

Deism: Throughout history, deists have believed that God is distant from His creation. They suppose that God is like a divine watchmaker—He built the universe, wound it up, and let it go. We cannot know God because of the great distance between God and His people. Deism is a distortion of Scripture. Jesus is God in human flesh walking, talking, living, and breathing in creation. God is near. God is close. God is present: "God is our refuge and strength, a very present help in trouble" (Psalm 46:1).

Hate: Theological bloodletting can also result in hate. Everyone who believes differently is just plain stupid. If you do not agree with me, then I hate you. Hate confuses everything. It destroys communities. It ruins lives. It is opposite the heart of God. Infantile beliefs lead to hatred and violence: "First of all, then, I urge that supplications, prayers, intercessions, and thanksgiving be made for all people, for kings and all who are in high positions, that we may lead a peaceful and quiet life, godly and dignified in every way" (1 Timothy 2:1–2).

Drained. Empty. Confused. Many Christian communities have theologically bled themselves to death. The pursuit of open-minded theology has caused their brains to fall out of their heads. Anemic doctrine has left their hearts cold and merciless. Death is imminent. Gasping to breathe, these congregations stumble in confusion and despair.

Lutherans are not immune. We do not have some special inoculation protecting us from theological bloodletting. Being Lutheran does not guarantee freedom from confusion. Even though we have a heritage of clear confession, we have no promise for future faithfulness—no promise that that heritage will continue. Postmodern relativism invites us to open a vein and drain our confidence in the Gospel. Academia beckons us to deconstruct our beliefs in Jesus. Society wants to puncture our confidence in God's Word. Bleed a pint here and a quart there. Drain some belief and we will feel better. Confess a little less and settle a little more.

We are not immune.

Being Lutheran is resisting confusion. We stand with those who have always resisted theological bloodletting. Luther refused to idly watch confused Christians. Luther refused to pour out his beliefs on faith, grace, and Scripture. He would not drain the power of Word and Sacrament ministry. Lutherans are not content with anemic beliefs. We make clear confessions of our faith. We know what we believe and why we believe it. We are not confused about these topics:

Sin: Adam and Eve rebelled against God's will. And all human creatures continue in that rebellion. Sin bends us away from God and into ourselves. Although sins have varying earthly consequences, they are all capable of destroying our relationship with God. Pretending that sin is no big deal is dangerous. Pretending that sin can be dealt with apart from Jesus Christ is even more dangerous. And pointing fingers at other sinners is like rearranging the deck chairs on the *Titanic*, "for all have sinned and fall short of the glory of God" (Romans 3:23).

Jesus: True God and true man, Jesus is God in human flesh. Jesus redeemed God's creation through His life, death, and resurrection. Eternal life comes through faith in Jesus. He spoke with authority. He did miracles. He was dead. He is alive. Jesus is not *a* way to God. He is *the* way to God: "And there is salvation in no one else, for there is no other name under heaven given among men by which we must be saved" (Acts 4:12).

Grace: Sinners are bent away from God. We cannot bend ourselves back to Him. Our own strength, merit, or works do not make us right before God. Christ's grace bends us back to God and makes us right with Him: "For by grace you have been saved through faith. And this is not your own doing; it is the gift of God, not a result of works, so that no one may boast" (Ephesians 2:8–9).

Scripture: The Bible is the Word of God. The Bible does not merely *contain* the Word of God. Scripture is not myth, magic, or metaphorical. Lutherans believe Scripture. Not just some of it; Lutherans believe all of it. It is God's Word through human authors. The Bible did not come from heaven on the back of a Pegasus; instead, believers openly and transparently deliberated the biblical canon. Jesus treated Scripture—even Genesis—as historically true and authoritative: "He answered, 'Have you not read that He who created them from the beginning made them male and female' " (Matthew 19:4).

Truth: God is truth. Right and wrong exist. Morality is more than personal preference. Lutherans believe that truth is revealed in God's creation, God's Word, and God's Son. Humans do not create truth(s) for a fleeting period of time. There are not infinite equal variations of truth. Something can be true for all people when it is revealed by God: "Teach me Your way, O LORD, that I may walk in Your truth; unite my heart to fear Your name" (Psalm 86:11).

Church: The Church is the Bride of Christ, the Body of Christ, and the Church of Christ. It is where the Word and Sacraments are rightly administered. That means it is not a bingo club or a spiritual affinity group. The Church is not merely for great praise music or sausage suppers. The Church is the locus of the Gospel. Proclaiming the Gospel of Jesus Christ is the only essential task of the Church: "And He is the head of the body, the church. He is the beginning, the firstborn from the dead, that in everything He might be preeminent" (Colossians 1:18).

Later chapters of this book will explore these topics further. However, it is important to know that Lutherans are not confused about these basic Christian beliefs. Others are confused about where they stand on the resurrection of Jesus. Others are confused about how much effort one needs to make in order to be saved. Some are confused about the authority of Scripture. Not Lutherans. We make a clear confession of what we believe. And we articulate why we believe it.

CONCLUSION

Bloodletting was once a medically approved practice. It turns out that generations of doctors were confused about blood. Removing blood did more harm than good. Yet this has not stopped the practice of intellectual bloodletting. Academia has doubted everything and deconstructed all knowledge. Society is incredulous toward any truth claims. Beliefs are considered unverifiable opinions. We live in a confused culture.

God is not confused. God is truth. Jesus leads us from confusion to confession. We boldly confess our beliefs. We have no need to hide behind postmodern gibberish. We refuse to confess a doughy blob of doctrine. Instead, Lutherans actually know what they believe. Being Lutheran requires intellectually grappling with the Gospel. If you have questions about your faith, then figure it out: Read the Bible. Attend a Bible study. Discuss with other Christians. Pray for the Holy Spirit's wisdom. Lean in to your beliefs and learn more. Being Lutheran is confessing in a world of confusion.

Vignette: María

She was baptized at forty years old. New life in Christ came with an entirely new life for María.

For thirty-nine years, she tried to prove that God does not exist. Her faith was firmly planted in logical proofs and physical explanations of the universe: "Pain is proof that God is indifferent to human suffering." "God is nothing more than an imaginary grandfather in the sky." "Praying to God does not heal sick people. Doctors and medicine heal sick people." "Religion is the opium of the masses." "God is dead."

In her twenties, she majored in biology and minored in chemistry. María wanted to be a scientist. After graduation, she worked briefly in a laboratory as a technician. A lifetime of menial chores such as measuring samples, charting results, and mating fruit flies was not her ideal career. Earning her doctorate would mean that María could have a slightly better position in the hierarchy of the laboratory.

In her thirties, she enrolled in a doctoral program to earn a terminal degree in analytical chemistry. Now she was the one telling people to mate the fruit flies and measure the chemicals. However, all she was really doing was relaying the orders from the primary investigator to the lab technicians. Nevertheless, it surprised her how much she liked being off the bottom of the beaker in the laboratory.

It also surprised her how much she liked one of the other students in her program. Gabe was also studying analytical chemistry. He was different from María in every way imaginable: She was loud and he was quiet. She was from the West Coast and he was from the Midwest. She was from a big family and he was an only child. She was an outspoken atheist and he was a committed Christian.

María and Gabe made an immediate personal connection. Choosing research stations as close to each other as possible, they became fast friends. And then they became more than just friends.

They saw each other in the lab. And then they would see each other at the coffee shop until closing time. She went to meet Gabe's family over Christmas break. She even went to church with the family. (But that was only to impress the family.)

They frequently talked about Christianity. María appreciated how Gabe gave her room to disagree and raise counterpoints. Most of the time, he gave a clear and cogent response to the issues María raised. Occasionally, he would admit that he did not have a good answer or did not know. He told María that he would get back to her after he researched the question and had a response. Even if it was six months later, he always came back with a thoughtful response. Long after she had forgotten the question, Gabe would call her up and say: "Remember when you raised that question about the Book of Jonah? I just finished reading a book that discussed that very question . . . "

Marriage was not part of her graduate school plans. But then again, becoming a Christian was not in her graduate school plans either. She emphatically agreed when Gabe asked if she would be his bride. And during their engagement, something else happened to María: she became a Christian. She came to faith in Jesus Christ. The Holy Spirit led her to trust in Jesus for her eternal salvation. It was a very quiet trust at first. She did not tell anyone that she had become a Christ follower. She kept it secret from her friends and parents. She even kept it secret from her soon-to-be husband.

Gabe found out eventually. He found out when María was baptized. As they drove to church one Sunday, María told Gabe that she was really excited for worship that day. They arrived, and María led Gabe to the front row of pews. He looked in the bulletin and saw her name next to some bold words: **The Sacrament of Holy Baptism**.

After her Baptism, María struggled with many questions from a lifetime of atheism. She would find an answer to one question and stumble upon ten more questions. She muddled through her daily Bible reading. She would read a verse, become confused, look at the study notes in her Bible, go to the verse referenced in the study notes, read that verse, become confused, and then look at the study notes. She would continue doing this until she had a headache. The next day, she would go back to the initial verse and reread it. It was always a little less confusing on the second day.

Praying was equally confounding. She tried improvised prayers. She tried praying prayers written by other people. She tried praying the Psalms. She tried praying with a specific outline. She landed on simply praying the Lord's Prayer and adding additional prayers on to the end. María preferred this way of praying because it was biblically based, historically practiced, and taught by Jesus. She had researched the different options and determined the Lord's Prayer to be a better practice than praying the Prayer of Jabez or offering up a litany of confused thoughts.

Once in worship—on Trinity Sunday—the congregation confessed the Athanasian Creed. María noticed that everyone around her appeared a bit confused by what they were confessing. It bothered her for the rest of the day. The next day, she emailed her pastor and arranged to borrow a book on Church history. She spent the next week learning all about Athanasius, Arius, and the Trinitarian Controversy.

María would not remain confused. She wanted to know what she believed, why she believed it, and how she could rationally defend it. She always approached her scientific research in the laboratory with seriousness. Before her Baptism, María determined that she would always take her Christian faith with an even greater seriousness. Her rationale for this decision was cogent and clear: mating fruit flies is temporary, but knowing Jesus is eternal.

Chapter 3
Discussion Questions

1. Relativism claims that truth is confined to a specific cultural or historical context. How might relativism benefit Christianity? How might relativism hinder Christianity?

2. Read Matthew 21:23–27. Why did Jesus refuse to tell the chief priests and elders the source of His authority?

3. Read Luke 9:1–6. Jesus gave His authority to the disciples. Why were they told to not bring anything (no staff, bag, bread, or money) for the journey? What was Jesus trying to teach the disciples by sending them out with nothing more than His authority?

4. Augustine moved from confusion to confession by the work of the Holy Spirit. Read 1 Corinthians 2:6–16. What is the wisdom of this age in 1 Corinthians 2:6? What is the wisdom of God in 1 Corinthians 2:7? Are these different types of wisdom in opposition to one another?

5. Luther did more than simply give his barber a quick answer. Why did Luther encourage him to develop his own articulation of prayer? What is the benefit of using the Lord's Prayer, Ten Commandments, and the Apostles' Creed as a guide for prayer?

6. Read Matthew 22:23–33. Theological bloodletting is nothing new; Jesus confronted the Sadducees regarding their skepticism of the resurrection. What did Jesus use to correct their confusion? Why was the crowd astonished at His teaching?

7. Read Matthew 19:1–9. Why is it important to recognize that Jesus treated the Old Testament as historically and theologically reliable? What does that reveal about how Jesus viewed Scripture?

8. What does it mean to intellectually grapple with the Gospel? Does embracing Jesus with your brain replace embracing Jesus with your heart?

9. Reread the vignette. Do you know anyone like María? Read 1 Corinthians 3:18–23. What does Paul mean when he tells his readers to become a fool in order to become wise?

Chapter 4

LAZY

But Jesus answered them, "My Father is working
until now, and I am working." (John 5:17)

Why work when there is the Internet? The World Wide Web
has everything you could possibly need to avoid working forever.
Hours can be spent analyzing desktop wallpaper pictures of nuzzling
puppies. Days of lip dubs, music videos, and epic fails are available
online. Months of television episodes are accessible to binge-watch
on demand. Years of gossip, memes, and selfies are waiting for you
on social media. Centuries will pass before playing all the games
offered on the Web. The Internet is infinitely amusing.

Smartphones have taken the Internet one step further. In the
age of AOL discs, people accessed the Internet by using a landline.
(If you do not know what a landline is, then you should look it up
on your smartphone.) Technology has now mobilized our efforts to
avoid working. Riding an elevator, walking to class, or dining with
loved ones used to require the difficult work of human engagement.
Smartphones have solved that problem by allowing portable amusement. Now you can avoid work no matter where you go.

And the Internet is just the beginning. Certainly work can wait
when there are amusing athletes to watch. Game day rolls around, and
fans don their sweatpants and slippers, fry pounds of chicken wings,
and stagnate on the couch. Yet others make a pilgrimage to the stadium
for tailgating. For some, the "work" of setting up a tailgate is serious:

charcoal must be lit, beverages need to be cooled, and lawn chairs need to be anchored by warm bodies. Pregame preparation is exhausting.

Vacations are the same way. The "work" of tabulating frequent flyer miles, studying weather patterns, and examining travel brochures can be strenuous. Laboring to fill an empty suitcase is grueling. Breaking in flip-flops is arduous. And then there is flying to the destination, walking around the amusement parks, and rolling over on the beach to even your tan.

I am getting tired just writing about this.

Amusement takes many forms—television shows, movies, smartphone apps, sports, tailgating, vacations, casinos, concerts, and theme parks. Despite the many forms of amusement, its meaning is singular. The word literally means to be without a muse. In the ancient world, a muse was believed to be the source of creativity, ingenuity, and invention. Muses were supposed to generate thought and inspiration for poets, musicians, and writers. New ideas were thought to be a gift of the muse. Amusement, therefore, is actively trying to be without a muse. It is choosing to be mindless, thoughtless, unengaged, and checked out.

Based on the meaning of the word *amusement*, all we really want is a vacuous brain. We want someone else to do the work for us. We buy amusement park tickets so that we can stop thinking. We binge-watch television shows so that we can disengage our imaginations. We check in to the resort to mentally check out. We like sporting events because shoving popcorn in our mouths is the only work required. We play video games because someone has already done all the creative thinking. We pay to be mindless.

PEOPLE ARE LAZY

Why are we so fixated on amusement? Why do we work hard to avoid hard work? Why is everybody working for the weekend?

The answer is simple: people are lazy. It is not that some people are lazy and others are hard workers. It is not that some people have a drive to work hard while others do not. Nope. All people are lazy. I am lazy. You are lazy.

Before you put the book down because I have just insulted you, let me explain. Being lazy is the result of sin. God did not make human creatures to be lazy. Rather, we became lazy as a result of rebellion against God. Sin threw sand in the cogs of creation. Sin alienated us from fruitful labor. Sin forced us to sweat and toil just to scratch out a living. Double the effort reaps half the reward because of sin. Hacks, shortcuts, and instant gratification flourish in a world distorted by sin.

Work was part of God's creation in the beginning. Genesis begins with God at work. In the beginning, God worked to design and build His creation. At the end of each productive day, God reflected on His work and declared it to be good (Genesis 1:4, 10, 12, 18, 21, 25). On the sixth day, God reflected on all the work He had accomplished and declared it to be very good (Genesis 1:31). Six days of work were followed by a seventh day of Sabbath rest: "And on the seventh day God finished His work that He had done, and He rested on the seventh day from all His work that He had done" (Genesis 2:2).

However, God was not the only one working in the beginning. Adam and Eve engaged in fruitful work in the garden. Humans were given the responsibility to continue God's creative work (Genesis 1:26–30). God gave them the work of marriage, family, and parenthood. God gave them the work of planting, harvesting, and cooking. God gave them the work of land management, city planning, leadership, and zoology. Man was placed in the garden to work: "The LORD God took the man and put him in the garden of Eden to work it and keep it" (Genesis 2:15).

Seeds sprouted and grew into sturdy plants. Vegetables weighed heavy on the vine. Fruit tugged downward on tree branches. Flavorful food simmered to a perfect melody of taste. Bread adorned the dinner table of Adam and Eve. Harmony filled their marriage, and intimacy flourished through their conversations. Joy permeated all their work. Adam planted seeds into black soil, and Eve picked tomatoes barefoot. Unity shined into every nook and cranny of God's creation. Life was good. Work was good.

Destruction came into this perfect creation. Sin shouldered its way into the garden. Work changed forever as a result of human rebellion. Adam and Eve bit into the forbidden fruit. And sin bit back. Work was frustrated as a result of their sinful rebellion:

> And to Adam He said, "Because you have listened to the voice of your wife and have eaten of the tree of which I commanded you, 'You shall not eat of it,' cursed is the ground because of you; in pain you shall eat of it all the days of your life; thorns and thistles it shall bring forth for you; and you shall eat the plants of the field. By the sweat of your face you shall eat bread, till you return to the ground, for out of it you were taken; for you are dust, and to dust you shall return." (Genesis 3:17–19)

Vegetables shriveled on the vine. Rich soil became sand. Farming was exasperating. Baking bread was a burden. Sin separated Adam and Eve from God, complicated their work, and made everything harder. God's judgment on sin alienated Adam and Eve from their labor. The curse made planting seeds and growing food a wearisome project. Childbirth became a challenge and cooking became a chore. Joyful labor for the Lord changed into mindlessly punching a time clock. Death gnawed away at human creatures as they toiled under the sun. Life was toil. Work was toil.

Adam and Eve's rebellion caused work to rebel against all people. Generation after generation fruitlessly labored to grow food, raise a family, and scratch out a living. This legacy of fruitless labor extends to us today. Sin invites us to be lazy. Sin bids us to be apathetic. Sin makes us weary. Sin frustrates our labor so that sweat and struggle offer minimal reward and temporary satisfaction. We see the frustration of sin in daily life:

Food: Plant a garden and watch it wither with drought and disease. Pluck the weeds and find more growing twice as long the next day. Wait patiently for vegetables to grow only to find a groundhog munching away on them. Give up and go eat a gas-station hot dog.

Health: Start an exercise routine and sprain an ankle on the first day. Go to the doctor and she tells you that you need to stop running but continue exercising. Pay for a gym membership only to find that every machine is occupied except for the treadmill. Give up and go sit on the couch.

Work: Enroll in college and find it is crazy expensive. Take out student loans to cover the cost of tuition. Switch majors from one you love to one that will pay your loans. Graduate with a degree you did not really want and look for a job. Apply, interview, and no call back. Repeat this a dozen times with the same results. Take an hourly job outside of your degree to pay your loans. Give up and go play Frisbee golf.

Family: Find a spouse and plan a wedding. Find out that weddings cost more than college. Add to your student loan debts by purchasing invitations, flowers, and cupcakes. Get married and realize that being husband and wife is difficult. Have children and start a family. Realize that parenting is difficult. Spend the rest of your life tired with a house that is forever cluttered. Give up and join the circus.

Hard work is often unrewarded. Experience tells us to give the minimum amount of effort. Scarcity encourages us to put our needs ahead of others. No matter how hard we work, our efforts will be frustrated. Take one step forward and two steps back. Gain a few inches and lose a few feet. Pay off one debt and open the mailbox to find ten more. Sin teaches us to never work harder than is necessary. Sin creates a world in which we must work smarter, not harder. Sin bids us cut corners, do the bare minimum, and always take the easy way out.

THE WORK OF JESUS

God could have taken the easy way out of sin. He could have looked the other way on Adam and Eve's rebellion or hit rewind the moment sin entered into creation. He could have swiped the fruit from their hand before they sank their teeth into sin.

But He didn't.

God refused to take the easy way out of sin. Instead, His plan of salvation required work. Hard work. God's redemption of His people took generations of work. His plan of salvation in Christ Jesus required steadfast labor, persistent promise keeping, and incredible sacrifice. Jesus Christ is proof that God loves work.

Immediately after sin entered into creation, God began the work of salvation

Immediately after sin entered into creation, God began the work of salvation. While sin was still dripping from the mouth of Adam and Eve, salvation began pouring from the heart of God. He promised that He would work to undo the curse: "I will put enmity between you and the woman, and between your offspring and her offspring; He shall bruise your head, and you shall bruise His heel" (Genesis 3:15). This is the first mention of the Gospel in Scripture (*protoevangelium*). It is God's promise to get busy with the work of salvation in Jesus Christ.

Words turned into action as God worked in creation. God worked through Noah to keep mercy afloat through the flood (Genesis 6–8). Detailed plans and instructions for an ark were created by God and dispatched to Noah. The work went according to God's careful design. Noah planed wood, fitted it together, used pitch to seal the joints, and layered thatch for the roof. Working toward the fulfillment of the promise made to Adam and Eve, God labored to keep the promise of Jesus afloat.

The work of God continued through Abraham. The promise of redemption made to Adam and Eve came up again in God's promise to Abraham: "And I will establish My covenant between Me and you and your offspring after you throughout their generations for an everlasting covenant, to be God to you and to your offspring after you" (Genesis 17:7). Refusing to take the easy way out, God worked through His people to ensure their salvation. Resisting laziness, God actively engaged creation to deliver His promise of salvation.

Abraham, Isaac, and Jacob were the instruments of God's work. The work of salvation continued through Joseph, Moses, Aaron, Joshua, and the prophets. God never resorted to salvation hacks, quick fixes, or shortcuts. He refused to slap some duct tape on sin and call it good. He refused to cover human rebellion with a thin coat of paint. Rather, God took the long way to redemption through Jesus Christ. It took generations of work to fulfill the promise made to Adam and Eve. It required patience, perseverance, and perspective to work redemption through human flesh.

"Behold, the Lamb of God, who takes away the sin of the world!" (John 1:29). It took a lot of work to get to the point in which John the Baptist could speak these words. God had worked for generations to deliver the promise of salvation in Jesus Christ. The Gospel of Matthew begins with a long genealogy documenting the generations of God's work leading up to Jesus (Matthew 1:1–17). And the birth of Jesus was not the end of God's work. God's work in Christ Jesus is for all eternity.

Jesus worked. He worked hard to restore creation. He set about the task of undoing death, healing disease, and forgiving sins. Like a skilled craftsman, Jesus removed the varnish of sin through words of forgiveness (Matthew 9:2–5; 26:28; Mark 2:5–12). Like an expert carpenter, Jesus reworked broken bodies to make them function again (Matthew 4:23; Mark 7:31–37; Luke 4:38–40). Like a master chef, Jesus prepared feasts that others could not (Matthew 14:13–21; Mark 8:1–10; John 2:1–11). Performing the work of the divine physician, Jesus raised the dead to new life (Luke 7:11–15; 8:41–55; John 11:1–44).

The work of Jesus, unlike our work, actually accomplishes something. We labor in vain; Jesus labors in victory. We struggle to complete a simple task; Jesus makes it happen instantly. We seldom see results from our efforts; Jesus' work overflows with results. Our work is slow, tedious, and often frustrating; His work is fruitful, successful, and eternally productive.

The miracle at Cana offers an example of Jesus' fruitful labor. While attending a wedding, Jesus performed the work of a winemaker. Human winemakers spend a lifetime working on the perfect bottle of wine. Season after season, winemakers grow, prune, graft, and trellis grapes so that they are suitable for winemaking. Harvesting and crushing the grapes takes strenuous labor. Fermenting and aging the wine requires tremendous patience. Lastly, pairing the completed wine with the right meal and occasion is the careful work of a sommelier.

At a wedding in Cana, Jesus accomplished all of this work imme-diately. Jesus did the work of a viticulturist, vintner, and sommelier when He turned water into wine. Jesus completed years of hard work in the amount of time it took to pour a glass. And His work had delectable results:

> When the master of the feast tasted the water now become wine, and did not know where it came from (though the servants who had drawn the water knew), the master of the feast called the bridegroom and said to him, "Everyone serves the good wine first, and when people have drunk freely, then the poor wine. But you have kept the good wine until now." (John 2:9–10)

The kingdom of God was at work in and through Jesus. Every day of His earthly ministry was marked by diligent and fruitful labor. Preaching and teaching, serving and caring were His daily work. Sabbath rest was filled with prayer, not mindless amusement. Jesus performed the fruitful work of God with every step, every word, and every heartbeat. And even when His heart stopped beating, Jesus was working: "When Jesus had received the sour wine, He said, 'It is finished,' and He bowed His head and gave up His spirit" (John 19:30). Refusing to take the easy way out, Jesus finished the work of salvation promised to Adam and Eve.

FREE FROM LAZY

Jesus frees us *from* working to earn salvation. Jesus frees us to work *for* our neighbor. Sadly, the Church has not always taught this way. Prior to Luther's reforms, there was tremendous confusion about the role of work in the Christian life. Before the Reformation, the Church taught that good works were vital to salvation. The predominant teaching of the day was that grace empowered believers to perform good works and thereby earn salvation. Walking an old lady across the street was an opportunity to win God's favor. Caring for neighbors was a way to gain eternal salvation. Laziness was considered a sin because it squandered opportunities to earn forgiveness through good works.

The Church's teaching on works concerned Luther. He wanted people to understand that the work of Jesus frees them to work for others. Luther clarified the role of work in the Christian life through his treatise *On Christian Freedom*. Rather than working to earn salvation, Christians are able to work for the well-being of their family, friends, and neighbors. Luther makes two central arguments throughout the treatise:

A Christian is a perfectly free lord of all, subject to none.

A Christian is a perfectly dutiful servant of all, subject to all.[22]

These appear to be contradictory statements. How can someone be free and bound, subject to none and subject to all? Luther explains how both of these statements originate in Scripture (1 Corinthians 9:19; Romans 13:8). Luther uses Scripture to argue that Christians are free from working for their salvation yet bound to work for others.

Faith alone unites us to Christ's perfect work of salvation

Christ's righteousness does not depend on our work. Jesus has done all the work through His life, death, and resurrection. There is no more work to be done. All the work has been done for us. Before God, we are free in Jesus: "This is that Christian liberty, our faith, which does not induce us to live idleness or wickedness but makes the law and works unnecessary for any man's righteousness

---

22   LW 31:344.

and salvation."[23] No work of human hands can improve our standing before God; faith alone unites us to Christ's perfect work of salvation.

Take note: Luther says that the work of Jesus is not license to be lazy. The work of Jesus for our salvation leads us to work hard for the good of others. There should be no confusion about the purpose of our hard work; our labor does not earn God's fortune, favor, or forgiveness. Made new in Christ, our labor is now directed at the well-being of others. New life in Christ frees us to fulfill our God-given responsibility of working and keeping creation. Even when we work for our own well-being, we are working for the good of others:

> This is what makes caring for the body a Christian work, that through its health and comfort we may be able to work, to acquire, and lay by funds with which to aid those who are in need, that in this way the stronger member may serve the weaker, and we may be sons of God, each caring for and working for the other, bearing one another's burdens and so fulfilling the law of Christ [Gal. 6:2].[24]

This clear understanding of work allowed Luther to speak clearly on the topic of laziness. Although sin made us lazy, salvation makes us busy in service to one another. Our old self is selfishly lazy, apathetic, and focused on amusement. Our new self is empowered by Christ Jesus to perform fruitful work for the kingdom of God. The old self, fraught with selfish apathy and laziness, has been crucified with Christ (Romans 6:6). Luther understood the old self to be entirely corrupt:

> But what is the old man? It is what is born in human beings from Adam: anger, hate, envy, unchastity, stinginess, laziness,

---

23   LW 31:349–50.
24   LW 31:365.

arrogance—yes, unbelief. The old man is infected with all vices and has by nature nothing good in him [Romans 7:18].[25]

Thankfully, Jesus frees us from our old self and creates the new life of faith. This new life in Christ frees us to work for the good of others, protect their life and safety, and guard their property. The good work of salvation was done on the cross, while the good work of neighborly love is never done.

You should know that Lutheran theology has been misconstrued as encouraging laziness and rejecting the work of God's Law (*antinomianism*). This claim is not a stretch: being Lutheran is proclaiming salvation by grace apart from works. Some theologians have claimed that this means Lutherans reject doing any good works for others and are spiritually and physically lazy. Sadly, we have often lived up to this claim. There is a constant temptation to abuse our Christian liberty and neglect our earthly work. Lutherans have often stood behind the forgiveness of Jesus to justify their apathy, complacency, and laziness.

This is wrong, wrong, wrong.

As with other aspects of Lutheranism, we are not always perfect in living our theology. To be certain, Luther never claimed that the work of Jesus frees us from working for others. Lutherans *reject* good works when the aim is to earn salvation. Yet we wholeheartedly *embrace* good works when the aim is to serve others in faith. This is a fine line. We do not always walk the line well.

SANCTIFIED SWEAT

Being Lutheran is working hard for others. Securing salvation does not compel Lutherans to work. Gaining grace is not the motivation

---

25   Large Catechism, Part IV, paragraphs 66–67.

for our efforts. Using unsuspecting people to earn points in heaven is not the hidden goal lurking behind our labor. Being Lutheran is about sanctified sweat.

Faith in Jesus declares that sinners are holy and blameless new creations. This happens immediately when the Holy Spirit leads a person to saving faith in Jesus. There is no probationary period for salvation. Saving faith delivers Christ's forgiveness to sinners instantly. The theological term for this is justification. Broken souls are made just right through faith in Jesus. Justification is instantaneous. Sanctification continues for a lifetime. The process of becoming a holy and new creation, known as sanctification, is far from instantaneous. Rather, the Holy Spirit is constantly working in the lives of believers to make them holy. The sweat we offer in service to others is the work of the Holy Spirit.

The Lutheran reformers explained sanctification as the work of the Holy Spirit making believers holy after being restored in Christ Jesus:

> Therefore, when we have been justified by faith and regenerated, we begin to fear and love God, to pray to Him, to expect aid from Him, to give thanks and praise Him, and to obey Him in times of suffering. We also begin to love our neighbors, because our hearts have spiritual and holy movements.

> These things cannot happen until we have been justified through faith and regenerated (we receive the Holy Spirit).[26]

Lutherans resist laziness. Being lazy is part of the old self. Being lazy comes from sin, selfishness, and spiritual depravity. Offering sanctified sweat for others is central to new life in Christ.

---

26 Apology of the Augsburg Confession, Article V (III), paragraphs 4–5 [125–26].

Lutherans today work for the good of others in many different ways:

Family: Being Lutheran celebrates the work of family life. When everyone else disparaged parenthood, Luther lauded the merit of this hard work. He preached on the work of the family saying, "But this at least all married people should know. They can do no better work and do nothing more valuable either for God, for Christendom, for all the world, for themselves, and for their children than to bring up their children well."[27] Mothers and fathers do the important work of caring for God's dear children. Lutherans believe that the work of marriage, family, and parenting is a foundational service to others.

Education: Being Lutheran is providing quality education to all people. Soon after the Saxon immigrants came to America, congregations established schools to provide Christian education. Elementary schools came first. High schools, colleges, and seminaries soon followed. Hard work led to Lutheran schools spreading throughout the country and the world.

Emergency Relief: Being Lutheran is offering a cup of cool water to someone in need. The devastation of World War II led to the formation of Lutheran World Relief (LWR). Providing food, water, medical care, and relief efforts has kept LWR busy since its inception. Their work began in Europe and rapidly expanded to the Middle East, Asia, and Africa. National and global crises have Lutherans working hard for others.

---

27   LW 44:12.

Hospitals: Being Lutheran is caring for the physical needs of others. Christ proclaimed the forgiveness of sins and healed broken bodies. Following in the pattern of Jesus, Lutherans have a long legacy of establishing hospitals to promote healing. Luther understood that caring for souls also meant caring for the whole body. Lutheran hospitals work to serve others in body and soul through medical care.

Farming: Being Lutheran is feeding others. Jesus fed people not only with the bread of life but also with actual bread (John 6). Lutherans work to feed others with the Word of God and the bread of the earth. Following the immigration from Saxony, Lutheranism in America flourished in farming and agricultural communities. Providing food for others is a tangible way in which Lutherans work for the well-being of others.

This is clearly an incomplete list. There are many other ways in which Lutherans work for the well-being of others. These are simply some of the historic ways in which Lutherans have served their neighbors through hard work. Nevertheless, you can offer sanctified sweat in your own daily work. In Christ Jesus, the work that fills your day is an offering of love and service for others.

You can add to this list by asking yourself what sort of work you do on an average day. Are you a student studying for exams and completing assignments? Are you a parent raising children, cleaning spaghetti sauce off the ceiling, and working to stay awake through story time? Are you a cashier working through an endless line of customers, helping with returns, and bagging purchases? Do you bail hay, bill medical tests, or buy steel for a manufacturing company? Whatever work you do, do it knowing that you are made new in Jesus: "And whatever you do, in word or deed, do everything in the name of the Lord Jesus, giving thanks to God the Father through Him" (Colossians 3:17).

CONCLUSION

Amusement is not a bad thing. Spending time on the Internet is not a sin. Movies, vacations, sporting events, and concerts are wonderful gifts of God's creation. They are good gifts to be celebrated. Nevertheless, sin has an unhealthy attachment to these gifts. The old self craves more mindless amusement, vacations, and gossip on social media. The old self will find any way to cut corners, do as little as possible, and get back to being lazy.

Made new in Christ Jesus, the new self welcomes hard work for the well-being of others. Justified through faith in Jesus, the Holy Spirit works holiness within you. In Christ, the work that you do is holy work. In Christ, the sweat from your labor is sanctified sweat. Jesus turns your work into something more than drudgery: Parenting is a holy sacrifice for the well-being of others. Studying for a test is preparing to serve your neighbor with a future career. Bagging groceries is helping to provide the daily bread for a family. Work as drudgery is dead and buried in the tomb. Work as a labor of love is alive and risen with Jesus. Chapter 9 (Purpose) will go into greater detail on how God works through the daily work of Christ followers.

Being Lutheran is resisting lazy and embracing work. We believe that God made us to engage in joyful and fruitful work. Sin alienates us from work and distorts our efforts. Jesus frees us from working for our salvation so that we can work for the well-being of others. We welcome dirty hands that earn clean money. We believe that tired muscles and worn-out jeans are a gift of the Holy Spirit.

Vignette: Bessie

The young girl was perplexed. She watched intently as the doctor worked. Yet, she could sense that something was not right. She was certain that only women wore dresses. And she knew that only men were doctors. Watching as this doctor took care of her brother, she was befuddled by what she saw: a doctor wearing a dress.

The little girl could not help but call this oddity to the attention of her mother: "Mother, isn't that a funny doctor? He has no beard and wears dresses like a woman."[28]

The year was 1904. The beardless doctor wearing a dress was Dr. Bessie Efner. After graduating from Morningside College and Sioux City School of Medicine, she hung out her shingle in Hinton, Iowa. In a time when beards and medicine went together, Dr. Bessie confounded many people as a female doctor in a rural farming community.

When Dr. Bessie first began practicing medicine, many male patients were vehemently opposed to a female doctor. Women were hesitant at best. Very few people were inclined to trust Dr. Bessie as a competent doctor. Her first few months of practicing medicine were dreadfully slow, and she barely met her financial obligations.

That soon changed.

A transient, drunken worker was brought to her clinic after being dragged for some distance by a runaway horse. The man was still drunk and completely unable to give intelligible answers to the questions asked of him. He had sustained a double fracture in his right jaw, making it impossible to put on an ordinary cast. Dr. Bessie studied the case and set out to perform a creative procedure: she pulled one of his molars to provide an opening so that he could be fed by means of a tube. Then she set the edges of the bones together completely

---

28   Alfred Rehwinkel, *Dr. Bessie* (St. Louis: Concordia, 1963), 21.

by touch alone since she did not have the aid of a fluoroscope or x-ray. Finally, she wired the upper and lower teeth together to keep the jaw from moving.

Weeks later, when the wiring and bandages were finally removed, the man's face and jaw had healed completely. Although the man refused to pay Dr. Bessie for her services, he served as a walking testimony of the young female doctor's abilities. The community slowly forgot their prejudices against having a female doctor, and Dr. Bessie's practice grew.

Work was plentiful. She was called on to deliver babies, dress wounds, and set broken bones. And work was difficult. She had to talk young mothers out of having abortions and confront adulterous spouses for spreading sexually transmitted disease. Despite the difficulties, Dr. Bessie always worked hard to provide competent care for her patients.

Adding to her already large workload, Dr. Bessie became a mother through adoption. She was confronted with the opportunity to adopt her three young nieces after her brother and his wife died within months of each other. After much prayer and consideration, Dr. Bessie decided to have her three nieces live with her. She knew that she had no other choice in the matter; she could not stand to see the girls raised in an orphanage. Trusting that God would daily and richly sustain her, Dr. Bessie committed to the work of being both rural doctor and single parent.

Life went on for Dr. Bessie. She was more than competent to heal all kinds of ailments: hemorrhaging cowpokes, breached babies, and sobbing young mothers. Nevertheless, economic downturn was beyond her medical abilities. The Panic of 1907 was a time of widespread financial crisis. The year saw excessive bank failures, freezes on new loans, and a panicky stock market. Patients were unable to pay for services, and her bank refused access to her deposits. Dr. Bessie was forced to leave Iowa. Like many others in the day, she took Horace Greeley's advice and moved west to homestead in Wyoming.

Work was even harder in Wyoming. There were fewer patients, yet somehow that amounted to more work. Dr. Bessie practiced medicine along with having to chop wood, grow vegetables, tend the household fire, and help to build a frontier city. Rugged land extended clear to the mountains. Craggy wilderness went on for miles.

After moving her practice and nieces west, Dr. Bessie had seventy-five cents to her name. The land in which she was to begin homesteading was almost entirely uninhabited. The town of Carpenter consisted of nothing more than railroad tracks and Dr. Bessie's newly built house. That first year of homesteading, patients came to town as often as tumbleweeds.

Her first patient in Wyoming was a horse. Seriously.

The frontier town slowly grew. The train delivered more people than it took away. Houses and stores sprouted from the dusty earth. Dr. Bessie served the community by becoming the first postmistress of Carpenter in 1908. She became a central figure in the burgeoning new community. She was well respected for her medical abilities. She loved her job. She could not imagine that any other work could be more fulfilling than being a doctor.

Dr. Bessie was wrong. She soon discovered that there was one thing more fulfilling than being a doctor: being a wife and mother. While practicing in Wyoming, Dr. Bessie cared for the wounds of a young student pastor named Alfred Rehwinkel. He was studying to be a Lutheran pastor and had been assigned to be a vicar in the frontier of Wyoming. Late one evening, while riding home from one of his congregations, Alfred's horse ran into a barbed-wire fence. The horse wildly bucked back and forth, sawing Alfred's leg into the fence. The cut went down to bone. He was brought to Dr. Bessie's practice, and she treated his extensive wounds. He did not seem to mind that she was cutting through his flesh; he was fixated on having a conversation with her.

Meeting Alfred changed her life. After years of courtship, Bessie married and became a wife. She then soon became a mother to children of her own. In the autumn of 1912, the new family moved to Alberta, where Alfred served as a frontier pastor to multiple Lutheran congregations. Two years later, the Rehwinkel family moved from the frontier to Edmonton, where Alfred was pastor at St. Peter's Church.

Work changed profoundly for Bessie. Now she was caring for her family as mother, caring for her congregation as pastor's wife, and caring for the medical needs of immigrants in Edmonton. Later in life, Bessie returned to medicine when she worked as a campus doctor at St. John's College in Winfield, Kansas.

Reflecting back on her life, Bessie wrote:

> I lived a long life, an active life, a rugged life, a most interesting life, and I trust it may also be called a useful life.

> I was a pioneer lady doctor on the Western frontier, a pioneer minister's wife on the Canadian frontier, and a college president's wife on an academic frontier.

> I was blessed with the joy of motherhood, and my life was enriched immeasurably in the wonderful companionship of my preacher-professor husband. . . .

> And as I now survey the eventful years through which I have lived, I clearly recognize in it all a most wonderful pattern, and I can see that even my sorrows, reverses, and heartaches all had to work together for my good in God's providential design.[29]

---

29 Rehwinkel, *Dr. Bessie*, 163–64.

The work of Jesus freed Dr. Bessie to work for others. Her life was a life of neighborly love, sanctified sweat, and hard work for others. And this was all because Jesus had done the far greater work of earning her eternal salvation.

Chapter 4
Discussion Questions

1. Read Genesis 2:1–3. God worked in order to make His creation. What do the six days of creation reveal about God's nature? Is work part of God's plan for creation or a result of sin?

2. Jesus Christ is proof that God loves work. What work did Jesus do before the cross? What work did Jesus do after the resurrection? Read John 4:31–38.

3. The wedding in Cana shows Jesus doing the work of viticulturist, vintner, and sommelier immediately. What are some other miracles in which Jesus performs human work immediately? Read John 6:5–14.

4. Read Luke 10:25–37. For what purpose did Jesus tell the parable of the Good Samaritan? Is this parable an encouragement to work for others or a glimpse into God's work for us? Could it be both?

5. Read Matthew 5:17–20. What does it mean that Jesus came to fulfill the Law, not to abolish it? What is the role of God's Law now that Jesus has fulfilled it through His life, death, and resurrection?

6. Antinomianism means rejecting the role of God's Law in the Christian life. Are Lutherans antinomians? If not, what is the role of the Law in the life of a Christ follower?

7. Sanctification is the lifelong process of becoming holy. Read 1 Corinthians 12:1–11. Who is the primary actor in sanctification? Does the work of the Holy Spirit in sanctification look the same for everybody?

8. Read Matthew 7:15–20. In Christ, the work that you do is holy work. Does it always appear that way? Is the work of a Christian fundamentally different than the work of an unbeliever?

9. Dr. Bessie led an incredibly productive and compassionate life. How did her relationship with Jesus shape her daily work for others? How does your relationship with Jesus shape your daily work for others?

Chapter 5

PASTEL

Those who look to Him are radiant, and
their faces shall never be ashamed.
(Psalm 34:5)

What makes Lutherans unique? Umm . . . that's a good question. Lutherans have potlucks. Nobody else in all of Christendom has devised a communal meal with various people bringing a dish to pass. Layered Jell-O, creamed corn, German potato salad, and ham sandwiches served in a fellowship hall is uniquely Lutheran.

On second thought, that's not unique to Lutherans. Walk in to any congregation from any denomination and they will boast about having the best potlucks since the Early Church. Potlucks do not make Lutherans unique.

Lutherans never sit in the front row of pews. Only Lutherans are truly pious enough to refrain from the seat of honor in the sanctuary. Other denominations are full of proud people fighting over the front pew, but we have people fighting not to sit in the front row.

Like potlucks, this is not unique to Lutheranism either. Every denomination has people resisting the front row. Even university classrooms, movie theaters, and synagogues have a row of empty seats in the front. Refusing to sit in the front pews does not make Lutherans unique.

Even our soup suppers, never-ending committee meetings, and propensity to argue fail to make Lutherans unique. There is nothing special about any of these practices. The Methodists do it. The Presbyterians do it. Catholics, Pentecostals, Calvinists, and Baptists know all about these. Even the Mormons have potlucks, empty front pews, and committee meetings. "A Mighty Fortress" is a favorite of the Mormon Tabernacle Choir.

Relying on superficial details to set us apart from other denominations has made Lutherans painfully pastel. We've become a soft shade of Protestant pastel. We resemble every other Christian Church around us. We offer shallow reasons for being Lutheran: "Be Lutheran because we have great potlucks!" "Be Lutheran because we have committee meetings." "Be Lutheran because we sing 'A Mighty Fortress.'" We have become just another hue in the Protestant crayon box. We have colored ourselves with all the wrong shades. Lutherans have become remarkably unremarkable. This is a problem.

To be certain, being pastel is not a marketing problem for Lutherans. We are not worried that our lack of a unique selling proposition will hurt our bottom-line membership. Looking like every other denomination is not an issue of product differentiation. We do not fear that our brand will perish if we cannot stand out from the other Christian franchises. Carving out a corner of the Christian market is simply not our concern.

Rather, being pastel risks our confession of faith. If being Lutheran is about hymns, potlucks, and meetings, then we will soon resemble many other non-Christian religions. Lutherans and Mormons sing songs in worship; therefore, they must be similar faiths. Lutherans and Jehovah's Witnesses have committee meetings and take an offering; therefore, they must have similar beliefs. When those who are not Christian can come off as Christians (the Church of Jesus Christ of Latter-day Saints, Christian Science, Jehovah's Witnesses, most any New Age philosophy), how can we ever say, "I intend to continue steadfast in this confession and Church and to suffer all, even death, rather than fall away from it"?[30] Being pastel makes it hard to differentiate one shade from another.

THE COLOR OF JESUS

Can you tell the difference between rich mauve and deep mauve? Can you delineate baby blue from pale blue? Are your eyes able to separate mint green from spring green? I didn't think so. Slight differences in color are imperceptible. Minor variations in shade are lost on the untrained eye. Designers and other trained professionals may be able to differentiate the shades of pastel. Most of us cannot.

First-century Judaism was a colorful mixture of beliefs. The different shades of Judaism were not minor gradations; the various sects had substantial differences in both belief and practice.

Perhaps the most well-known Jewish group during the time of Jesus was the Pharisees. They were a scholarly shade of Judaism. They placed great emphasis on studying the Torah, keeping its mandates perfectly, and creating additional mandates as a hedge around the Laws of Moses.

The Sadducees were another shade within the Jewish spectrum. They painted their beliefs in a very different color. They were known for their political and economic involvement, high social standing, and rejection of many foundational Jewish beliefs. For instance, the Sadducees did not believe in a bodily resurrection (Matthew 22:23).

The Essenes were yet another colorful group within the Jewish people. They colored Judaism with a unique form of asceticism; the Essenes lived in voluntary poverty, communal settlements, and often took vows of celibacy.

---

30 See the Rite of Confirmation in *Lutheran Service Book* (St. Louis: Concordia, 2006), 273.

These groups constituted the three primary colors of first-century Judaism.

However, there were many other shades adding to the color of Judaism. The Zealots were a group intent on armed rebellion against the Roman Empire. The Sicarii were extreme revolutionaries within the Zealots. These Jewish revolutionaries were known for their violence against anyone opposing their calls for an uprising. Neither Romans nor Jews were safe from the daggers of the Sicarii. Opposite the Zealots and Sicarii on the color wheel of Judaism were the masses of Jewish people dutifully living under Roman rule. Many first-century Jewish people did not strongly align with any of the major sects—Pharisees, Sadducees, Essenes, and Zealots—and instead lived according to the traditional beliefs of Judaism, desiring to simply work and worship faithfully without aligning with a particular sect.

Judaism during the time of Jesus, a period known as Second Temple Judaism (516 BC–AD 70), was a colorful mixture of religious beliefs, spiritual practices, and political ambitions. It was hard to stand out amidst this panoply of colors.

The unique color of Jesus stood out from the crowd. Jesus' teaching painted a vivid picture of the kingdom of God. Beige beliefs were recolored at the Sermon on the Mount (Matthew 5). Israel had relaxed Scripture and made it a guide to pastel piety. Jesus restored vivid color to the teachings of Scripture: "Therefore whoever relaxes one of the least of these commandments and teaches others to do the same will be called least in the kingdom of heaven, but whoever does them and teaches them will be called great in the kingdom of heaven" (Matthew 5:19).

Vivid actions accompanied the vivid teaching of Jesus. Jesus brought the color back to the deathly pale skin of Lazarus. Although Lazarus was the ashen hue of death, Jesus raised him to new life. Warmth returned to his flesh and color returned to his cheeks. Jesus dazzled Peter, James, and John at the transfiguration as he shined bright white (Matthew 17:1–13). Brilliant colors accompanied this momentous event with His face shining like the sun and his clothing becoming white as light. Jesus did not live a pastel life. He lived with the vibrant color of truth.

Jesus engaged a full spectrum of colorful people in His ministry—tax collectors, prostitutes, children, fisherman, zealots, and foreigners. The Pharisees took offense at this (Matthew 9:11; Mark 2:16; Luke 7:34). But they were not the only ones objecting to the colorful people Jesus chose to engage with God's mercy; the disciples were equally offended (John 4:27; Luke 18:15–17). Even though the disciples had learned directly from Jesus, they still tried to sift the colorful characters from God's kingdom.

Nevertheless, Jesus did not come only for vivid teaching, vibrant actions, and colorful people. Jesus came to paint the wooden cross red with the blood of sacrifice. A scarlet robe around His shoulders and tawny thorns around His head, Jesus went to the cross. The sky darkened, and red blood flowed for the sins of the world. Although there were two criminals on crosses next to Jesus, He stood out from the others. Even the Roman soldiers guarding Jesus on the cross noticed Him: "When the centurion and those who were with him, keeping watch over Jesus, saw the earthquake and what took place, they were filled with awe and said, 'Truly this was the Son of God!' " (Matthew 27:54).

His dead body was placed in a stony tomb. Three days later, God raised Jesus from the dead: His cold heart again perfused with warm blood. Dead neurons ignited with human heat. Cells reactivated, organs reheated, and airways reopened. And breath—the holy breath of God—filled the vacuous lungs of Jesus. He appeared throughout Jerusalem and the surrounding area. He came to the disciples in a locked room and displayed His crimson marks of nails and spear: "Then He said to Thomas, 'Put your finger here, and see My hands; and put out your hand, and place it in My side. Do not disbelieve, but believe' " (John 20:27). Thomas stained his finger with the vividness of Jesus. Before long, the whole earth would be witness to the unique color of Jesus.

UNITED WITH CHRIST

Jesus stood out from the crowd. His teaching was a different shade than all the others. His actions were a different hue than other religious teachers. His companions were not variations of one color. God dwelt among us in vivid mercy, vibrant compassion, and vital truth. The unique color of Jesus is impossible to overlook.

And God calls us to be the color of Jesus. Painted with the blood of Jesus, washed with divine truth, and perfected with the gift of salvation, believers share in the vibrant color of Christ Jesus. We stand out from the crowd, because Christ dwells in us: "I have been crucified with Christ. It is no longer I who live, but Christ who lives in me. And the life I now live in the flesh I live by faith in the Son of God, who loved me and gave Himself for me" (Galatians 2:20).

God calls us to be the color of Jesus

Believers are unique because the triune God—Father, Son, and Holy Spirit—dwells within us in a mystical union (*unio mystica*). Luther saw in Scripture a clear teaching that Christ's presence dwells within Christians. Believers reflect the color of Jesus because He is truly present within us:

> Christ is my "form," which adorns my faith as color or light adorns a wall. (This fact has to be expounded in this crude way, for there is no spiritual way for us to grasp the idea that Christ clings and dwells in us as closely and intimately as

light or whiteness clings to a wall.) "Christ," [Paul] says, "is fixed and cemented to me and abides in me."[31]

Luther believed that Christians are united with Christ. He found Scripture depicting Jesus as being intimately present in the life of believers (Romans 8:10–11; Ephesians 3:14–19). This teaching, though clearly present in the Early Church, was neglected during the Middle Ages. Prior to the Reformation, the Church was deeply confused about how Jesus acted in the life of the believer.

The prevailing belief before Luther was that Jesus is the distant, unapproachable Son of God. The perfect holiness of Jesus kept sinful people from drawing near to Him. Rather than dealing directly with Jesus, people went to the saints as intermediaries. Praying to the saints became a popular expression of piety. Since the saints were holier than thou, Jesus was more likely to hear their requests on your behalf.

Appealing to the saints grew out of a belief that Jesus was angry about the crucifixion. Jesus died for your sins, and He is not happy about it. St. Dorothy, on the other hand, did not die for your sins, so she kind of likes you. Drawing near to Jesus had become a spiritual pyramid scheme: Jesus was at the top; ordinary believers were at the bottom; and the pope, priests, and saints resided somewhere in the middle.

Holy Communion was the rare time in which Jesus was present in the lives of believers. The Church developed many traditions surrounding Holy Communion. One of these traditions was the Corpus Christi procession. Developed in the Middle Ages, this feast day included a public procession through the streets with the body and blood of Christ. After speaking the Words of Institution, the body would be placed in a monstrance. The monstrance, also known as an ostensorium, was a glass case attached to a long pole.

31   LW 26:167.

This allowed the body of Christ to be paraded through the church and around town. This was a rare moment for believers to be near the presence of Jesus Christ.

Scripture depicted something very different, according to Luther. He could not find scriptural proof to support the belief that Christ was distant and aloof. Luther found nothing in the Bible suggesting that saints and priests must mediate Christ's presence in the life of believers. Instead, Scripture taught that Christ's presence abounds in the life of faith. Being close to Jesus does not require an epic pilgrimage to gaze upon the spear that pierced His side; through the work of the Holy Spirit, faith in Jesus is the intimate union of God and His children.

For Luther, faith in Jesus went beyond just salvation and the forgiveness of sins. He believed that faith was the one-flesh union of the soul with Christ. Being united with Christ is a blessed exchange of God and mankind, salvation and sin; Christ receives our sin, and we receive His abundant gifts. Luther depicted this blessed exchange as a divine marriage in which faith unites the soul with Christ as a bride is united with her bridegroom.

> Let us compare these and we shall see inestimable benefits. Christ is full of grace, life, and salvation. The soul is full of sins, death, and damnation. Now let faith come between them and sins, death, and damnation will be Christ's, while grace, life, and salvation will be the soul's; for if Christ is a bridegroom, he must take upon himself the things which are his bride's and bestow upon her the things that are his.[32]

Bride and groom share life together. Husband and wife share joy, pleasure, and wealth with each other. They also share in each

---

32   LW 31:351.

other's burdens, brokenness, and debts. If the bride is hurting, then the groom is hurting as well. If the groom prospers, then the bride prospers as well. Luther used this to illustrate the intimate relationship between Christ and individual Christians. Jesus gives His perfect holiness to the individual believer. In exchange, the individual believer gives sin and brokenness to Jesus. Jesus offers joy, pleasure, and the wealth of God's kingdom to the sinner. And the sinner offers Jesus burdens, brokenness, and debts. Needless to say, we are getting the better end of the deal.

Being married has a transformative power. Ask anyone married for a decade or more and the response will be the same: marriage changes you. A meaningful relationship has the power to change your entire life. Marriage alters your priorities and preferences, personality and perspective, expectations and experiences. Intimate union with another will never leave you the same. Luther emphasized the transformative power of being united with Christ. Faith in Christ transforms a believer. Christians are regenerated through faith in Christ, revived to a new life of neighborly love, and restored to reflect the perfect color of Jesus.

Luther believed that Christians should therefore stand out from the crowd. Lutheran theology teaches that God dwells within His people: "We unanimously reject and condemn . . . [that] God does not dwell in believers, only God's gifts dwell in them."[33] Lutherans believe that not only the gifts of God (i.e., grace, love, wisdom) dwell in believers, but God Himself dwells in believers. This led Luther to boldly assert that Christians possess far more than just the name of Christ:

We are altogether ignorant of our own name and do not know why we are Christians or bear the name of Christians. Surely

---

33 Formula of Concord, Solid Declaration, Article III, paragraphs 59, 65.

we are named after Christ, not because he is absent from us, but because he dwells in us, that is, because we believe in him and are Christs one to another and do to our neighbors as Christ does to us. But in our day we are taught by the doctrine of men to seek nothing but merits, rewards, and the things that are ours; of Christ we have made only a taskmaster far harsher than Moses.[34]

Being a Christian means being different. Believers stand out from the crowd because Christ dwells within them. His royal blood purges our sin and recolors our soul. His perfect mercy colors our actions. His bold truth tints our words. And you can be certain that Christ's holy hue will not leave you a soft pastel easily overlooked by others.

CULTURAL DISOBEDIENCE IN THE PAST

The world loves Christians. That is, as long as Christians soften their beliefs to a pleasing pastel, conform to the culture, and keep quiet about Jesus. People begin to look suspiciously at Christians when there is a whiff of cultural disobedience:

- Nobody else is praying for the food at the restaurant. Why do you insist on making us uncomfortable like that?

- We all go golfing on Sunday mornings. Are you silently passing judgment when you refuse to join us?

- It is weird when you go silent once the conversation turns to gossip. Why are you so awkward when it comes to talking about others?

---

34 LW 31:368.

- We all complain about our wives; why can't you just be one of the guys?

The world loves Christians as long as they act like everyone else. This is nothing new. Jesus sent the disciples out with words of warning:

Behold, I am sending you out as sheep in the midst of wolves, so be wise as serpents and innocent as doves. Beware of men, for they will deliver you over to courts and flog you in their synagogues, and you will be dragged before governors and kings for My sake, to bear witness before them and the Gentiles. (Matthew 10:16–18)

Lutherans have a heritage of cultural disobedience. To be certain, this is not synonymous with civil disobedience. Lutherans have never condoned refusing to pay taxes or breaking laws. We take the Fourth Commandment seriously and strive to honor civil authority. However, Lutherans have always refused to be colored by anyone other than Jesus. We resist the culture when it tries to soften the Christian faith into a more palatable pastel. Being Lutheran is confronting the culture.

Lutheran theology resists the culture when it is in opposition to God. Speaking out against the culture of his day placed a bounty on Luther's head. During the time of the Reformation, the Church and culture were deeply intermingled. The Church was the culture, and the culture was the Church. Certainly, there were some power struggles between church and state (most notably the Investiture Controversy of the eleventh and twelfth centuries). Still, the Roman Empire had a fairly harmonious relationship between church and state. When Luther resisted the practices of the Church, he was also resisting the practices of the culture.

Resisting the culture put a bull's-eye on Luther's back. He was a wanted man for speaking out against selling indulgences and other vacuous church practices. He was condemned for resisting the belief that the pope was the earthly substitute for Jesus (Vicar of Christ). Pushing against the church's teaching on purgatory pushed Luther into harm's way.

A tribunal of the Catholic Church, known as the Diet of Worms (1521), led Emperor Charles V to issue the Edict of Worms. This was an imperial death sentence:

> We have declared and made known that the said Martin Luther shall hereafter be held and esteemed by each and all of us as a limb cut off from the Church of God, an obstinate schismatic and manifest heretic. . . .

> We say, in the name of the Roman and imperial majesty . . . you shall refuse to give the aforesaid Martin Luther hospitality, lodging, food, or drink; neither shall anyone, by word or deed, secretly or openly, succor or assist him by counsel or help; but in whatever place you meet him, you shall proceed against him; if you have sufficient force, you shall take him prisoner and keep him in close custody; you shall deliver him, or cause him to be delivered, to us or at least let us know where he may be captured. In the meanwhile you shall keep him closely imprisoned until you receive notice from us what further to do, according to the direction of the laws. And for such holy and pious work we will indemnify you for your trouble and expense.[35]

Luther stood up to the Holy Roman Empire. And the whole Roman Empire stood against him. Luther's cultural disobedience

---

35   James Harvey Robinson, *Readings in European History*, vol. 2 (Boston: Ginn and Company, 1906), 87–88.

led to assaults on his character and teaching. The Edict of Worms asserted the following about Luther:

> Indeed, he writes nothing which does not arouse and promote sedition, discord, war, murder, robbery, and arson, and tend toward the complete downfall of the Christian faith. For he teaches a loose, self-willed life, severed from all laws and wholly brutish; and he is a loose, self-willed man, who condemns and rejects all laws; for he has shown no fear or shame in burning publicly the decretals and canon law. And had he feared the secular sword no more than the ban and penalties of the pope, he would have committed much worse offenses against the civil law.[36]

The presiding officer at Worms, a theologian named Johann Eck, directed sham accusations at Luther. He lumped Luther's name in with notorious heretics such as Pelagius (AD c. 354–c. 418) and Arius (AD 256–336). They colored Luther as a fanatic intent on overthrowing the church and society. Nevertheless, Luther did not conform to the color of the culture. He kept the color of Jesus.

Following in Luther's pattern, generations of Lutherans have engaged in cultural disobedience. The second generation of Lutherans—notably led by Martin Chemnitz and Jacob Andreae—helped maintain Lutheran theology amid pressures to soften the color of their beliefs. Lutheran princes formed an alliance known as the Schmalkaldic League to defend Lutheranism from being overtaken by the Holy Roman Empire. On February 27, 1531, Philip I, Landgrave of Hesse, and John Frederick I, Elector of Saxony, pledged to defend each other should their territories be attacked for being Lutheran. The Schmalkaldic

---

36 Robinson, *Readings in European History*, 85–86.

League became a formidable defender of Lutheranism as an increasing number of rulers subscribed to the Augsburg Confession.

Similarly, many Lutherans immigrated to America when the culture demanded that they stand down in the face of governmental changes in the church. They chose to leave everything behind rather than become a muted mixture of government-approved beliefs. They refused to simply become a boring shade of Protestant pastel. C. F. W. Walther followed in the pattern of other Lutherans by preserving the unique color of Lutheran theology in a land far from home.

The early part of the twentieth century (1900–1920) witnessed many church bodies softening their beliefs. Liberal theology swept through Protestant churches, turning every belief into some shade of ecumenical ecru, metaphorical mauve, or Schleiermacher soft blue. Lutherans were pressured to soften their beliefs on creation, resurrection, miracles, and the inerrancy of Scripture. Nevertheless, they held their true colors. Led by a dogged defender of the faith, Francis Pieper (1852–1931), the Lutherans resisted the soft hues of liberal theology. Pieper wrote a robust three-volume work (*Christliche Dogmatik*) articulating orthodox Lutheran theology.

These were all acts of cultural disobedience. These were not acts of civil disobedience or wanton disregard for civil authority. They were, however, acts of resistance against the pressure of the culture. When the culture told him to recant, Luther would not. When the culture told them to give up on the Reformation, Chemnitz, Andreae, and the Schmalkaldic League would not. When the culture told them to become a boring share of government-approved beliefs, the Lutherans would not. When the culture told them to loosen their belief on the resurrection, the Lutherans would not.

When the culture asks you to just be like everyone else, what are you going to do?

CULTURAL DISOBEDIENCE IN THE PRESENT

What can you do to boldly reflect the color of Jesus? What can you do to be Christ to your community? How can you stand out from the crowd because Christ dwells within you? There are many ways to enact cultural disobedience through our obedience to Jesus:

Pray in Public: When a friend tells you that she is going through a hard time, resist the urge to say, "I will keep you in my prayers." Rather than offering a sugary platitude, actually pray with her right then and there. Sure, it might make her uncomfortable. The people near you will stop and stare. Do it anyway. Other opportunities include praying a blessing before a meal at a restaurant, taking time at work to pray, or engaging complete strangers in prayer as opportunities arise. Praying in public is a way that you can reflect the bold color of Jesus.

Say Something: When others dogpile on Christianity, speak up and say something. It is not wrong to let people know that you find their words offensive. When people speak about Christians with gross generalities, call them out on it. When a colleague makes an erroneous claim about the Christian faith, provide accurate information in a respectful manner. When a group conversation turns to mocking believers, tell them that you rejoice in the foolishness of the cross (1 Corinthians 1:18).

Tithe: If you want to stand out from the crowd, give your money to a local congregation. Tithing slays the idol of wealth and forces you to rely on God's sustaining gifts. The culture tells us to live beyond the amount on your paycheck. Tithing tells the culture that you are going to live by faith in God: "For where your treasure is, there your heart will be also" (Matthew 6:21).

Posting Proclamation: Social media offers numerous opportunities to be bold in your faith. Rather than posting a picture of the awesome dinner you made, post a picture of your home group meeting together for Bible study. Instead of sharing mindless dribble about some reality television show, share a Bible verse. Rather than just "liking" a post about a friend mourning a death in the family, go talk with your friend over a cup of coffee. Boldly bear the color of Jesus as you engage in social media.

Think for Yourself: Everyone wants to think for you. Companies claim to have your best interests in mind. Television shows want to tell you what is right and wrong, normal and weird. Science says that it has done the research and crunched the numbers on your behalf. Doctors have thought it all through and deemed various procedures ethical. Think for yourself. Ask your doctor to explain exactly what occurs with the fertility treatment she is suggesting. Find out where your local grocery store purchases its produce. Learn about the political-campaign financing practices of your favorite coffee shop.

Again, these are not acts of civil disobedience. These are, however, clear ways that you can swim upstream against the flow of culture. Being united to Christ will transform you. Knowing Jesus will not leave you the same person. The presence of God dwelling within you is the unique gift of faith. Lutherans have engaged in cultural disobedience for generations. And yet today, being Lutheran is obedience to Jesus over the culture.

CONCLUSION

Let's return to the question at the beginning of this chapter: what makes Lutherans unique? We can safely rule out potlucks, committee meetings, and "A Mighty Fortress." These are not defining features of Lutheranism. We cannot trust that these features will distinguish the Lutheran confession from other confessions. We must figure out what makes Lutherans unique lest we join the ranks of Protestant pastel.

The first part of this book has explored what Lutheran theology resists. These are the human tendencies that we challenge. We push against a closed culture with a radical openness to sharing God's grace. We reject apathy and actually defend our faith. We refuse to be ignorant by actually knowing what we believe. We resist the urge to work for God's love and instead work for our neighbor's well-being. We detest being pastel like every other church body. Lutherans are unique because we are willing to challenge these broken human tendencies.

However, there is a problem here: even though we challenge these inclinations, we often engage them both individually and collectively:

- We are often closed to sharing the Gospel with people who are different; if they do not speak the same language as us, then we are not willing to tell them about Jesus.

- We have become lukewarm about defending our faith; we want to follow Jesus, but we keep our distance just in case He asks us to take up a cross of our own.

- We are confused about what to believe; many others have drained the Bible of its authority, and we consider opening a vein and joining them.

- We often use the Gospel to be lazy; our salvation does not depend on works, so let's go ahead and put on our sweatpants and do nothing for our neighbors.

- We have softened our beliefs and practices to a pleasing pastel; people find soft-pink theology less offensive than bold black-and-white beliefs.

- We will never be unique as long as we continue to reject the faith handed down to us. Reading a book about Lutheran theology does nothing unless we actually embody these beliefs. Before we can differentiate this confession from other confessions, we have to actually start being Lutheran.

We can start by living our beliefs.

More than simply knowing what we believe, we can do what we believe. The first part of this book has started us on the path to being Lutheran by exploring the broken human tendencies that we challenge. Now, the second part of this book will address what Lutheran theology cherishes.

We will examine the distinct works of God that we cherish. Richer than potluck pudding, we savor a salvation that comes from beyond ourselves. Stranger than the ever-empty front pew, we marvel at the mystery of how God uses ordinary material to deliver Christ's extraordinary grace. Unlike the melodic resolution in our hymnody, we recognize that certain tensions in Scripture are better left unresolved.

Beyond the committee meetings, we celebrate Christ working in and through us. Stronger than the urge for congregational infighting, we cling to the worship of the local congregation, where God dwells in the midst of the community. Being Lutheran is cherishing the peculiarities of the Gospel.

Vignette: Jack

Memorable hardly begins to describe Jack. His neighbors knew him as the "tomato guy" before they knew he was a pastor. He planted a vegetable garden behind his church: cucumbers, rutabaga, potatoes, tomatoes, lettuce, peppers, and herbs. After service during the late summer and early fall, Jack would check on the garden to see what was ripe. He would then go door-to-door at an apartment complex a few blocks away handing out the free vegetables from the garden. Before long, he was known throughout the community simply as the "tomato guy." Only a few people in the entire apartment complex knew he was pastor of the local Lutheran church.

Serving a congregation in a small college town, Jack is the kind of guy that defies stereotypes. He is a vegan and a Confessional Lutheran. He writes poetry and has a tattered, well-worn Book of Concord. He goes on silent prayer retreats and reads through the Bible yearly. He quotes Wendell Berry and Martin Chemnitz in the same conversation. When he is not preaching a sermon at his congregation or growing vegetables in the garden, he is in Kenya working at a Christian orphanage. Trying to categorize Jack is impossible. He is crunchy but not a hippy. He is an environmentalist but rejects biocentrism. He is a Bible-reading, sandal-wearing, granola-munching, mission-minded, Confessional Lutheran.

Jack's faith in Christ directs every aspect of his life. Who he is and what he does is centered on his life in Christ Jesus. Jesus encouraged His disciples to give people something to eat; Jack encourages his congregation to work in the garden and give the community something to eat. Jesus went on quiet prayer retreats; Jack goes on quiet prayer retreats. Jesus had a heart for widows in Judea; Jack has a heart for orphans in Kenya. Jesus knew Scripture and applied it to His daily life; Jack studies Scripture and applies it to his daily life.

Jesus confessed divine truth; Jack confesses his faith in Christ Jesus and the beliefs of Lutheran theology.

The young man eventually died in Portland at a homeless camp. He developed an infection and refused to seek medical attention from a clinic. He left behind an ex-girlfriend and two young kids. Jack went to visit the family after he heard that his friend had died. After visiting with them, his friend's two-year-old son ran after Jack and wanted to be picked up. When Jack picked up the young child, the child kissed him right on the mouth.

Both drifters and toddlers are drawn to Jack. And so are complete strangers. They sense the peace that he has within him and want to know more. They recognize that there is something different about him. Within minutes of meeting Jack, people cannot help but feel loved by him. People want to know what makes him so unique. And he gladly tells them: Jesus. People ask why he is so calm, and he tells them it is because of Jesus. People ask why he cares for the environment, and he tells them it is because of Jesus. People ask how he came to be known as the "tomato guy," and he tells them it is because of Jesus. People ask him why he became a pastor, and he tells them it is because of Jesus. Jack is the way he is because of Jesus. Radical discipleship and vividly reflecting the color of Christ Jesus ensures that Jack is not pastel.

Jack does, however, have his share of struggles. It is hard following Jesus. He is constantly tempted by others to give up. His congregation wants him to be more like normal pastors. It is difficult to have a successful potluck when your pastor does not eat ham sandwiches. It is a little awkward having to worship next to a homeless man with no teeth. It is embarrassing having your pastor known around town as the "tomato guy."

There are times when he begins telling himself he should give up. It is demanding to take up a cross and follow Jesus. Being dedicated to reading Scripture does not get any easier over the years. It gets harder. Jack always has an uneasy feeling in his stomach before he sets out on a silent prayer retreat; being alone with God for a whole day is not a walk in the park. It would be easier for Jack to change his practices, buy a set of golf clubs, and "spend some time with God" while he waits for the beverage cart to arrive.

Jack refuses to give up.

He knows that his life of faith is a gift from God. He trusts that the Holy Spirit will give him endurance as he follows Jesus. He prays that the Spirit would sustain his faith every new day. He asks God to guide his actions so that he can clearly reflect the color of Jesus in all that he does.

Chapter 5
Discussion Questions

1. Read Matthew 5:1–12. How does Jesus recolor conventional thinking through this teaching? Why might other religious teachers resist this colorful teaching of Jesus?

2. Read Matthew 17:1–13. What is the meaning behind Jesus becoming radiantly white? Why did Peter, James, and John respond with terror when they saw Jesus transfigured?

3. Jesus engaged a whole array of colorful people with the mercy of God. Did Jesus discriminate against certain ethnicities? Was racism an issue during that time in history? Read Matthew 15:21–28.

4. Christians carry Christ with them wherever they go. How does this change your perspective on daily life? Are menial tasks made holy because of Christ's presence?

5. Luther taught that Christians are "Christs one to another and do to our neighbors as Christ does to us" (LW 31:367). What does this look like in your life? How do you bring Christ's love, forgiveness, and peace to the people around you?

6. Read Matthew 10:16–18. Jesus prepared His disciples to stand out from the crowd. How does your faith in Jesus lead you to stand out from the crowd? What are some ways that you blend in with the crowd? Is this necessarily a bad thing?

7. Luther faced public ridicule for opposing the culture of his day. Have you ever faced public ridicule for your faith in Jesus? How can you face persecution in a godly way? Read Matthew 10:19–25.

8. How is cultural disobedience different than civil disobedience? Read 1 Peter 2:13–17.

9. Jack vividly reflects the color of Jesus. How much do your actions, lifestyle, or practices reflect the color of the culture?

Part 2

Being Lutheran:
What We Cherish

Chapter 6

NEW

And He who was seated on the throne said, "Behold,
I am making all things new." Also He said, "Write this
down, for these words are trustworthy and true."
(Revelation 21:5)

Born to Slovak immigrants, Jaroslav Pelikan (1923–2006) found a home in American academia. Although his father was pastor at Trinity Slovak Lutheran Church in Chicago, Illinois, and his grandfather was a bishop of the Slovak Lutheran Church in America, he did not follow their lead by becoming a parish pastor. Instead, Pelikan spent his career as a university professor. He taught Lutheran theology for many years at Valparaiso University and Concordia Seminary. He also translated a tremendous amount of Martin Luther's writings into English. In 1962, Pelikan took a professorship at Yale University teaching in the history department. There he continued to lecture on the history of Lutheran theology.

In 2005, Pelikan developed lung cancer. Finally, after a long struggle with the illness, Pelikan died in May 2006. His last words were easily his greatest: "If Christ is risen, then nothing else matters. And if Christ is not risen, then nothing else matters."

These words encompass the extremes of empty despair and resurrection hope. Pelikan, as with all believers in the resurrection of Jesus, placed his trust in the former half of these words. Everything hinges on Christ's resurrection. Everything else in all of creation is secondary to the empty tomb. Pelikan's words echoes the words of Paul in 1 Corinthians 15: "If Christ has not been raised, your faith is futile and you are still in your sins. . . . But in fact Christ has been raised from the dead, the firstfruits of those who have fallen asleep" (vv. 17, 20).

Imagine just for a moment that the second half of Pelikan's statement was true. Suppose that Christ was not raised from death to life. What if Jesus was just a great teacher who simply lived and died? What if we were left to save ourselves? What would still matter if Christ were dead and in the ground?

Nothing.

Nothing else matters if Christ is not risen. Without the hope of God in Christ Jesus, there is nothing of lasting worth. Without His resurrection, there is only despair, decay, and **Nothing else matters if Christ is not risen** death. There is only the bane, blight, and brokenness of sin. Humanity would have to save itself from death and brokenness. If God were dead and in the tomb, then our lives would be a steady march toward the vacuous pit of death. This is what human existence would look like if the stone had never been rolled away from Christ's grave:

Death: Life ends in death. That is it. Meaningless molecules came together to form life, and soon they will come apart in the grave. Do not try to find meaning in life because there is no lasting meaning to be found. Happiness, joy, and laughter are eclipsed by the vast nothingness of mortality. Brokenness abounds, death is inevitable, and suffering is inescapable. Every possible remedy to overcome death is impotent. We toil to extend our lives by mere minutes only to face an eternity in which we don't exist.

Medicine: The medical arts have no cure for death. Cancer multiplies faster than researchers can develop new treatments. And even if doctors cure cancer, death will surely come from some other source. Viruses spread as fast as a contaminated plane can fly. Perennial medical problems—infertility, miscarriages, and the common cold—still haunt humanity. Researchers promise a brighter future by locating every gene in the human body, yet countless children are concerned with locating their absentee fathers. Why squeak out a few more years if life is but a drop of water in the vast sea of death?

Technology: Technological progress is equally hopeless. New technology promises a new life of happiness and peace. Yet, these advancements in technology only reflect and magnify our human brokenness. Smartphones boast of perfect connectivity; yet, all they really do is promote distracted driving. The greatest technological achievement of the twentieth century was the atomic bomb. The greatest technological achievement of this century will likely be just a better bomb.

Racism: Bigotry has no permanent remedy in education, activism, or public service announcements. Any progress made by these efforts is quickly erased by one protest, one bullet, or one bomb. Slavery is not an entry in a history book; entire tribes and nationalities continue to work against their will for others. Terrorism utilizes everyday technology—planes, computers, and social media—to create a worldwide web of violence. All a person needs is a few hundred dollars and some household items to inflict unimaginable brutality. Why toil to make social progress if the next generation is going to undo it all anyway?

Wealth: Economic progress claims to create a better world for all people. Yet, the only apparent progress is precariously stacking the financial house of cards higher and higher and higher. A lifetime of savings depends on a menagerie of circumstances including the price of oil, the direction of the wind, and the current turmoil in some Eastern European country ending in "stan." The economy climbs and debt deepens. The American dream is paying off student loans before you default in death. Why scrimp and save for a lifetime when death is just going to take it all away?

In the words of the French philosopher Michel de Montaigne, "Live as long as you can, you shall by that nothing shorten the time that you are to lie dead."[37] If Christ is not risen, then nothing else matters. Sin abounds. Brokenness breeds more brokenness.

This chapter is shaping up to be a bit of a bummer, huh?

JESUS: MAKING ALL THINGS NEW

Here is the good news: God is not dead. Christ is risen. And everything else orbits around the gravity of the empty tomb. The truth is that we cannot save ourselves. Every attempt at our own salvation—every human effort to stop death—comes up wanting. Rescue from the brokenness of life can come only from outside of us. God comes into our midst with the remedy. Salvation is from beyond us.

---

37   William Hazlitt, *The Complete Works of Michael de Montaigne* (New York: Worthington Company, 1869), 59.

Jesus Christ makes all things new. The last book of the Bible, Revelation, gives us a glimpse into the new creation of Christ:

> Then I saw a new heaven and a new earth, for the first heaven and the first earth had passed away, and the sea was no more. And I saw the holy city, new Jerusalem, coming down out of heaven from God, prepared as a bride adorned for her husband. And I heard a loud voice from the throne saying, "Behold, the dwelling place of God is with man. He will dwell with them, and they will be His people, and God Himself will be with them as their God. He will wipe away every tear from their eyes, and death shall be no more, neither shall there be mourning, nor crying, nor pain anymore, for the former things have passed away." And He who was seated on the throne said, "Behold, I am making all things new." Also He said, "Write this down, for these words are trustworthy and true." (Revelation 21:1–5)

This new creation began when God entered the old creation. The long-awaited incarnation of Jesus Christ marked the moment in which God put on human flesh for all eternity (John 1:14). The word *incarnation* comes from the Latin word *carnis*. This word translates into "meat" or "flesh." The incarnation (in-*carnis*-ation) of Jesus is God taking on meat and bones, muscles and sinew, flesh and blood. God came from outside creation to dwell inside the womb of Mary. Salvation came from outside of us (*extra nos*) and entered into our midst. God entered into humanity to deliver the salvation that we so desperately need.

Therefore, it is no mistake that the Gospels include detailed genealogies of Jesus of Nazareth. He is fully human with a fully human lineage. Jesus had a family: aunts, uncles, cousins, grandfathers, and grandmothers. His mother's cousin Elizabeth undoubtedly pinched His cheeks and used her own spittle to clean His holy face. Establishing Jesus' lineage within humanity is crucial. Human flesh was the source of sin plaguing creation. God went to the source of the problem to bring about His new creation.

The Creator entered His creation. This mystery has confounded Christendom for centuries. Many people have ended up in error trying to make sense of the incarnation. For instance, there was a group of people in the first century that claimed Jesus only appeared to be human (Docetism). They refused to accept that God would assume human flesh into the Holy Trinity. Others thought that Jesus only appeared to be divine (Arianism). They refused to accept that God would personally enter the messiness of creation.

The truth confounds the false teachers. God entered His creation, took on human flesh for all eternity, and made all things new through Jesus Christ. Jesus did not just make some things new. He did not just make human things new. He made all things new. Jesus Christ is the harbinger of the new creation. Thus all of God's creation—humans, angels, animals, heavens, and mountains—rejoiced at Christ's arrival. He was born amid a symphony of bleating barnyard animals. Mary draped rags woven from organic matter around the newborn Jesus' body (Luke 2:7). These humble Christmas linens became the first outfit ever worn by Christ. The sky above proclaimed God's handiwork as a star announced the birth of this newborn Christ Child (Matthew 2:2). Shepherds and angels, human and nonhuman creatures (Luke 2:8–12), rejoiced at the news of Jesus' birth.

From the animals and celestial signs to the shepherds and angels, it is clear that all of creation rejoiced at Christ's birth. Notice God did not exclusively use human beings to herald Christ's birth; instead, God used the panoply of the created world to signal the Savior had arrived. Christ came to bring a new creation and therefore all of creation rejoiced at His coming.

Bleating barnyard animals are rejoicing in the presence of the Lord? A star twinkling in the sky is praising its Creator? All creatures great and small are worshiping Jesus? I don't think so. That sounds a little bit out there. That sounds like some sort of new age slop . . .

Or it sounds like Scripture. Psalm 19 sings about the heavens and sky declaring the glory of God. Psalm 96:11–13 exudes a similar message:

> Let the heavens be glad, and let the earth rejoice; let the sea roar, and all that fills it; let the field exult, and everything in it! Then shall all the trees of the forest sing for joy before the LORD, for He comes, for He comes to judge the earth. He will judge the world in righteousness, and the peoples in His faithfulness.

Elsewhere in Scripture, the prophet Isaiah proclaims that in the presence of God, "the mountains and the hills before you shall break forth into singing, and all the trees of the field shall clap their hands" (Isaiah 55:12). The apostle Paul makes it clear that all of creation longs for the new creation of Christ: "For the creation waits with eager longing for the revealing of the sons of God" (Romans 8:19).

Jesus is the arrival of the new creation. Everywhere Jesus went, the new creation unfolded at His feet. At His Baptism, a glimpse of the new creation occurred when the heavens opened and God spoke (Matthew 3:13–17). Jesus then went into the wilderness to take on Satan's temptation. While going toe-to-toe with the old evil foe, the new creation was made manifest as Jesus literally hung out with wild animals (Mark 1:13).

After His Baptism and temptation, Jesus went about the work of publicly making all things new. New creation occurrences accompanied the ministry of Jesus.

- New peace came to an old sea when Jesus stilled the storm on command (Mark 4:39).

- New sustenance came from old bread when Jesus miraculously fed thousands (Mark 6:41).

- New health came to old bones when crowds touched the hem of Jesus' garment (Mark 6:56).

- New light came to old darkness when Jesus corrected human traditions with divine truth (Matthew 5).

- New hope came to an old widow when Jesus raised her son back to life (Luke 7:11–17).

- New ways surpassed old ways when Jesus stooped to wash the feet of the disciples (John 13:14–15).

The old creation came to ruin by sin; the new creation radiantly bloomed in Jesus.

JESUS: MAKING YOU NEW

Christ is risen. His victory over death has made all things new. And Christ makes *you* new. Jesus brings peace to stormy seas *and* peace to your stormy soul. Jesus sustains the masses with bread *and* sustains you for eternity with the bread of life. Jesus heals broken bodies *and* heals your brokenness. He forgives your sin, shines truth into your darkness, and makes you a new creation: "Therefore, if anyone is in Christ, he is a new creation. The old has passed away; behold, the new has come" (2 Corinthians 5:17). New life came to the whole creation through Jesus. And new life comes to you through faith in Jesus.

The global work of God is made local through faith in Christ. God provides new life to all of creation through the death and resurrection of Jesus (objective justification). Since Christ is risen, nothing else matters more than the empty tomb. The rock is rolled away for the sins of the whole world. Yet, God gives new life to you individually through faith in Jesus (subjective justification). The rock is rolled away for your sins. New life in Christ is personally grasped through faith. Just as the prongs of a ring hold tight to a diamond, faith holds tight to the salvation of Jesus. The Holy Spirit creates faith and allows individual believers to personally take hold of salvation.

Faith holds tight to the salvation of Jesus

Scripture is teeming with examples of new life coming to individuals through faith in Jesus:

- There is the woman with chronic bleeding. Her faith led her to reach out and touch Jesus' garment, and she was made new by Jesus. He said to her, "Daughter, your faith has made you well; go in peace, and be healed of your disease" (Mark 5:34).

- There is the Samaritan leper healed by Jesus and made well through faith. Jesus healed ten lepers in a village between Galilee and Samaria. Nevertheless, only one of the healed lepers returned to worship Jesus. As the Samaritan leper returned, Jesus spoke words of new life, saying, "Rise and go your way; your faith has made you well" (Luke 17:19).

- There is blind Bartimaeus who asked in faith that Jesus would have mercy on him. Jesus responded by giving him the new life that comes through faith: "Go your way; your faith has made you well" (Mark 10:52).

Made well in Jesus. The disease of sin is made well by grace through faith in Christ. The weight of sin is removed by calling upon the name of Jesus in faith. God counts Christ's righteousness as our righteousness. Broken people are justified by grace, receive the forgiveness of sins, and take hold of eternal salvation through faith in Jesus Christ.

This may not seem all that radical. These statements may seem almost commonplace among Christian beliefs. That is because of Martin Luther. Do not be mistaken: These teachings were at one time so radical that they could get you killed. These teachings were so vehemently rejected by the Church that people were put to death over the issue. Luther sparked a revolution when he used Scripture to show that believers are justified by grace through faith in Jesus. He took a stand for the Gospel and articulated how we receive new life in Christ apart from human efforts. And the world has never been the same since.

There was a time when Luther did not know the Gospel. He thought that new life in Christ was something he had to earn through good living. If he wanted to be made well for all eternity, then he had better start living a life devoted to healing his sin. He dedicated himself to the Augustinian order as a monk in the Roman Catholic Church. This monastic life had Luther fasting for days, praying for hours, and frequenting the confession booth.

Although he went through all the pious motions, Luther daily questioned his salvation. He struggled through many dark nights of fear. He was never fully sure that his efforts were enough to warrant eternal life. He questioned if his motives were genuine and acceptable to God. His was not a nihilistic fear of a universe without meaning; rather, it was a fear of eternal damnation for his sins. Luther did not question whether or not Christ was risen; instead, he questioned whether or not he was worthy to stand before the risen Lord on the Last Day. He was afraid of death, condemnation, and Satan. Even more, Luther was afraid of Jesus. He feared standing before Jesus and having to prove why he was worthy of eternal life.

During this time of inner struggle, Luther was teaching theology at the University of Wittenberg. His primary task as theology professor was to teach the Bible. He lectured on the Psalms (1514–15), Romans (1515–16), Galatians (1516–17), and Hebrews (1517–18). Being in God's Word daily had a profound impact on Luther, and lecturing on Scripture forced him to reexamine the basis of his beliefs. Rather than study Aristotle or Aquinas, Luther was studying God's Word.

A curious thing happened while Luther was studying Scripture: he discovered the Gospel.

A CONFUSED GOSPEL

Medieval theology had lost the Gospel. The clear teaching of Scripture that sinners are justified by grace through faith was buried under heaps of philosophical tradition. During the Middle Ages, theologians were more interested in the works of Aristotle and Aquinas than Scripture. Philosophical reason had authority over God's Word; theologians were taught to read the Gospel of Matthew only after years of studying the gospel of Aristotle.

As a result of valuing philosophy over Scripture, many peculiar beliefs grew within the Church. Sins were subdivided into different categories:

- Mortal sins were sins that separated a person from God and threatened eternal damnation.

- Venial sins were lesser sins that, while not worthy of eternal damnation, did threaten to harm a person's relationship with God.

Medieval theology also divided sins into eternal and temporal consequences. A sin had the eternal consequence of separation from God and the temporal consequence of penance. Even when the eternal consequence of sin was forgiven, the temporal consequence remained. Christians had to perform acts of penance in order to repay their sins.

With philosophy at the forefront of theology, Scripture fell into the background. The belief in purgatory flourished during this period of Church history. Purgatory became an official Church doctrine at the Second Council of Lyon (1274). The Council determined that a waiting room for the dead should be an official belief; it stated that those who died in the faith, yet had not made complete satisfaction for their sins, would have their souls purified by "cleansing pains." Furthermore, the Council stipulated, these pains could be lifted by the actions of the living, such as the sacrifices of masses, prayers, giving of alms, and other pious work established by the Church.

Purgatory relies on the premise that nothing unclean or unholy can enter heaven (Revelation 21:27). However, it assumes that Christ's forgiveness of sins is not enough to remove the temporal consequences of sin. Purgatory is a place of refinement for believers preparing for heaven. It is a place for those destined for heaven yet waiting for their paperwork to clear.

The Gospel somehow had to fit into this complex system of philosophical categories. Luther was raised believing that the Gospel was God setting you on the path of holiness. Sinners were infused with grace (infused righteousness), which allowed them to obtain new life through holy living. The life of faith was a progressive justification between Baptism and Judgment Day.

Luther, however, feared that his self-justification was never enough. He doubted his personal holiness. He was skeptical that his motives for praying and fasting were pure enough. He questioned the sincerity of his charitable giving. He wondered if he had truly repented or had just spoken hollow words in the confession booth.

This inner struggle of doubt, coupled with his attentive study of Scripture, led Luther to reexamine the Gospel. As previously discussed in chapter 2, Luther studied the Book of Romans and realized that Christ's righteousness is the free gift of faith. New life in Christ does not come slowly by a life of good works through infused grace. Rather, new life in Christ comes immediately by grace through faith. Christ alone makes all things new. Human hands and hearts help nothing. God's grace does it all.

Luther found that Scripture teaches that Christ's righteousness was freely given through faith (imputed righteousness): a totally new heart, totally new holiness, and totally new life come simply by the grace of God in Christ Jesus. The Reformation was founded on this central belief. Luther lived and breathed this reality. He cherished this biblical truth. He centered his whole existence on the new life that comes from grace alone through faith alone in Christ alone.

This confession pushed against many established beliefs about sin, grace, and the Gospel. Luther's confession of the Gospel threatened to disrupt everything.

And it did.

The Roman Catholic Church demanded that Luther and the other Wittenberg reformers give an articulation of their beliefs on how sinners are made new. Thus, the Augsburg Confession proudly proclaimed that sinners are saved by grace through faith:

> Our churches teach that people cannot be justified before God by their own strength, merits, or works. People are freely justified for Christ's sake, through faith, when they believe that they are received into favor and that their sins are forgiven for Christ's sake. By His death, Christ made satisfaction for our sins. God counts this faith for righteousness in His sight.[38]

---

38   Augsburg Confession, Article IV, paragraphs 1–3.

This confession was a departure from the Roman Catholic belief in a human-directed process of justification. The Lutherans freely confessed that human strength, merits, or works contribute nothing to salvation; rather, people are freely and instantaneously justified through faith. Faith alone makes all things new, forgives all sins, and delivers eternal life in Christ Jesus:

> Through faith, as St. Peter says, we have a new and clean heart [Acts 15:9–11], and God will and does account us entirely righteous and holy for the sake of Christ, our Mediator [1 Timothy 2:5]. Although sin in the flesh has not yet been completely removed or become dead [Romans 7:18], yet He will not punish or remember it.[39]

Being Lutheran is confessing new life in Christ. This confession of new life recognizes an old life of sin and death. This old life is the nothingness of being "dead in the trespasses and sins" (Ephesians 2:1). The old life is bondage to the devil and slavery to fleshy desires. New life in Christ is being made alive in Him (Ephesians 2:5). And this new life in Christ comes by grace through faith: "For by grace you have been saved through faith. And this is not your own doing; it is the gift of God, not a result of works, so that no one may boast" (Ephesians 2:8–9).

NOTHING ELSE MATTERS

Nothing matters more than new life in Christ. We enter the empty tomb through faith. Our only hope is being made alive in Christ. Being Lutheran is confessing new life by grace through faith in Christ. We obsess over this because the Gospel is at stake. We refuse to turn

---

39 Smalcald Articles, Part III, Article XIII, paragraph 1.

justification by grace into a human project. We will not let Scripture be twisted and contorted so that the gift of Christ's resurrection must be completed by human efforts. Being Lutheran is receiving a different, new, clean heart through faith in Christ.

Rightly understanding new life in Christ leads to rightly understanding all other beliefs. Luther made it clear that nothing else matters if our understanding of new life in Christ is confused: "For if the doctrine of justification is lost, the whole of Christian doctrine is lost."[40] He further elaborated on this by saying,

> (For by this doctrine alone and through it alone is the church built, and in this it consists.) Otherwise we shall not be able to observe true theology but shall immediately become lawyers, ceremonialists, legalists, and papists. Christ will be so darkened that no one in the church will be correctly taught or comforted.[41]

You are made new by grace through faith in Christ Jesus. This truth has tremendous implications on your daily life. Being a new creation in Christ changes everything:

Today: God's grace through faith in Jesus makes you new today. Not tomorrow. Not someday. Today. The very moment the Holy Spirit works saving faith is the very moment of salvation. There is no probation period for justification. God does not take six to eight weeks to process your paperwork. You are made new on the very day and hour of saving faith. As quick as the paralytic stood and walked, Jesus replaces your old life of sin with the new life

---

40   LW 26:9.
41   LW 26:10.

of salvation: "Take heart, My son; your sins are forgiven" (Matthew 9:2). In Christ Jesus, you are a new person today. The way you relate to your family and friends, co-workers and neighbors is immediately and forever changed by new life in Christ.

Hope: Your hope is in Christ alone. Your hope is not in health or happiness, money or mankind. Your hope is not in the goodness of your heart or the merits of your hard work. Your hope is in Jesus. Daily life is forever changed when your hope is in Jesus. Have I done enough to please God? What can I do to be worthy of God's love? Am I a good person? These questions are all answered in Jesus. The cross of Jesus has eternally pleased God in your stead. God looks at you and sees one worthy of His love and His life. You are a good person because of Christ's righteousness given to you through faith. Your hope is no longer in yourself. Careers will come and go. Health will fade and diminish. Morality will offer fleeting confidence. Your eternal hope is in Jesus.

Confidence: Daily life will shake your confidence. Hurtful words, failed endeavors, and poor performance will leave you feeling like a failure. Past mistakes and buried sins keep cropping up in your life. Satan will hang sin after sin over your head and remind you of all the times you have failed. Salvation by grace through faith means that your confidence is in Christ. No matter how sinful your past, Jesus makes you a new creation. Luther taught that Christian confidence is anchored in Jesus: "Little is gained against the devil with a lengthy disputation; but a brief word and reply such as this is effective: 'I am a Christian, of the same flesh and blood as my Lord Christ, the Son of God. You settle with Him, devil!' Such a retort would soon make him depart."[42] Your self-confidence may be shaken by a strong wind. However, your confidence in Christ cannot be shaken.

Glory: Being Lutheran is giving glory to God alone (*Soli Deo Gloria*). You have been made new simply by the grace of God. You did nothing to earn salvation or merit forgiveness. New life in Christ is a gift of God. The Small Catechism puts it this way: "I believe that I cannot by my own reason or strength believe in Jesus Christ, my Lord, or come to Him; but the Holy Spirit has called me by the Gospel, enlightened me with His gifts, sanctified and kept me in the true faith."[43] Being Lutheran is giving God all the glory. Even your own salvation is to the glory of God. Praise God for giving you saving faith. Rejoice in Christ's righteousness over your own self-righteousness. Let all your actions give glory to God for the salvation given to you in Christ Jesus.

Tomorrow: The future may seem uncertain. Will my job still be there tomorrow? Will my relationships remain the same years from now? What happens if we have global war and more terrorism? As uncertain as tomorrow may seem, your future is certain in Christ Jesus. Your future is as certain as the empty tomb. Since Christ is risen, nothing else matters. Poverty, cancer, terrorism, and death do not own your tomorrow. Future fear, failure, and fatigue are stripped of

---

42 LW 22:106.

43 Small Catechism, Explanation of the Third Article.

their power because you have new life in Christ. Face the future knowing that your sins are forgiven, your salvation is certain, and you forever have new life in Christ.

CONCLUSION

Look around and you will see brokenness. Broken bodies. Broken homes. Broken relationships. Broken communities. Every attempt at our own salvation comes up wanting. We have proven that we simply cannot do it. We cannot save our bodies from death, our relationships from demise, or our communities from decay. Help must come from outside of us.

And help does come in Christ Jesus. Our inability to save ourselves from the inside requires a Redeemer from the outside. The empty tomb makes all things new as God came in human flesh to bring new creation. God's grace is the life, death, and resurrection of Jesus Christ. His sacrifice has covered the sins of the world and His resurrection makes all things new. Salvation came to creation in the Word made flesh.

Salvation comes to you through faith. The Holy Spirit creates faith and delivers new life in Christ. By grace through faith you are an entirely new creation. God gives you Christ's righteousness, forgives your sins, and makes you new. A totally new heart, new holiness, and new life come simply by the grace of God in Christ Jesus. Nothing matters more than God's gift of new life.

Being Lutheran centers on justification by grace through faith in Christ Jesus. This confession will shape the rest of the book. The remaining chapters revolve around this one truth. Baptism, Holy Communion, vocation, and worship orbit around the gravity of grace given through faith. New life comes by grace alone, through faith alone, in Christ alone. Without new life in Christ, nothing else matters.

Vignette: Ben

Ben was kind of a big deal. He was in charge of sales for a manufacturing company in Detroit. His job was to wine and dine big customers. Making customers feel special was a nightly occurrence: *"We do not order the most expensive bottle of wine for all our clients." "Not everyone gets this sort of treatment." "We especially want your business."* Every night it was the same story with different characters.

His company bankrolled all his expenses. A five-hundred-dollar tab at a restaurant was nothing when it could secure a deal worth millions of dollars. Ben had a membership at the nicest country club so he could secure tee times on the nicest golf courses. He had a penthouse suite for cocktail parties. He was allowed to charge booze to the company credit card. The only thing he had to buy himself was the yacht.

There was one drawback to Ben's job: he could not say no to a customer. He did whatever the clients wanted to do. If the clients wanted to play golf, then Ben wanted to play golf. If the clients wanted sushi, then Ben wanted sushi. If the clients wanted to get sloshed, then Ben wanted to get sloshed. If the clients wanted to do cocaine, then Ben wanted to do cocaine. He did not *have* to do it. However, it made closing big deals that much easier. The more he said "yes" to the customers, the more they said "yes" to the deal—and the more the commission checks grew.

It did not take long for Ben to develop an addiction. His addiction was initially relegated to work outings, but it slowly crept into his home life as well.

Ben's wife soon noticed that he would average five drinks a night . . . on a Tuesday. Children's soccer games were missed. Marital arguments grew louder. Hand tremors became shakier. And the big paychecks kept coming.

Ben was losing it.

His wife told him she was leaving. She moved in with her sister. Their three sons went with her. The boys kept in contact with Ben for a while. Then they stopped answering his calls. The job was the last thing to go. Ben pushed drugs and alcohol on an unwilling customer, and the president of the company heard about the incident. The paychecks stopped, and the memberships were canceled.

The months after that became foggy. Ben aged considerably in less than a year. He lost part of his thumb in a fight. He also lost his driver's license after driving under the influence. He started chain-smoking cigarettes and lost a lot of weight. He drank cheap whiskey in the morning and weak coffee at night. Ben was stumbling to the grave.

God stopped Ben's death march. New life in Christ Jesus came to Ben one evening in a hotel room. A week before, he had made some Christian friends at a support group for alcoholics. They were talking about how their faith in Christ was the source of their new life. Although Ben was not particularly interested, he enjoyed the conversation. (Not many people talked to him anymore.) Later that same week, Ben was in a hotel room drinking alone. He threw up in the toilet and noticed blood. He had thrown up some blood before, but never as much as this. He looked at the scarlet-red water and panicked.

Before he could think clearly, he prayed. And then he realized that he did not know how to pray. He had been baptized and raised in the church over forty years ago. He ran to the bed and pulled out the Bible from the nightstand. He opened it up and leafed through some pages. He tried to remember verses that were meaningful from his childhood. Nothing came to mind. He went to the beginning of the New Testament and started with Matthew. He skipped over all the names that were hard to pronounce. And then he found something he recognized: "Now the birth of Jesus Christ took place in this way" (Matthew 1:18).

Ben read as long as he could stay awake. He fell asleep somewhere around chapter 2. The next morning, he picked up where he had left off. He finished the Gospel of Matthew. He prayed again that day. He made a point of telling the others in his support group what had happened. Some of them stayed after the meeting and prayed with him that God would continue to grow and strengthen Ben's faith.

Life was made new for Ben. New life in Christ Jesus changed everything. He was not the same man. He never drank again after that night in the hotel room. Coming to know Jesus was the turning point in his addiction. He kept going to group meetings. He had to take the bus or walk to get there, because he still did not have a driver's license. Yet, he did not mind waiting for the bus. It was his time to pray or reflect on the blessings God had shown him that day.

One day, Ben took the bus across town to attend a support-group meeting. One hour and three transfers later, he arrived only to find that the meeting had been canceled. No problem. Ben decided that he would get something to drink at a coffee shop across the street. He walked into the coffee shop and looked at the menu: Latte, Espresso, Americano, Chai, Mocha, and Biscotti. Ben was confused.

The barista sensed his confusion and asked him politely, "Do you know what you want?"

Ben replied with a chuckle and said, "No. I have no idea what I want."

Keeping the playful banter going, the barista replied, "If you don't know what you want to drink, then how will you ever know what you want out of life?"

Ben's face turned serious. He said, "I know exactly what I want out of life: I want to live in the new life that I have been given in Christ Jesus. I want to live every day and enjoy the many blessings of God. That is what I want out of life."

The barista was stunned. After a confused pause, she responded: "You mean to tell me that you do not know what sort of coffee you want to drink, but you know exactly what you want out of life?"

Ben smiled and shook his head. And then he ordered a black coffee.

Chapter 6
Discussion Questions

1. Read 1 Corinthians 15:12–19. There is nothing of lasting worth without the hope of God in Christ Jesus. What is the difference between hope and optimism?

2. Many people have ended up in error trying to make sense of the incarnation of Jesus Christ. Read 1 Timothy 3:16. What do many people erroneously believe about the incarnation? Is this erroneous belief intentional or accidental?

3. All of creation rejoiced at the coming of Jesus. Did all of creation come under the curse of sin? What happened to the ground and animals as a result of human sin? Read Genesis 3:17–21.

4. Scripture is teeming with examples of new life coming to individuals through faith in Jesus. Besides those mentioned in the chapter, are there other individuals in Scripture who have been made new through faith in Christ? Read 1 Timothy 1:12–17.

5. Read Ephesians 2:8–9. What is grace? What does it mean to be saved? Why are accurate definitions for these words so important?

6. Why might Luther teach that if the article concerning justification falls, then everything falls? Why is salvation by grace through faith such a vital confession for Lutherans?

7. Even your own salvation is to the glory of God. How is your salvation to God's glory? What are some ways that people diminish God's glory in salvation? Read 1 Corinthians 10:31–33.

8. Brokenness abounds. What sort of brokenness abounds around you? How does new life in Christ change this brokenness? Read Isaiah 25:6–9.

9. Ben received new life from Christ Jesus. Do you know anyone like Ben? Is new life in Christ always a dramatic conversion?

Chapter 7

ORDINARY

Then the LORD *God formed the man of dust from the*
ground and breathed into his nostrils the breath of life,
and the man became a living creature. (Genesis 2:7)

The earth weighs roughly 5.972 x 10^{24} kg. Less than thirty grams
of the entire weight of the earth is an element known as astatine. It
is the rarest naturally occurring element on the periodic table. It has
never been seen directly because gathering enough of it together
would cause it to self-vaporize from its own radioactive heat. Astatine
has eighty-five protons packed into its nucleus, creating an extremely
unstable configuration. As soon as the protons come together to
form this element—poof!—it immediately disappears as the protons
reconfigure into a stable state.

Were God to use physical material to deliver salvation, He would
surely use something extraordinary to do it. God would use only
precious substances to do His work, right? Eternal life would come
by means of exceedingly rare elements. Forgiveness of sins would be
delivered by means of a million-dollar medication. Salvation would
come through the powder of ground-up unicorn horns . . .

Wrong.

God uses the most ordinary material to perform the most extraordinary works. God works through stuff. He takes ordinary stuff,
combines it with the power of His Word, and does the extraordinary.

No unicorn horns. No ointment made in a laboratory. No rare elements. Salvation comes to us by means of Word and Sacrament.

This is how God has always worked. In the beginning, God made all things. He declared every gram of the six million billion billion kilograms of earth very good. Although separate and distinct from His creation, God worked in and through His creation. God got His hands dirty embracing creation to do His work. We see this from the very beginning with the creation of Adam.

God scooped up a handful of dirt. He formed it and shaped it. God took a deep breath and breathed life into this otherwise lifeless clump of dirt.

Mud + the Power of God = Life

Dirt was miraculously transformed into human life. Adam was called out of the ground, made in God's image, and given the breath of life. God took something ordinary and made it extraordinary.

Out of all the infinite ways God could have made Adam, He chose the dust of the earth. The crowning accomplishment of creation was formed out of mud. God could have cobbled Adam together with gold and diamonds, rubies and marble. God could have woven a beautiful human tapestry out of silk. God could have painted a picture of Adam with brilliant colors and shades of paint. Instead, God used mud. God took something ordinary and made it extraordinary.

And then God continued to work through ordinary stuff. God used wood to keep hope and humanity afloat through the flood (Genesis 6–8). God used thorns to catch a ram and provide a sacrifice to save Isaac (Genesis 22). God came to Moses through a bush (Exodus 3). God delivered the Israelites from captivity by means of a wooden staff in the hand of Moses (Exodus 14). God gave military victory to Gideon by means of clay pots and trumpets (Judges 7). God used stones and water to turn people away from worshiping

Baal (1 Kings 18). This is simply what God does: He takes ordinary stuff and performs extraordinary works.

WOOD, NAILS, AND ROCK

Jesus continued God's practice of embracing the ordinary. At the beginning of His ministry, Jesus went to be baptized by John the Baptist in the Jordan River. John momentarily refused to baptize Jesus, thinking it would be too ordinary for the extraordinary Son of God: "John would have prevented Him, saying, 'I need to be baptized by You, and do You come to me?' " (Matthew 3:14). Nevertheless, Jesus was baptized to fulfill all righteousness. As He emerged from the ordinary water of the Jordan River, the heavens were opened, and God spoke an extraordinary blessing upon Jesus.

This pattern of ordinary-turned-extraordinary continued throughout Jesus' ministry. Harkening back to what God did in the beginning to make Adam, Jesus used mud to miraculously heal a blind man. This miracle likely happened sometime around the celebration of the Festival of Booths. This celebration was one of the three that required Jewish people to make a pilgrimage to Jerusalem. While Jesus was there in Jerusalem, he encountered a man born blind.

The disciples asked Jesus what appears to be a rather odd question: "Rabbi, who sinned, this man or his parents, that he was born blind?" (John 9:2). There was, however, a good reason for their question. Many people in that day believed that specific ailments were connected to specific sins. The Jewish people directly linked sickness and sin. They thought that if you had a cold, then God might be judging you for a specific sin. Thus, the disciples wanted to know if this blindness was the result of his sin or the sin of his parents.

Jesus responded to their question by saying: "It was not that this man sinned, or his parents, but that the works of God might be displayed in him" (John 9:3). Jesus was asked about the cause of the man's blindness, but He answered in terms of its purpose. The purpose of this miraculous moment was for the works of God to be displayed for all to see. And then Jesus took the ordinary and did the extraordinary:

> Having said these things, He spit on the ground and made mud with the saliva. Then He anointed the man's eyes with the mud and said to him, "Go, wash in the pool of Siloam" (which means Sent). So he went and washed and came back seeing. (John 9:6–7)

Jesus reached down to the ground and scooped up a handful of dirt. He spit on the dirt and made mud. Jesus took ordinary, plain old dirt; the same sort of ordinary, plain old dirt that God used to make man. Jesus took ordinary, plain old saliva. He took this ordinary, plain old mud and put it on the man's eyes. He told the man to go to the pool of Siloam and wash the mud off. This was an ordinary pool of water. It was not special water. It was not holy water. It was not medicinal water. This was the public drinking fountain. At the command of Jesus, the man washed in this ordinary, plain old water.

And then something extraordinary happened. Sight was restored. Light and color flooded his eyes. The man could see. Jesus miraculously healed this man born blind. He did not perform ophthalmological surgery on him. He did not give him some extraordinarily expensive medication to repair his eyesight. Jesus took mud, spit, and water. Through the power of God, He took these ordinary elements and turned them into something extraordinary.

This was not an isolated event in the ministry of Jesus. He did this sort of stuff all the time. Ordinary fishermen caught an extraordinary haul of fish at the command of Jesus (Luke 5:1–11). Ordinary saliva extraordinarily restored the hearing and speaking of a deaf man (Mark 7:31–37). An ordinary coin in the mouth of a fish proved the extraordinary power of Jesus' teaching (Matthew 17:24–27).

As the end of His life approached, Jesus used ordinary bread and wine to deliver an extraordinary blessing to His followers: His body and blood for the forgiveness of sins. As they were celebrating the Passover, Jesus took bread and gave it to His disciples. He told them, "Take, eat; this is My body" (Matthew 26:26). He then took wine and gave it to them saying, "Drink of it, all of you, for this is My blood of the covenant, which is poured out for many for the forgiveness of sins" (Matthew 26:27–28). This was ordinary bread and wine delivering the body and blood of Jesus Christ. Plain old wheat and grapes offering extraordinary grace through the forgiveness of sins.

Every miracle Jesus performed, every sin He forgave, and every sermon He preached was a reason for the Pharisees to kill Him. Every crowd that gathered around to hear Jesus teach, every dispute among the Jewish people as to whether He was the Messiah was proof that the Roman Empire had to kill Him.

Time ran out. They killed Jesus.

As Isaac did generations before, Jesus carried the wood on which He would soon die (John 19:17). Before it was a wooden cross, it was a seed. The seed grew into a small shoot. The shoot grew into a tree. The tree grew to the point that it was cut down and milled into a cross. Jesus carried ordinary wood on his back up to Golgotha. Ordinary metal harvested from the earth was forged into nails. These nails pierced the flesh of Jesus and pinned Him to the cross. Blood—ordinary red and white cells, platelets, and plasma—flowed from His veins.

When Jesus died on the cross, the soldiers pierced His side with a spear: "But one of the soldiers pierced His side with a spear, and at once there came out blood and water" (John 19:34). Ordinary elements—blood and water—poured from His lifeless body.

They took Him off the cross, and a man named Joseph of Arimathea put His body in a tomb made of rock: "Then he took it down and wrapped it in a linen shroud and laid Him in a tomb cut in stone, where no one had ever yet been laid" (Luke 23:53). Not a marble tomb. Not a mausoleum. Not a cathedral. They took His body and put it in a tomb made of ordinary rock.

And that is when the power of God did something extraordinary. God raised Jesus from the dead. He conquered sin through His resurrection. Using the ordinary things of creation, God performed a miracle. God used dirt to make Adam. God

God uses the ordinary to do the extraordinary

used mud to heal a blind man. God used wood, nails, and blood to restore all humanity. Ordinary things become extraordinary in the hands of God. God has always worked in this way. From the dust of the earth in the beginning to the empty tomb of Jesus, God uses the ordinary to do the extraordinary.

Nevertheless, human sinfulness resists this simple truth. Extraordinary grace coming by means of ordinary objects goes against sinful inclinations. Sinful hearts want to be satiated by means of extravagant and expensive, glitzy and glamorous objects.

GOLD, RELICS, AND MAGIC

At various points in history, the Church has rejected the ordinary in order to chase after extravagant and expensive, glitzy and glamorous objects. The Crusades are a prime example. Beginning in 1096, the Roman Catholic Church engaged in a number of sanctioned Crusades to the Holy Land. The purpose of the First Crusade, under the leadership of Pope Urban II, was to restore Christian control to Jerusalem. The First Crusade succeeded in this endeavor with the successful recapture of Jerusalem in 1099. Subsequent Crusades followed for nearly two centuries as captured territory exchanged hands between Christians and Muslims.

The Council of Clermont (1095) promised that anyone participating in the Crusades would receive plenary indulgences. As discussed in chapter 6, the Church had developed a distinction between eternal and temporal consequences of sin. The Church taught that even when the eternal consequences of sin were forgiven, the temporal consequences still remained. Christians had to perform acts of penance in order to repay the earthly consequences of their sins. Ordinary forgiveness from Jesus was not enough to cover the whole problem of sin; extraordinary human efforts had to pay off the full burden of sins. Crusaders received total forgiveness, known as plenary indulgences, as a sort of one-and-done repayment for sin. Go on a crusade, and you were covered for life.

Plenary indulgences gave the Crusades a religious motivation. Crusaders claimed to be fighting in the name of Jesus for the forgiveness of their sins. Nevertheless, the Crusades quickly digressed into a hunt for extravagant and expensive, glitzy and glamorous objects. The Fourth Crusade (1202–04) included many of the worst atrocities committed by the crusaders. The original intention of this Crusade was to wrestle Jerusalem back from Muslim control. The crusaders instead chose to sack Constantinople, the capital of the Byzantine Empire and the heart of Christianity in the East. They attacked fellow Christians. The crusaders ransacked the city of its gold and silver, looted their artwork, and pillaged the churches.

Extraordinary relics flowed from the east to the west as a result of the Crusades. Medieval Christianity had a canine appetite for these "holy" objects. Crusaders brought home loads of extraordinary relics and sold them to the highest bidder.

Extraordinary relics soon filled churches throughout the Roman Empire. Portions of the True Cross, wood from the cross of Jesus' crucifixion, were brought home from the Crusades. Multiple churches claimed to have the index finger that St. Thomas the apostle thrust into Jesus' wounds. Fragments of the Scourging Pillar, the pillar to which Jesus was tied and beaten, were on display at numerous cathedrals. The perfectly preserved tongue of St. Anthony of Padua was displayed in Italy.

Extraordinary occurrences were also believed to accompany the relics. Stories about miraculous flows of blood pouring out of relics circulated throughout Christendom during the Middle Ages. The Holy Prepuce, the foreskin from Jesus' circumcision, supposedly dripped blood once during Mass. (Yes, you read that correctly.) Around this same time in history, the blood of St. Januarius in Naples began to spontaneously liquefy at various times throughout the year.

Relics and miraculous occurrences were just a few of the ways that Christendom rejected the work of God through ordinary means. Private Mass, a special service beyond the ordinary public service, became a very popular practice in the Middle Ages. Roman Catholic theologians had developed a belief that the worship service, known as Mass, involved re-sacrificing Jesus. Holy Communion was believed to be a sacrificial work performed by the priests on behalf of the congregation. Better than the ordinary Mass offered on behalf of all people, the Private Mass (*Missa privata*) was available for a special fee. People diverted their offerings from the ordinary Mass to the Private Mass. These private services were bought and sold as an extraordinary blessing for weddings, birthdays, anniversaries, illnesses, or deaths. Priests often performed these services as quickly as possible because they were paid per Mass. They sprinted through the liturgy.

Medieval theology also developed a nearly magical understanding of the sacraments. Scholastic theology taught that Baptism and the Eucharist worked apart from the faith of the recipient. Sacraments delivered grace simply by performing the action (*ex opere operato*). The faith of the recipient did not matter; all that mattered was that the work of the sacraments was performed.

This led to some strange beliefs about the extraordinary power of the sacraments. The Scholastic theologian John Duns Scotus

(c. 1266–1308) argued for the forcible Baptism of Jewish children; the rationale for this practice was that the waters of Baptism would confer eternal salvation simply by doing the work of Baptism. Communion wine was regarded by laypeople as a powerful remedy. Many average people believed that it was able to stop a woman's menstrual cycle and treat epilepsy. Sacramental bread was also used for all sorts of magical purposes by laypeople; rather than chewing the bread, some people would keep scraps in their mouths for later use as a remedy for sick children or animals, to protect themselves, or even to harm others. Some people would use the ground-up body of Christ in love potions.

None of this was biblical.

God's Word presented a totally different view of God's work through the material world: Dust and the breath of God brought about human life. Soil and spit healed a blind man. Bread and wine delivered forgiveness. Wood and nails brought eternal salvation. God uses ordinary things for His extraordinary purposes. Christendom rejected the ways in which God uses the ordinary to do the extraordinary. For generations, God's people chased after gold in faraway lands, costly relics, private services, and magical sacraments. This practice was not good, right, or salutary.

Change was coming soon.

WORD, WATER, BREAD, AND WINE

Luther served as a monk during this period of Church history. He made a pilgrimage to Rome in order to gaze at relics brought back from the Crusades. Like all ordained monks in his day, Luther performed the sacrifice of the Mass frequently. He performed extraordinary penance—crawling up the Holy Stairs in Rome on his knees—in the hopes of releasing family members from purgatory.

Luther was part of the frenzied celebration of extraordinary relics, penance, and sacraments.

Nevertheless, Luther found no peace in these things. He gazed at the relics, yet he struggled to experience God's grace through these extraordinary objects. He purchased indulgences with their extraordinary claims of forgiveness, yet he still felt the weight of sin upon him. He performed the private services, yet he questioned the value of his work in performing the sacrifice of the Mass. These inner struggles drove Luther to seek answers in Scripture. Rather than finding his answers in the pope or Scholastic textbooks, Luther went to the Word of God.

Scripture made it clear that God does extraordinary work through ordinary substances:

- God embraces the ordinary stuff of creation through Word and Sacrament.

- God's Word, though spoken by ordinary people, accomplishes extraordinary work.

- The Sacraments, though composed of ordinary substances, deliver extraordinary grace.

Normed by the authority of Scripture, Luther reassessed Church teachings on Word and Sacrament. He realized that God delivers the grace of Jesus Christ through basic things like the Word of God, water, bread, and wine. Lutherans argued that Scripture teaches that the Holy Spirit, faith, forgiveness, and eternal salvation come by means of Word and Sacrament:

Through the Word and Sacraments, as through instruments, the Holy Spirit is given [John 20:22]. He works faith, when and where it pleases God [John 3:8], in those who hear the good news that God justifies those who believe that they are received into grace for Christ's sake. This happens not through our own merits, but for Christ's sake.[44]

Lutherans also found that relics, indulgences, and private services were curiously nowhere to be found in Scripture. This quickly put Lutheran beliefs in opposition to the official beliefs of the Roman Catholic Church. Luther and others soon rejected the extraordinary claims concocted by tradition over the centuries. He encouraged people to stop purchasing private Mass, visiting relics, and buying indulgences.

As Luther questioned the validity of these human traditions in the Church, he also began to question the traditional understandings of the sacraments. Along with relics and indulgences, the sacraments had become a rather murky topic through the Middle Ages. The Roman Catholic Church had determined that there were seven sacraments: Baptism, confirmation, the Eucharist, penance, anointing of the sick, marriage, and ordination. These sacraments were considered necessary for salvation; however, not every believer had to receive every single sacrament. Believers could take part in either marriage or ordination; however, all believers were expected to take part in Baptism and penance.

The Lutherans, working from Scripture instead of Church tradition, resisted the Roman Catholic understanding of sacraments. They called for a biblical definition of a sacrament:

If we call Sacraments "rites that have the command of God, and to which the promise of grace has been added," it is easy to decide what are true Sacraments. For rites instituted by

---

44 Augsburg Confession, Article V, paragraphs 2–3.

human beings will not be called true Sacraments. For human authority cannot promise grace.[45]

This brought the number of sacraments down to three: Baptism, the Lord's Supper, and Absolution. The Roman Catholic Church vehemently opposed defining sacraments as rites commanded by God with the promise of grace. Nevertheless, the Lutherans held to their position that Scripture ought to be the norm of all beliefs:

> Therefore, Baptism, the Lord's Supper, and Absolution (which is the Sacrament of Repentance) are truly Sacraments. For these rites have God's command and the promise of grace, which is peculiar to the New Testament. When we are baptized, when we eat the Lord's body, when we are absolved, our hearts must be firmly assured that God truly forgives us for Christ's sake.[46]

This biblical definition of sacrament left churches to deliver God's grace by ordinary means. Ordinary water and the Word of God could wrestle a person back from the clutches of Satan and deliver new life in Christ. Plain old bread and wine join with the power of God's Word to deliver the extraordinary forgiveness of sins. Words of forgiveness spoken by an ordinary person have the same power as if Jesus Himself had said them. Being Lutheran is receiving God's extraordinary grace through ordinary means:

Baptism: Jesus spoke of Baptism in extraordinarily simple terms, saying, "Whoever believes and is baptized will be saved, but whoever does not believe will be condemned" (Mark 16:16). Peter reiterated the simplicity of Baptism by saying, "Repent and be baptized every

---

45 Apology of the Augsburg Confession, Article XIII (VII), paragraph 3.

46 Apology of the Augsburg Confession, Article XIII (VII), paragraph 4.

one of you in the name of Jesus Christ for the forgiveness of your sins, and you will receive the gift of the Holy Spirit. For the promise is for you and for your children and for all who are far off, everyone whom the Lord our God calls to Himself" (Acts 2:38–39).

Luther used the clear teaching of Scripture to prioritize Baptism over human traditions: "Now, the *first* thing to be considered about baptism is the divine promise, which says: 'He who believes and is baptized will be saved' [Mark 16:16]. This promise must be set far above all the glitter of works, vows, religious orders, and whatever else man has introduced, for on it all our salvation depends."[47] God delivers the forgiveness of sins, rescues from death and the devil, and gives eternal salvation through the waters of Baptism. Ordinary water, combined with the Word of God and faith that trusts in the promises of God, results in something extraordinary.

Ordinary water, combined with the Word of God and faith that trusts in the promises of God, results in something extraordinary

Baptism is never distant in the life of the believer. Being baptized in the name of the Father, Son, and Holy Spirit is adoption into the kingdom of God. This delivers an entirely new identity to the baptized believer. Our baptismal identity surpasses our sexual, social, and cultural identities. Making the sign of the cross is a daily reminder of how God used ordinary water to deliver extraordinary gifts to you through Baptism. Long after the physical water has dried, the new life of faith remains soaked in baptismal grace.

Jesus gave the extraordinary gift of His body and blood through ordinary bread and wine

47   LW 36:58.

The Lord's Supper: Jesus also spoke clearly and simply about the Lord's Supper. He commanded nothing about Corpus Christi processions or the magical properties of the bread and wine. Rather, Jesus gave the extraordinary gift of His body and blood through ordinary bread and wine:

> Now as they were eating, Jesus took bread, and after blessing it broke it and gave it to the disciples, and said, "Take, eat; this is My body." And He took a cup, and when He had given thanks He gave it to them, saying, "Drink of it, all of you, for this is My blood of the covenant, which is poured out for many for the forgiveness of sins." (Matthew 26:26–28)

Relying on Scripture alone, Luther offered a clear and simple understanding of the Lord's Supper in the Small Catechism: "It is the true body and blood of our Lord Jesus Christ under the bread and wine, instituted by Christ Himself for us Christians to eat and to drink."[48] Through ordinary bread and wine, the Word of God delivers the true body and blood of Jesus.

This extraordinary gift of Christ's body and blood delivers the forgiveness of sins, eternal life, and salvation. Faith hears and trusts in the words of Jesus when He says, "Given for you" and "shed for you for the forgiveness of sins." Through faith, we receive both the body and blood of Jesus and the assurance of the resurrection. Since Christ's body and blood dwells in us, we will be raised with Him to new life.

Absolution: God spoke the creation into existence. Jesus spoke the forgiveness of sins. The Holy Spirit spoke through a crowd of people at Pentecost to proclaim the Gospel. God's Word is power. Just as God breathed into a clump of dirt and made Adam, God breathes

---

48   Small Catechism, The Sacrament of the Altar.

life into the Word (2 Timothy 3:16). And God has given this Word to His people. Jesus gave the Church the authority to speak on His behalf: "If you forgive the sins of any, they are forgiven them; if you withhold forgiveness from any, it is withheld" (John 20:23). God forgives sins by means of the Word spoken through a simple human mouth. No incantations. No special Latin words. No penance to complete the forgiveness. The grace of God comes to us by means of the spoken Word.

Luther taught that Confession and Absolution is a gift of God. The confession of sins involves speaking words of repentance. The Holy Spirit leads sinners to turn away from sin in repentance. This does not mean listing every individual sin; rather, the confession of sins is a completely and totally repentant heart. Upon this confession, the words of Absolution are spoken. Luther described this as "the other part is a work that God does when He declares me free of my sin through His Word placed in the mouth of a man."[49]

> In Absolution, God's extraordinary forgiveness is placed in the mouth of an ordinary person

In Absolution, God's extraordinary forgiveness is placed in the mouth of an ordinary person. The forgiveness of sins is not some vague feeling floating somewhere out there. God's people do not have to hope for a murky feeling of forgiveness. Freedom from guilt is not somewhere in the cloud. Rather, God speaks clear and confident forgiveness through Absolution. When the pastor declares Absolution—"Your sins are forgiven"—it is as if Jesus Himself had spoken.

---

49   Large Catechism, A Brief Exhortation to Confession, paragraph 15.

EMBRACING ORDINARY

Our culture invites us to overlook God's work through ordinary stuff. The prevailing opinion within our culture is that ordinary stuff performs ordinary work and extraordinary stuff performs extraordinary work. Basic is boring, modest is monotonous, and ordinary is overlooked. Bigger is better, extravagant is exciting, and extraordinary is enticing.

The music industry gets it. Larger tour busses haul larger quantities of pyrotechnics. (And everyone knows that the best musicians have the best pyrotechnics.) Popular musicians are called stars because they constantly try to outshine the others. Gaudier outfits, louder concerts, plus bigger scandals equals extraordinary music.

The movie industry gets it. Special effects can suffice in the absence of a plot. There is no need for a script when you can depict King Kong climbing the Empire State Building. Blow up more stuff, show more skin, and add more zombies, and you will have a successful film. The movie premier must have an expensive red carpet, actresses in flashy dresses, and looooong stretch limos. Put it all together, and you have an extraordinary movie.

And we get it. Nobody wants to be ordinary. We all want to be extraordinary. We want the best house on the block with the greenest lawn and the whitest picket fence. We want the coolest job with the best perks and the biggest paycheck. We stand in line for the newest gadgets that are in the highest demand. We want to take the most extreme vacations, post pictures of the tastiest food, and have the cutest kids. We want to be extraordinary.

God's work through the ordinary stuff of creation is countercultural. Extraordinary work through ordinary means is foreign to society. The Sacraments are weird. Nobody would expect the forgiveness of sins to be delivered through the water of Baptism. Not one person would anticipate Jesus giving His precious body and blood to us through simple bread and wine. Who would think that the plain words of Absolution spoken by a pastor carry the same weight as if Jesus had spoken them?

This is the mysterious work of God.

God has established the Means of Grace. The extraordinary work of God comes to us through the ordinary stuff of creation. Being Lutheran is being sacramental. It means embracing God's magnificently countercultural work through Word and Sacrament.

There are many ways that you can practice a life that embraces God's extraordinary work through ordinary means:

Baptismal Identity: People search for lasting identity in their sexuality, career, family, or a political party. Establishing an identity in anything other than Baptism will certainly disappoint. If your identity is in your sexuality, then your identity will have to change as the culture's definition of male and female changes. If your identity is in your career, then you will have to find a new identity when you are laid off or decide to retire. If your identity is in your family, then you will struggle when death separates the family.

If your identity is found in the Father, Son, and Holy Spirit, then you will have a steadfast identity. Who you are will be normed by who God is. God's name will be your name. God's heritage will be your heritage. God's future hope will be your future hope. Being Lutheran is making the sign of the cross, remembering your Baptism, and embracing the extraordinary gift of baptismal identity.

Commune with God: New-age spirituality searches for a close connection with the divine. Holy Communion is the closest connection with God one could ever desire. Through bread and wine, God personally visits His people. God visibly comes to us with His body and blood and is truly present. Scripture tells of God appearing to His people (theophany). Holy Communion is an ongoing theophany. God visits His people every week at the Communion rail.

You do not have to channel your inner light through yoga. You do not have to take a trip across the globe for a religiously moving experience. God is not hiding somewhere on the golf course or in the silence of a morning sunrise. God has promised that you will find Him in, with, and under the bread and wine of Holy Communion. Being Lutheran is approaching the altar and communing with God.

Extraordinary Forgiveness: You have absolute certainty that God has forgiven your sins. God has promised forgiveness in the Sacraments. You have felt forgiveness in the water of Baptism. You have tasted forgiveness in the body of Christ. You have smelled the aroma of forgiveness in Christ's blood. You have heard God's forgiveness spoken for you. Being Lutheran is not about waiting around for some inner feeling of forgiveness. Rather, being Lutheran is about the external work of God coming to you in Word and Sacrament. You have certain forgiveness through the Means of Grace. If you ever doubt whether or not God forgives you, then all you need to do is look to the sacramental promises of God. Being Lutheran is receiving God's extraordinary forgiveness through ordinary water, bread, and wine.

Be Countercultural: Believing that God delivers the Holy Spirit and salvation through Word and Sacrament puts you in opposition to the culture: "The reason why the world does not know us is that it did not know Him" (1 John 3:1). It is more glamorous to believe that God works through some spark of the divine dwelling within us. It is more culturally acceptable to claim that you must forgive yourself before God will forgive you. It is countercultural to believe that God works through the very ordinary proclamation of the Gospel. It is weird to find such power in the simple waters of Baptism. It is not cool to have a deeply religious experience in an ordinary sanctuary in the presence of ordinary people. Embracing God's work through Word and Sacrament ministry is faithful to Scripture. It goes *against* all cultural expectations. And it goes *with* the clear work of God. Being

Lutheran is embracing the countercultural work of God through Word and Sacrament ministry.

CONCLUSION

God works through stuff. God works through the very ordinary means of Word and Sacrament ministry. The Word of God spoken by ordinary people creates extraordinary faith clinging to the precious forgiveness of Christ Jesus. Baptism and the Lord's Supper—composed of ordinary water, bread, and wine—deliver extraordinary grace. Absolution delivers Christ's forgiveness through a human mouth. God has given these gifts to the Church as the Means of Grace.

Being Lutheran is embracing God's mercy through ordinary means. The flashiest thing you will find among Lutherans is an overly polished pectoral cross. We have no place for rare relics, private Mass, or internal attempts at forgiveness. The Means of Grace are not flashy like the gold-plated bones of a saint. They do not cost lots of money like private Mass. They are not a solitary experience like doing yoga atop a mountain. Nevertheless, embracing God's work through Word and Sacrament is faithful to God. The Means of Grace—ordinary as they may appear—are more precious than the bones of a saint, more costly than a private Mass, and more spiritual than doing yoga on top of a mountain. They are extraordinary grace through the most ordinary means.

Daily life is shaped by God's work through ordinary means. The external Word of God breathes life into our lives and turns our dusty old life into new life in Christ. The waters of Baptism deliver an eternal identity that does not ebb and fade with the changes of life. The real presence of Jesus in the Lord's Supper allows us to commune with God. Ordinary stuff accomplishes the extraordinary work of God.

Vignette: Sharon

Tubes connected her to medicine. Cords connected her to monitors. And monitors connected her to a team of doctors and nurses. Proprietary technology kept her alive. Thousands of insurance dollars paid for her care. It was an extraordinary sight.

Sharon came close to dying of sepsis. It began with an infection in her lungs. It spread. And it spread. Organs began shutting down just one day after the infection hit her bloodstream. It progressed with startling speed. Doctors soon started using words like *palliative care*, *hospice*, and *comfort*.

Nobody thought that Sharon would recover. But she did. As she recovered from infection, many people came to visit her. Visitors brought flowers and cards, pictures of her puppy, and books to read. One of the many visitors was a pastor from her parents' congregation. More accurately, this was the pastor from her parents' former congregation; both Sharon's mother and father had recently passed away. They were well along in years and died within six months of each other. She had met this pastor at her mother's funeral. And then again at her father's funeral.

They had a pleasant conversation. Sharon told the pastor about everything that had happened with the infection and how it turned into sepsis. She told him all about the team of specialists working on her case and the proprietary technology used to administer the medication. It was a truly incredible story.

After she was finished explaining everything that had happened, the pastor asked her a question: "How are you doing with all of this?"

Sharon was a bit perplexed by the question. She had just told him all about her blood cultures and medication changes. She had already explained that the discharge date was set and she would be moving to a rehabilitation facility. Yet, she sensed by the inflection in the pastor's voice that he was not asking how she was doing physically. Sharon stopped and thought for a moment.

She confessed that it was really scary to be that close to death. She was fearful of what would be next for her after her life ended. Sharon hoped that God would welcome her into His presence. She always tried to do the right thing. She usually felt like she was on God's good side.

After listening to her talk, the pastor then asked if she had been baptized. She said no. And then she realized that she had not considered that question since she was a child. She attended church infrequently. Mostly just funerals. She would occasionally hear the pastor at the funeral talk of the person's Baptism. And she remembered hearing that this same pastor had baptized her parents a few years before they passed away.

The pastor asked, "Sharon, may I lift up a word of prayer?"

She was deep in thought and the pastor's question startled her. She agreed to pray with him and folded her hands. After he concluded the prayer, he told her that he would come back and visit her soon. As he was leaving, he also mentioned that he would be glad to talk more with her about Baptism and see if she had any questions.

Sharon did have questions. She called the pastor the next day, and they scheduled for him to visit that afternoon. They talked about Baptism, and he shared some Scripture readings with her. The last one that he shared with Sharon was the account of Philip baptizing the Ethiopian eunuch:

> And as they were going along the road they came to some water, and the eunuch said, "See, here is water! What prevents me from being baptized?" And he commanded the chariot to stop, and they both went down into the water, Philip and the eunuch, and he baptized him. (Acts 8:36–38)

After thinking for a moment, Sharon announced, "I want to be baptized. Can we do it here in the hospital?"

The pastor gladly agreed. He went and asked a nurse for a cup. She could not find one, so she gave the pastor a sterile specimen cup. He went to the bathroom faucet and got some water. Sharon was baptized there in the hospital. In the midst of extraordinary technology and resources, ordinary water and God's Word made her a child of God.

Salvation came in the most ordinary way: God's Word and a few ounces of water. Right after the pastor left, Sharon called her husband and told him about the Baptism. Then she called her sister. They both agreed that their mother and father would be very glad to hear that she was baptized.

She was released from the hospital and eventually returned home. She and her husband lived on a hobby farm. Sharon bought the farm so that she could run an animal rescue. Abused animals were brought to the farm until they were adopted. Although the number of animals on the farm was in a constant state of flux, she generally had over thirty donkeys, a few chickens, and some dogs. And there was always one sad goat that nobody wanted to adopt.

Her health, however, continued to deteriorate. Her pastor continued to visit with her on a regular basis. She was too weak to attend worship or even walk out to the barn to bring the donkeys in for the night. When her pastor would visit, they would chat for a bit before it was time for prayer and Holy Communion. Occasionally, one of the donkeys would bray so loudly that it could be heard in the house. Sharon would immediately identify which donkey made the sound: "That is Eddie fussing about something." "Sounds like Daisy is hungry." "Mae wants to come inside." She knew her donkeys simply by the sound of their voice.

The last time her pastor came to visit, Sharon was hardly able to sit upright. She wore dirty sweatpants and slumped back on the couch. Even though the donkeys were braying, she was in no mood for identifying which donkey it was. She knew that death was imminent. The grinding pain made her long for it to come quickly. Her pastor shared a Scripture reading with her: "I am the good shepherd. I know My own and My own know Me, just as the Father knows Me and I know the Father; and I lay down My life for the sheep" (John 10:14–15).

The pastor took out ordinary bread and wine and spoke the Words of Institution. He communed Sharon in the living room as she slumped on the couch and received the very body and blood of Christ Jesus given for the forgiveness of her sins. That afternoon on the farm, the Good Shepherd came to take one of His precious sheep home.

Chapter 7
Discussion Questions

1. God created man out of a clump of dirt. How was the creation of humans different than the rest of creation? How did God utilize ordinary material in the creation of woman? Read Genesis 1:24–25 and 2:7, 21–22.

2. Read John 9:1–7. What are some other ways that Jesus could have performed this miracle? Why do you think He performed it the way He did?

3. Read Mark 6:30–44. What are some other ways that Jesus used the ordinary to perform the extraordinary?

4. The Crusades were a hunt for extravagant and expensive, glitzy and glamorous objects. Crusaders were seeking a once-in-a-lifetime experience that would solidify their salvation. How do Christians today chase after these sorts of once-in-a-lifetime experiences?

5. Read Philippians 3:17–21. Luther found no peace in relics. Where do people look for peace today? How are these modern objects of comfort different than religious relics? How are they similar?

6. Lutherans believe that it does not belong to human authority to promise grace. What does this say about the Lutheran understanding of Sacraments? What do they deliver?

7. Jesus gave the Church the authority to forgive sins. Are there other places in Scripture in which God has given His people great responsibility? Read Genesis 1:28 and 2:15.

8. Baptism is never distant in the life of the believer. How does your Baptism impact your daily life? What can you do to remember the present impact of your Baptism? Read Galatians 3:23–29.

9. Sharon had to receive Holy Communion at home as a result of her illness. How is this different than the Private Mass of the Middle Ages?

Chapter 8

UNRESOLVED

It is the glory of God to conceal things,
but the glory of kings is to search things out.
(Proverbs 25:2)

It used to be that thirty minutes was all you needed. One half-hour time slot was enough time for a television show to introduce characters, establish a problem, and offer a resolution so that everyone lived happily ever after. Absolutely everything was resolved and tied up in a tidy package before the closing credits.

Deep family problems arose and were resolved in one episode. A television show would depict a family torn apart by divorce, yet the kids would inexplicably be all right within twenty-nine minutes. Soap operas depicted the pain of death as lasting roughly five minutes. Sitcoms portrayed a layoff as an opportunity to joke about eating beans and rice, but thankfully, a new job always came before the commercial break. Conflict and resolution were never far apart on TV.

Modern television is beginning to reverse this pattern. Viewers today refuse to believe that everything can be wrapped up in a matter of minutes. Producers are now running the closing credits with many loose ends still remaining. Television shows today end with more slow collapses than slow claps. Writers use the thirty-minute time slot to raise many questions and offer few answers. Conflict and resolution are increasingly far apart on television today.

And this reflects our own lives. Daily life is never tidy, time rarely heals all wounds, and problems often remain unresolved. Surgeries leave scars that do not go away. Layoffs sting for years after the new job begins. Miscarriages leave questions even after the next child is born. Painful experiences cause us to walk through life with a limp. The death of a loved one causes tears to linger right at the surface. Answers to life's deepest questions are elusive.

Your life is full of unresolved tensions. Everyone's life is full of unresolved tensions. On this we can agree.

But the universe is not this way, is it? Math and science are always orderly and tidy, right? Wrong. Math, the so-called purest form of science, is tainted by all kinds of messy details. The famous coastline paradox is an example of how even mathematics has unresolved tensions. If you measure the coastline of Great Britain using units 100 km long, then the length of the coastline is approximately 2,800 km. With 50 km units, the total length is approximately 3,400 km. The same coastline measured with different units of measurement produces an approximate 600 km discrepancy. Add the problem of daily erosion and hourly tidal changes and it becomes obvious: nobody knows the exact length of Great Britain's coastline.

Science has similar problems. The double-slit experiment in the field of quantum physics provides an example of how even science has unresolved tensions. The experiment involves shining a light on a barrier with two vertical slits cut into it. The light passes through the slits and gathers on the other side of the barrier. The way that the light passes through the two slits simultaneously proves that light moves as a wave and a particle. One experiment proves two contradictory claims about the fundamental nature of light. It is both wave and particle. Quantum mechanics has other unresolved tensions including Schrödinger's cat thought experiment and the Einstein-Podolsky-Rosen paradox.

Life is lopsided with more questions than answers, more confusion than clarity, and more mystery than revelation. Whether it is daily life and human emotions or math and science, we live in a universe of unresolved tensions.

CREATOR → CREATURES

Behind all of the unresolved tensions in life is one word: creature. Human beings are creatures made by a Creator. Creatures are wholly dependent upon their Creator. A creature does not come into being on his or her own. God gives life to creatures. Creatures live and move and have their being in God.

Creatures, unlike the Creator, have boundaries. Existence is the fundamental boundary surrounding creatures. Scripture begins in a time when creatures did not exist (Genesis 1:1–19). Scripture marks a specific time when the Creator brought creatures into existence (Genesis 1:20). God created living creatures and filled the waters, air, and land. These creatures were given specific boundaries according to the will of their Creator. Birds were confined to their specific habitats according to their kind. Fish remained within the boundary of the water according to their kind. Land animals dwelt on the land according to their kind.

Human creatures, like all creatures, are bound to their Creator. Adam and Eve lived according to certain boundaries that God had established. There was a time when Adam and Eve did not exist (Genesis 1:1–25). There were specific tasks uniquely given to Adam and Eve (Genesis 1:26). There were trees and fruit to which they had access (Genesis 1:29), but there was also a specific tree and fruit that was beyond the proper boundaries of Adam and Eve (Genesis 2:17). Creatures live and move and have their being according to the boundaries established by the Creator.

The limits of creatureliness are lucidly displayed in the Book of Job. After much speculation by Job and his companions, God responds to Job from the whirlwind, saying:

Where were you when I laid the foundation of the earth?
 Tell Me, if you have understanding.
Who determined its measurements—surely you know!
 Or who stretched the line upon it?
On what were its bases sunk,
 or who laid its cornerstone,
when the morning stars sang together
 and all the sons of God shouted for joy? . . .
Have you entered into the springs of the sea,
 or walked in the recesses of the deep?
Have the gates of death been revealed to you,
 or have you seen the gates of deep darkness?
Have you comprehended the expanse of the earth?
 Declare, if you know all this. (Job 38:4–7, 16–18)

The answer to God's questioning is obvious: creatures cannot possibly know the hidden mind of their Creator. Creatures depend on what the Creator chooses to reveal. Job was not there when God laid the foundation of the earth. Job knew nothing of the measurements God made to form the creation. He knew nothing of the springs of the sea, the gates of death, and the expanse of the earth. All he knew was what God had revealed to him. Creatures depend on the Creator for life and knowledge. God provides revelation to creatures according to His wisdom. And God intentionally allows some tensions to remain unresolved.

JESUS → UNRESOLVED TENSIONS

Jesus affirmed God's wisdom in unresolved tensions. Jesus addressed many questions that people brought to Him. Nevertheless, He purposefully left some questions unanswered so as not to overstep boundaries. Jesus gave answers to the questions that were right for

Him to answer. And Jesus resisted giving answers to the questions that were beyond the boundaries of what God's creatures could or should know. He did not degrade life by treating it like a poorly written sitcom. Jesus never tied everything up in a tidy little package before the commercial break.

Jesus affirmed God's wisdom in unresolved tensions

One tension that Jesus left unresolved had to do with suffering. Jewish thinking during the time of Jesus claimed that suffering was God's way of punishing specific sins. Leprosy was punishment for not offering the proper tithe. Premature death was God's judgment for bad living. Disease was punishment for using a friend's password to watch on-demand movies. This direct correlation between sin and punishment was a prevalent belief during the time of Jesus. On numerous occasions, people asked Jesus to elaborate on the cause of specific calamities. And each time, Jesus gave the same answer: that is beyond the boundaries of creaturely knowledge.

The tower of Siloam is an example of Jesus allowing certain tensions to remain unresolved. Jesus was teaching a group of people when some of them asked Him to resolve a theological tension for them. They asked about an incident in which Pontius Pilate, the Roman governor of Judea, had slaughtered some Galileans. Theological speculation had led the people to believe that this horrific event had occurred because these individuals were particularly sinful people. Jesus answered their speculation by saying, "No, I tell you; but unless you repent, you will all likewise perish" (Luke 13:3). Jesus went on to say, "Those eighteen on whom the tower in Siloam fell and killed them: do you think that they were worse offenders than all the others who lived in Jerusalem? No, I tell you; but unless you repent, you will all likewise perish" (vv. 4–5).

Jesus provided resolution to their question. Yet, He also left parts of their question unresolved. Jesus clearly told the people that these specific occurrences of suffering were not punishment for specific sins. He clearly taught that they, too, needed to repent of their sins. Nevertheless, He let the hidden work of God remain hidden. He did not elaborate on why these events occurred. He did not indulge them with a discussion on why bad things happen to good people. Jesus let this tension remain unresolved.

Similar tensions occurred elsewhere in the teaching of Jesus. While teaching about the Last Day, Jesus told the disciples: "But concerning that day and hour no one knows, not even the angels of heaven, nor the Son, but the Father only. For as were the days of Noah, so will be the coming of the Son of Man" (Matthew 24:36–37).

Unlike the question regarding the tower of Siloam, Jesus claims that even He does not know the answer to this question. Just as certain questions about suffering are out of bounds for human creatures to know, there are certain questions about the Last Day that are out of bounds for even the Son of God. As the Son of God, Jesus submitted Himself to God the Father. In His submission, Jesus allowed certain tensions to be unresolved. This hidden work of the Father is beyond the boundaries of even the Son of God.

To be certain, God does not always hide knowledge from His creatures. Rather, God delights in revealing knowledge to His creatures. Even though Jesus left certain tensions unresolved, He also answered many, many questions for His followers. Jesus shared all that He could rightfully reveal: "No longer do I call you servants, for the servant does not know what his master is doing; but I have called you friends, for all that I have heard from My Father I have made known to you" (John 15:15).

Revelation poured from the mouth of Jesus. He spoke, and truth was revealed to God's people. Although He left some questions unanswered, Jesus more often resolved the tensions in people's minds. He revealed to people that their sins were forgiven (Matthew 9:2; Luke 5:20; 7:48). He revealed the inner thoughts of people hidden to all others (Matthew 12:25; Mark 2:8; Luke 5:22). He revealed eternal salvation to believers (John 11:17–27; Luke 23:43).

And Jesus revealed the Creator to creatures. He revealed God to all people:

> For from His fullness we have all received, grace upon grace. For the law was given through Moses; grace and truth came through Jesus Christ. No one has ever seen God; the only God, who is at the Father's side, He has made Him known. (John 1:16–18)

Jesus sent the Holy Spirit to guide believers in all truth (John 15:26). Jesus spoke only what God the Father had given Him to speak. And the Holy Spirit speaks only what bears witness to Jesus Christ. The Holy Spirit came on Pentecost to guide believers in speaking the truth about Jesus. Believers do not receive the Holy Spirit so that some new revelation about God might be known; rather, the Holy Spirit directs believers to what Jesus Christ has already revealed.

LUTHER → UNRESOLVED TENSIONS

By the time of the Reformation, the Roman Catholic Church had spent generations attempting to resolve various theological tensions. Drawing on philosophers such as Plato and Aristotle, Scholastic theologians had developed an answer to every one of life's mysteries. The guiding assumption among these theologians was that human reason—church councils, philosophical inquiry, logical syllogisms, and dialectic reasoning—could reveal the truth about God.

For example, Thomas Aquinas (1225–74) wrote a theological treatise known as the *Summa Theologica*. This text, also known simply as the *Summa*, quotes nineteen church councils, forty-one popes, and forty-six philosophers. Aquinas relied on philosophers for numerous definitions and methodologies. He utilized Aristotle extensively as he attempted to untangle the mysteries of the existence of God, eternity, and human free will.

Drawing on Aquinas, theologians throughout the Middle Ages probed deeper into many unresolved tensions of the faith. One of those theologians, Desiderius Erasmus (1466–1536), attempted to resolve many of the mysteries surrounding free will. Erasmus wrote a treatise entitled *On the Freedom of the Will* (1524), in which he argued that the existence of God's commandments logically demanded free will. If humans had no free will, then there would be no purpose in God giving commandments.

Erasmus was attempting to resolve a persistent debate among theologians during that time: Why are some saved and not others? Why do some people enjoy eternal salvation while others suffer eternal damnation? This conundrum became known as the *crux theologorum* (the cross of the theologians). According to Erasmus, some people were saved because they exercised free will in choosing to receive salvation. Likewise, some people were damned because they exercised free will in choosing to reject salvation. Although God was capable of intervening in this human decision, He allowed humans to exercise their free will. This provided a perfect resolution to the *crux theologorum*: salvation and damnation depend entirely on how you decide.

Luther saw one glaring problem with the way Erasmus had resolved the tension of free will. Erasmus's argument was more logical than scriptural; it had resolved the tension of the *crux theologorum* at the expense of being faithful to Scripture. Luther responded by writing *On the Bondage of the Will* in 1525. Addressing the topic of free will, Luther argued that sin totally incapacitates human free will. Sin enslaves sinners. However, this bondage of the will does not negate God's commands; humans are still responsible for keeping God's commandments even though they are in bondage to sin. Satan possesses sinners and refuses to willingly release them to God.

Salvation, therefore, must come from God alone. Luther called this divine monergism; God is the sole actor in human salvation. Sinners do not choose God; God chooses them. God predestines His people for eternal salvation. Through the Holy Spirit, God creates faith when and where He pleases. This justifying faith is not a human decision but rather a divine decision. Nevertheless, God does not predestine people to eternal damnation; He desires all people to be saved (1 Timothy 2:4). Luther understood Scripture as teaching that humans alone are responsible for damnation and God alone is responsible for salvation.

This leaves many questions unanswered. How can God predestine some people to salvation without also predestining others to damnation? How can we be held responsible for something that we cannot possibly achieve? Luther's understanding of divine monergism is illogical. Yet, it is biblical. Rather than resolving the tension of the *crux theologorum*, Luther left the tension unresolved. Instead of unraveling the mysteries of God, Luther recognized that the creatures must live within the bounds determined by the Creator. God is God, and we are not. The work of the Creator is often beyond the comprehension of the creatures:

> We say, as we have said before, that the secret will of the Divine Majesty is not a matter for debate, and the human temerity which with continual perversity is always neglecting necessary things in its eagerness to probe this one, must be called off and restrained from busying itself with the investigation of these secrets of God's majesty, which it is impossible to penetrate because he dwells in light inaccessible, as Paul testifies [I Tim. 6:16].[50]

---

50   LW 33:145.

Understanding the mysteries of God is a fruitless endeavor. Luther encouraged people to resist the urge to probe into the unresolved hiddenness of God. Instead, he argued that Christian reason should focus on the revelation of God in Christ Jesus:

> Let it occupy itself instead with God incarnate, or as Paul puts it, with Jesus crucified, in whom are all the treasures of wisdom and knowledge, though in a hidden manner [Col. 2:3]; for through him it is furnished abundantly with what it ought to know and ought not to know. It is God incarnate, moreover, who is speaking here: "I would . . . you would not"—God incarnate, I say, who has been sent into the world for the very purpose of willing, speaking, doing, suffering, and offering to all men everything necessary for salvation.[51]

God has revealed everything necessary for salvation in Jesus. Yes, we still have questions. Yes, we cannot fully wrap our minds around divine election without divine damnation. Even though not all of our questions have been resolved, all of our sins have been forgiven. Luther's response to the *crux theologorum* is just one of many unresolved tensions within Lutheran theology. Nearly every strand of Lutheran theology contains some sort of theological tension. There are times when it seems like Lutheran theology contradicts itself. There are times when Luther equally emphasized two opposing points. There are places in the Book of Concord where the numbers simply do not add up correctly. Being Lutheran is faithfulness to Scripture even when it leaves unresolved tensions.

---

51   LW 33:145–46.

LUTHERAN THEOLOGY → UNRESOLVED TENSIONS

Lutheran theology is a logician's worst nightmare. It is teeming with paradoxical confessions and unsolvable mysteries. Rather than forcing Scripture to fit into tidy little boxes of doctrine, Lutheran theology builds its beliefs around the not-so-tidy teachings of Scripture. Instead of conforming God's Word to human reason, Lutheran theology conforms human reason to God's Word. Human reason is properly used when it is in service to God's revealed truth in Scripture (known as the *ministerial use* of reason). And human reason is improperly used when it tries to rule over God's revealed truth in Scripture (known as the *magisterial use* of reason).

Lutheran theology works from the premise that God is God and we are not. Creatures live best when they are living within the boundaries established by their Creator. There are numerous theological tensions that we simply cannot resolve while still being faithful to Scripture:

Sinner and Saint: Sinners are forgiven of their sins through faith in Christ Jesus. The righteousness of Christ transforms sinners into saints. We are completely perfect and blameless before God. Original sin, nevertheless, is woven into our DNA and occupies the marrow of our bones. Although Baptism drowns the old Adam, he is a mighty good swimmer. We are always sinners in need of a Savior. This side of eternity, there is never a time when we do not need the forgiveness of sins offered to us in Christ Jesus. Lutheran theology describes this as being both sinner and saint (*simul justus et peccator*). We are not *either* sinner or saint; we are *both* sinner and saint at the very same time.

Mathematically speaking, this makes no sense. It would make more sense to think that original sin starts us at 0 percent saint and 100 percent sinner and grace turns us into 100 percent saint and 0 percent sinner. In fact, this was the belief held by the Roman

Catholic Church during the time of Luther. The Roman Catholic Church taught that Baptism washed away original sin and only the inclination to sin remained. Assuming that this inclination to sin (concupiscence) was not acted upon, a person was entirely saint and not at all sinner. Instead, Lutheran theology holds the scriptural tension (Romans 7) that believers are 100 percent sinner and 100 percent saint at the very same time.

In, With, and Under: The Lord's Supper presents numerous theological tensions. While other theologians attempted to resolve the tensions, Lutheran theology maintains the tensions. The Roman Catholic Church developed a belief about the Lord's Supper known as transubstantiation. This teaching relied heavily on Aristotelian philosophy for its understanding of "substance." Transubstantiation claims that the substance of the Lord's Supper changes completely from bread and wine into Christ's body and blood when the priest speaks the Words of Institution. Even though it outwardly appears to be bread and wine, the substance of the elements has changed entirely into body and blood. Lutheran theology gave a clear response to this doctrine: "As for transubstantiation, we care nothing about the sophistic cunning by which they teach that bread and wine leave or lose their own natural substance so that only the appearance and color of bread remain, and not true bread."[52]

Other theologians made the exact opposite claim about the Lord's Supper. Instead of claiming the elements are entirely the body and blood of Jesus, some theologians denied any sort of real presence in Holy Communion. One reformer in particular, Ulrich Zwingli (1484–1531) of Switzerland, was on the vanguard of theologians making this argument. Luther and Zwingli engaged in a public debate, known as the Marburg Colloquy (1529), on the topic of Christ's real presence in Holy Communion. Zwingli argued that

---

52 Smalcald Articles, Part III, Article VI, paragraph 5.

the body of Christ must exist in a certain space since He is true man; Jesus cannot be truly present both in heaven and in the Lord's Supper. Luther argued that he rejects mathematical reasons for limiting what God can and cannot do. Instead, he took Jesus at His word when He said, "This is My body" (Matthew 26:26) and "This is My blood" (Matthew 26:28).

Lutheran theology continues to leave this tension unresolved: Christ is really present in, with, and under the bread and wine of Holy Communion. How is Jesus present at the right hand of God (Mark 16:19) and present at the Communion rail? How can ordinary bread and wine contain the precious body and blood of Jesus? Lutherans intentionally leave these questions unresolved and resolve to know nothing other than what Christ has revealed in Scripture.

Law and Gospel: Scripture is fraught with tension. Recognizing these tensions is a vital part of interpreting Scripture. God offers clear instructions for holy living in Scripture:

- You shall love the LORD your God with all your heart and with all your soul and with all your might (Deuteronomy 6:5).

- He has told you, O man, what is good; and what does the LORD require of you but to do justice, and to love kindness, and to walk humbly with your God? (Micah 6:8)

God also offers clear promises of divine mercy:

- For the Son of Man came to seek and to save the lost (Luke 19:10).

- I am the good shepherd. The good shepherd lays down His life for the sheep (John 10:11).

Rightly distinguishing God's commandments and promises, known in Lutheran theology as Law and Gospel, is vital to the Christian life. Using the Law as a path to salvation results in despair and disappointment. Trying to cure the curse of sin with holy living is like treating cancer as if it were a cold. Likewise, using God's promises to elicit holy living turns grace into guilt. Instead, Lutheran theology rightly distinguishes Law and Gospel:

All Scripture ought to be distributed into these two principal topics: the Law and the promises. For in some places Scripture presents the Law, and in others the promise about Christ. In other words, in the Old Testament, Scripture promises that Christ will come, and it offers, for His sake, the forgiveness of sins, justification, and life eternal. Or in the Gospel, in the New Testament, Christ Himself (since He has appeared) promises the forgiveness of sins, justification, and life eternal.[53]

Holding the tension of Law and Gospel is harder than it seems. The Holy Spirit must teach the believer how to apply Law and Gospel in the right situations. Does the child caught lying need to hear how God detests falsehood or the forgiveness of sins in Christ Jesus? Should an alcoholic hear of God's desire for sobriety or God's

---

53   Apology of the Augsburg Confession, Article IV (II), paragraph 5.

constant mercy for the weak? These are difficult tensions requiring prayerful discernment and the guidance of the Holy Spirit.

The Word: Just as God took on human flesh in Christ Jesus, God's Word has taken on human letters in Scripture. The Bible was not a contentious matter during the time of Luther. Roman Catholic, Lutheran, and Reformed theologians generally agreed that Scripture was the infallible Word of God written by human authors. Luther wrote about Scripture as the Word of God clothed in human letters:

> The Holy Scripture is God's Word, written and, so to speak, lettered and put into the form of letters (*gebuchstabet und in Buchstaben gebildet*), just as Christ, the eternal Word of God, is clothed in humanity. And men regard and treat the written Word of God in this world just as they do Christ. It is a worm and no book compared with other books.[54]

It was not until a few hundred years after the Reformation that Scripture came under attack. In the eighteenth century, during the Age of Reason, Lutheran theologians had to take a hard stance on the inerrancy of Scripture. Friedrich Schleiermacher (1768–1834), David Strauss (1808–74), and Ludwig Feuerbach (1804–72) developed a methodology for reading the Bible known as the historical-critical method. Their approach assumed that the claims of Scripture were mythological until proven historical. Since human authors wrote Scripture, the historical-critical method treated Scripture as if it were a purely human creation.

Lutherans maintain the theological tension of Scripture by confessing that it is fully God's Word yet fully written by human authors. While others resolve this tension by using the historical-critical method, Lutheran theologians utilize the historical-grammatical method. This

---

54   *WLS* § 214.

method of interpretation approaches Scripture as the Word of God clothed in the humanity of alphabetic language. The Bible can be approached through history, linguistics, and rhetoric since it is God's Word in human form. Nevertheless, these disciplines must submit to the greater work of the Holy Spirit since the Bible is truly God's Word.

Now and Not Yet: Hanging on the cross, Jesus victoriously proclaimed, "It is finished" (John 19:30). Yet, Scripture concludes as if the work of Jesus is unfinished: "Come, Lord Jesus!" (Revelation 22:20). Is the work of Jesus finished, or are we waiting for some future work of Jesus? The answer is yes. The work of Jesus is a reality now and not yet.

Luther kept this tension in his explanation of the Apostles' Creed in the Small Catechism. Explaining the Second Article, Luther wrote, "I believe that Jesus Christ, true God, begotten of the Father from eternity, and also true man, born of the Virgin Mary, is my Lord, who has redeemed me . . ."[55] Explaining the Third Article, Luther wrote, "On the Last Day He will raise me and all the dead, and give eternal life to me and all believers in Christ."[56] There is a tension in these explanations: Jesus has already redeemed, yet He will give eternal life. Salvation is here now. And salvation is not yet here.

This same tension occurs in other parts of the Christian life. We have been made new in Jesus now (2 Corinthians 5:17), though we are not yet the new creation that we will become (Revelation 21:5). Jesus heals us now (James 5:14–16), though we wait for the day when He will give us eternal healing (John 11:25). We live with Jesus now (Galatians 2:20), though we long for the day when we will be with Him (Philippians 1:23).

---

55   Small Catechism, Explanation of the Second Article.
56   Small Catechism, Explanation of the Third Article.

YOU → UNRESOLVED TENSIONS

You live with messy, mysterious, unresolved tensions. Life raises questions about the hidden work of God. Suffering and sadness, hardship and hurt raise many questions:

- "I believe that God works all things for the good of His people. Why would He let me lose my job on the very same day I bought my first house?"

- "I prayed constantly for this child. Why would God allow a miscarriage to happen?"

- "I've read in the Bible that God loves the whole world. Why does God allow people to die without ever hearing the Gospel?"

- "I have shared my faith repeatedly with my father. How is it possible that the Holy Spirit has not created the faith for him to believe?"

- "I did nothing to deserve the life that I live. Why does God bless me with food, water, and health, while so many others die of starvation and sickness?"

This is an incomplete list. Life provides many more questions just like these on a daily basis. Faithfully addressing these questions is the task of every Christ follower. Being Lutheran is providing answers according to what God has revealed. God has not created you to stoically accept life without question. Life in Christ is not about grinning and bearing through life without question. You were made to explore creation, ask questions, and be curious. God delights in

His creatures digging in the dirt, looking up at the sky, and searching for answers: "Great are the works of the LORD, studied by all who delight in them" (Psalm 111:2).

And as life raises complex questions, you will be called upon to provide faithful answers. This means knowing what God has revealed to His creatures. And this also means knowing what God has hidden from His creatures. Being Lutheran is speaking boldly about what God has revealed while resisting the urge to speak about the hidden mind of God. Hold the tension of boldly proclaiming what God has revealed while refusing to pry into the secret will of God.

For example, suppose a natural disaster brings widespread suffering to a nearby community. This event raises questions of why God permits this evil to occur (theodicy). Answering questions of theodicy requires you to speak only to what God has revealed in Scripture. God has revealed that this event, like all tragedies, is the curse of sin wreaking havoc on God's creation (Genesis 3:16–19). God has revealed that tragedies are the creation groaning with the pain of sin (Romans 8:19–22).

Cling to God's revelation and leave the hiddenness of God unresolved

However, God has hidden the reason for this specific tragedy. Although He has worked this way before (2 Chronicles 7:13–14), God has not revealed that this tragedy is a call to repent from a specific sin. Although God has previously used the threat of natural disasters to turn people from sin (Jonah 3:1–5), it remains hidden whether God was working the same way through this natural disaster. While it remains hidden as to why God allows such suffering to occur, God has revealed His salvation in Jesus. We cannot know why God permits sufferings, yet we know that God has eternally resolved suffering through the cross of Christ.

Being Lutheran means living faithfully with unresolved tensions. On the cross, God has revealed all that we need to live faithfully. He has kept certain mysteries of life hidden from our knowledge. Cling to God's revelation and leave the hiddenness of God unresolved. Here is what this looks like in your daily life:

Pray Hard: About a hundred times a day, you will find yourself pondering the hidden work of God. You will wonder why God allowed something to happen. You will wonder why God did what He did. You will theorize, speculate, and postulate why your friend has cancer. Your wandering mind will wonder about the future. When you find yourself prying into the hidden work of God, turn those moments into prayer. Pray that God would reveal His plans for you. Ask God to give you peace in the midst of wrestling with life's questions.

Know Scripture: You cannot answer life's difficult questions without knowing Scripture. When life gives you questions, search Scripture to see how God has already revealed His will for you. You will not find chapter and verse telling you what to study in college, where to work, or the name of your future spouse. Scripture will not reveal why you specifically suffered the hurt of a miscarriage, the sadness of divorce, or the turmoil of cancer. Scripture will, however, shine the light of God's revealed truth into the darkness of your confusion. When life leaves you with many questions, turn to what God has revealed in Scripture rather than pondering what God has chosen to keep hidden.

Trust God: Trusting in God means leaving some tensions unresolved. God invites you to be bold in your prayers.

You have an invitation from God to ask and expect that you will receive: "Ask, and it will be given to you; seek, and you will find; knock, and it will be opened to you" (Matthew 7:7). Nevertheless, faith trusts in God even when your prayers are answered contrary to your desires. Living by faith means embracing the tension between prayerfully asking God to act while faithfully accepting God's actions.

Love Others: God has revealed His will for you: "You shall love the Lord your God with all your heart and with all your soul and with all your strength and with all your mind, and your neighbor as yourself" (Luke 10:27). Although many questions remain, God has clearly revealed that we are to love Him and love one another. Gazing at our navels, paralysis by analysis, and unraveling the mysteries of God divert our ability to enjoy life. Luther explained it this way: "But God loved all, even His enemies, without making any difference. There, we, too, should love as brothers even those who are not loveable."[57] All you really need to know is that God has shown His love to you in Christ Jesus so that you can live love for others. What more do you really need to know?

CONCLUSION

Life is messy. God is not. Creatures have boundaries. God does not. Unresolved tension is simply part of being a creature living in a world messy with sin. Being Lutheran is admitting creaturely limitations and living with unresolved tensions.

---

57 *WLS* § 2586.

We proclaim paradoxes: sinner and saint, Law and Gospel, now and not yet. We tolerate tensions: Holy Communion is fully Christ's body and blood while also fully bread and wine. Scripture is fully the Word of God while also the work of fully human authors. Others traditions try to resolve these tensions with philosophical speculation, lofty reason, and historical proof. Lutherans tolerate the tension of God's revelation.

Being Lutheran is not made for TV. We refuse to resolve every theological question, fit our faith into tidy doctrinal packages, or chase after philosophical symmetry. We refuse to treat the mysteries of our faith as if they are riddles to be solved. Instead, we live faithfully as creatures of God. We cling to God's revelation of love in the cross of Jesus Christ.

Vignette: Hannah

Polite conversation turned into heavy silence. The ultrasound technician had been chatting about the weather, summer vacation plans, and how Hannah was feeling. The image on the screen caused the technician to stop talking entirely. She silently finished up the measurements and told Hannah that the doctor would be in to see her soon.

It might have been only two minutes. However, it felt like two hours. The doctor entered the room with a resident physician dutifully following behind. The doctor introduced herself to Hannah and then introduced the resident physician. After this very courteous exchange, the doctor shifted from plain language to highly technical medical jargon: "Hannah, the diagnostic sonography of your womb shows that you have a blighted ovum."

This statement was followed by a long pause.

Hannah's confused stare prompted the doctor to continue: "Anembryonic gestation occurs when there is a gestational sac present but no fetal pole. This is usually the result of embryonic death in the very early stages of growth."

Hannah understood many of the words that the doctor was saying. However, she was uncertain as to exactly what it all meant. Staring at the doctor, she said, "All right. What does that mean exactly?"

The doctor shifted back to plain language and said, "It appears that this pregnancy is going to be a miscarriage."

Those words sank in. And then they sank in some more. She suddenly felt very alone. The child in her womb was somehow no longer there. The doctor and resident sitting right next to her felt a mile away. She suddenly regretted not bringing anyone else to the appointment with her. All she wanted to do was call her husband.

Hannah got in the car and called her husband, Tim. He picked up the phone and asked how the appointment went. She tearfully explained that the doctor was fairly certain she was having a miscarriage. Those words sank in. And then they sank in some more. Tim had no response. He and Hannah knew that miscarriages happened frequently; yet, they never thought that a miscarriage could happen to them. They had prayed for friends going through a miscarriage, but this was different. This was their child.

Tim finally came up with a response: "Oh no. For real? Wow. Oh no."

Tim kept talking without really saying anything. He had nothing to say.

Prayer was their first response. They sat together on the couch and choked out a prayer: "God, You can undo this. You are the Author of all life. The doctor is not certain that this is a miscarriage. Reverse this and bless us with a child. God, we beg You to bless us with a happy and healthy child. This is our will. Thy will be done. Amen."

Hannah took the pills prescribed by the doctor. The medication was a pregnancy hormone that could possibly help save the child if the miscarriage was a result of her body not producing enough hormones. The pills made her drowsy and nauseous. It was hard to tell, however, if her drowsiness and nausea were the result of medication or depression. Hannah prayed constantly for her child: "Lord, work through this medication. Work through my body. Work any way that You can to save the life of our child. This is our will. Thy will be done. Amen."

God did not answer this prayer according to their will. Cramps came. Bleeding came. Hannah miscarried. Although the child was only six weeks old, Tim and Hannah buried their child in the backyard. Tim offered a prayer and Scripture reading: "For I consider that the sufferings of this present time are not worth comparing with the glory that is to be revealed to us" (Romans 8:18).

They thanked God for the time they had with their child. They prayed that in the mystery of God's mercy, they might be able to meet their child someday. They said amen and good-bye.

Three months later, Hannah found out she was pregnant again. Prayer was again their first response: "God, we thank You and praise You for this wonderful blessing. Be with this child. Bless our child. Bless Hannah's womb. Place Your hand of protection on her and on our child. Amen."

God did not answer this prayer according to their will. Cramps came. Bleeding came. Hannah miscarried for a second time.

Like a bad dream, they were standing in their backyard yet again burying yet another child. Again they prayed. They thanked God for this child whom they had never met. They placed their hope in God's mercy that they might be able to meet this child one day. They said amen and good-bye.

Six months later, Hannah found out she was pregnant again. Prayer was their first impulse: "God, we are here again. We know that You can do this. You have done this many times before. You did this for Adam and Eve. You did this for Abraham and Sarah. You did this for Isaac and Rebekah. Please do it for us. Amen."

This was their constant prayer.

Eight weeks into the third pregnancy, Hannah began bleeding. She feared that this pregnancy would also end in a miscarriage. Although they had done so twice before without their desired outcome, prayer was yet again their first response.

She went to the doctor's office. Instead of seeing an empty screen, she saw the flicker of a heartbeat. She called Tim. He wept. She wept. They were both exhausted from praying. They were deeply tired from a year of burying children, praying for God to reverse the obvious, and begging for healing. They were exhausted from living in the unresolved tension between God's infinite power and the reality of their profound suffering. Their hearts and knees were worn out from a year of unceasing prayer.

Yet, Hannah did not stop praying after the doctor finally gave her good news. She started praying more. She discovered that prayer is vital to the life of faith. Although God already knew the outcome, Hannah's faith still compelled her to pray. Although she could not understand why God allowed her to suffer, she still clung to the suffering of Christ Jesus on the cross for her salvation. Despite every sign pointing to bad news, Hannah sought good news from God. When God had answered every one of her prayers contrary to her desire, nevertheless Hannah prayed. Hannah lived in the unresolved tension of faith in Christ Jesus.

Chapter 8
Discussion Questions

1. Read Genesis 2:7. What comes to mind when you think of a creature? What is necessary for a creature to exist?

2. Hardship led Job to question the hidden mind of God. Does God not approve of creatures asking questions? Read Matthew 7:7–11.

3. Jesus referred to His disciples as friends. How are friendships formed? What does it tell you about God that He befriends human creatures?

4. Read John 1:14–18. How did so many people overlook God dwelling among them?

5. Read John 15:26–27. What are the two different names Jesus uses for the Holy Spirit here? What do these names tell us about the work of the Holy Spirit?

6. Erasmus concluded that people had the freedom to choose salvation or damnation. How does Scripture depict the human will? Read Ephesians 2:1–10.

7. God has revealed everything necessary for salvation in Jesus. What questions do you still have for God? Why might God have left these questions unanswered for you?

8. You cannot answer life's difficult questions without knowing Scripture. What is your practice of Bible reading? Do you read the Bible daily? How might a habit of Bible reading help you answer life's questions according to Scripture?

9. Tim and Hannah lived in the tension of trusting in God despite multiple miscarriages. Why should you pray even if God answers your prayers according to His will? Read Luke 18:1–8.

Chapter 9

PURPOSE

I cry out to God Most High, to God
who fulfills His purpose for me.
(Psalm 57:2)

He was a useful guy. Toting loads, lifting boxes, and sweeping floors: this guy did it all. He would show up, keep his nose to the grindstone, and quietly plug away at the to-do list. His boss found him very useful. Unlike many of the other workers, he was not noisy or disruptive. He just quietly went about his work.

Perhaps too quietly . . .

One day, the owner of the company came looking for his useful worker. He checked the warehouse and shop, closet and fields. Nothing. He asked the other workers if they had seen him. Nothing. He sat in the break room, waiting for him to come in and pour a cup of coffee. Nothing. He shouted out his name: "Onesimus! Onesimus! Where are you?" Nothing.

There was a good reason why Onesimus could not hear his boss yelling his name. He had skipped town. He had bolted in the night. He decided that his boss could take this job and . . . well, you get the point.

He landed in jail. Leaving in the night and running away from work—especially if you were a first-century slave in the Roman Empire like Onesimus—was a punishable offense. His boss, a man named Philemon, was also his owner. Philemon had purchased

Onesimus as a slave to work for him. He was most likely a slave from birth; the name Onesimus in Greek means "useful." He was born to be useful for someone else. Yet, locked up in jail, Onesimus was not very useful anymore.

Nobody knows why Onesimus left in the night. Nobody knows what led to his capture and imprisonment. Everything known about Onesimus comes from the apostle Paul in Scripture. Onesimus met Paul while in prison. He heard the Gospel and became a Christian. Onesimus told his new brother in Christ that he had a burden on his heart: he was a runaway slave. He had breached his master's trust by running away from his owner. His new brother in Christ offered a solution.

Paul decided that he would write a letter to Philemon seeking forgiveness for Onesimus. It appears that Philemon was also a Christian by the way Paul addressed the letter: "Paul, a prisoner for Christ Jesus, and Timothy our brother, To Philemon our beloved fellow worker" (Philemon 1). Paul knew that Onesimus had nothing to offer his owner to make things better. Instead, Paul offered to pay for the runaway slave's debts. Paul knew that Philemon had no reason to forgive his runaway slave, so he argued that he should be the reason to forgive him. Paul stood between an angry boss and a runaway slave.

Paul also knew that Onesimus's name meant useful. Ironically, as a jailed runaway, he was not useful to his owner. Locked up in jail, he was the exact opposite of his name. Paul wrote, "Formerly he was useless to you, but now he is indeed useful to you and to me" (Philemon 11). He knew something that Philemon did not know: Onesimus was now a Christ follower.

Made new by Jesus, he was useful in a far greater way. In Jesus, Onesimus was not just a runaway slave or a disgruntled employee who cheated and stole. Now he was a co-worker in God's kingdom. He was useful to neighbor and God alike as he labored with a joyful heart. He was useful whether he was performing daily tasks or proclaiming the Gospel. God used him to care for neighbors, embody divine mercy, and offer himself as a living sacrifice for others. Onesimus was useful in an entirely new way: Christ Jesus gave him eternal purpose.

Paul made it clear that Onesimus had received a new purpose in Jesus, "no longer as a bondservant but more than a bondservant, as a beloved brother—especially to me, but how much more to you, both in the flesh and in the Lord" (Philemon 16).

PURPOSE IN JESUS

This is what Jesus does. He comes to useless, purposeless, sinners and turns us into useful, purpose-filled workers for the kingdom of God. Although sin sucked the purpose out of life, Jesus came to revive it. He takes purposeless people and gives them eternal purpose.

Andrew received eternal purpose from Jesus. Before he met Jesus, fishing was just a job. Every day was the same: Punch in, push out, and pull up some fish. Punch out, prepare the fish for market, and hope to make a few shekels. Andrew's primary purpose in life was found in fish flopping around on the deck of a boat. Feeding his family and community through his labor was a noble task indeed. To be certain, God was at work feeding others through the fish that Andrew caught.

Nevertheless, Jesus came and anchored Andrew's labor to eternity:

Passing alongside the Sea of Galilee, He saw Simon and Andrew the brother of Simon casting a net into the sea, for they were fishermen. And Jesus said to them, "Follow Me, and I will make you become fishers of men." And immediately they left their nets and followed Him. (Mark 1:16–18)

Feeding people with fish is a noble task that lasts a lifetime; feeding people with fish and the Gospel is a noble task that lasts for all eternity. Jesus gave Andrew eternal purpose.

Zacchaeus also received eternal purpose from Jesus. Before Zacchaeus met Jesus, stealing from people was just a job. Like most tax collectors in the Roman Empire, Zacchaeus used his position of power for extortion. He made his riches at the expense of others. Every day was the same: get dressed, climb into his imported chariot, and drive to the office. Demand a denarius here and skim a shekel there; it was all in a day's work for Zacchaeus. His purpose in life was clinking coins in the coffer. Stealing from people was far from a noble task.

Nevertheless, Jesus came and invested new purpose into Zacchaeus's purposeless life: "And when Jesus came to the place, He looked up and said to him, 'Zacchaeus, hurry and come down, for I must stay at your house today' " (Luke 19:5). Jesus gave Zacchaeus an entirely new purpose in life. Rather than working for his own benefit, Zacchaeus found new purpose in working for the benefit of others. He told Jesus that he would begin by making right his many wrongs: "And Zacchaeus stood and said to the Lord, 'Behold, Lord, the half of my goods I give to the poor. And if I have defrauded anyone of anything, I restore it fourfold' " (Luke 19:8).

Jesus meets us in the midst of our purposeless life and gives us eternal purpose

Jesus sought out a lost and purposeless Zacchaeus and gave him eternal purpose.

From Andrew to Zacchaeus, literally from A to Z, Jesus gave people eternal purpose. He took what sin had made useless and made it useful again. And, like He did for Andrew and Zacchaeus, Jesus meets us in the midst of our purposeless life and gives us eternal purpose.

Jesus meets us in the midst of our uselessness, just like he met Onesimus in prison, and makes us eternally useful. Without Christ, we, too, are useless, runaway slaves. Left on our own, we are slaves to sin. We are born in bondage to sin (Romans 6:6). As slaves to sin, we are utterly useless to God. Our hands can produce nothing with lasting purpose; hands that should be serving others instead grab for more money or just remain idle. Eyes that should see the needs of others instead gaze over our neighbor's fence, seeing flaws in others and desiring their possessions. Ears that should listen for cries for mercy instead hear only gossip, slander, and bigotry. As slaves to sin, we are nothing more than useless runaways.

Like Onesimus, we need an advocate. We need an intercessor. We need someone to stand before our owner, make payment on our behalf, and restore our usefulness. And we have that in Christ Jesus. Christ stands before God, offering to pay the debts of useless runaways. Christ paid the debts that we owe. He paid them on the cross. Through His death and resurrection, Jesus declared us eternally useful again. Just as Paul said to Philemon, Christ stands before God saying, "Formerly he was useless to You, but now he is indeed useful to You and to Me."

You have new purpose in Christ Jesus. God purposefully uses you through everyday tasks. God uses your hands to feed, protect, and care for others. God uses your honest labor to bless your community. God uses your mouth to speak comfort, truth, and love. God uses your ears to hear the hurts and hopes, fears and failures of your neighbors. And God uses you to bring Jesus to other useless runaways, thereby making them useful again.

VOCATION: GOD CALLING

Medieval society had a truncated understanding of work. Theologians had divided work into two broad categories: sacred and secular. Only sacred work was considered to be a vocation. The word *vocation*, which comes from the Latin word *vocatio*, means calling or summons.

Clergy, monks, nuns, and anyone else with a formal vow of piety had a vocation and calling from God. Bakers, cobblers, farmers, mothers, and blacksmiths just had a job.

Working for the church meant you were serving the Lord and on the path to spiritual perfection. Working for your family meant you were serving man and coasting on the path of spiritual perfection. Working for the church came with the benefit of vocational fulfillment, societal respect, and active service for God; nevertheless, it required a vow of poverty, chastity, and dependence on others. Working a secular trade did not require any sort of self-imposed restriction on income, marriage, or personal piety; however, working for worldly gain was devoid of any serious spiritual benefit.

Luther struggled with the chasm between sacred and secular work. Luther's father, Hans Luther, had intended for his son to become a lawyer. Although the priesthood carried a high degree of societal respect, studying law carried both a high degree of societal respect and a substantial income. This was important to Hans Luther because children served as the primary support for aging parents. Having a child take a vow of poverty meant that the parents took an involuntary vow of poverty later in life. The sentiments of Hans Luther were not unique; similar to many modern parents, medieval parents were concerned about how their child's occupation would impact the well-being of the entire family.

Children, however, had concerns of their own. Medieval society belittled marriage and parenthood. Motherhood was characterized as dull drudgery and mindless monotony, plagued by helpless husbands and dirty diapers. Fatherhood was ridiculed as domestic death, besieged by crying children and whining wives. Children were either a tax on sex or cheap labor.

Luther, in his extensive treatment on marriage entitled *The Estate of Marriage*, characterized commonly held sentiments about family life:

Alas, must I rock the baby, wash its diapers, make its bed, smell its stench, stay up nights with it, take care of it when it cries, heal its rashes and sores, and on top of that care for my wife, provide for her, labor at my trade, take care of this and take care of that, do this and do that, endure this and endure that, and whatever else of bitterness and drudgery married life involves? What, should I make such a prisoner of myself? O you poor, wretched fellow, have you taken a wife? Fie, fie upon such wretchedness and bitterness! It is better to remain free and lead a peaceful, carefree life; I will become a priest or a nun and compel my children to do likewise.[58]

Yes. Medieval society had lowered daily work, marriage, and parenthood to unavoidable obligations. Conversely, churchly activities were elevated as the only activities that were truly pleasing to God. This sentiment created a severe rift between sacred and secular work. You could devote your life to either serving God or serving man; however, serving both God and man was not an option.

Vocations are the locus of God's active work in creation

Lutheran theology turned this paradigm upside down. Arguing from Scripture, Luther believed that serving others was serving God. Luther argued that vocation rightfully applies to all Christians. God calls believers to multiple vocations: mother, father, sister, brother, child, neighbor, citizen, worker, and church member. Vocations are the locus of God's active work in creation.

Luther taught that doing what God called you to do is a noble task no matter how simple the task. God cares for little ones through a father changing his child's diaper. God feeds people through the farmer harvesting wheat from the field. God provides peace and

---

58   LW 45:39.

order for a community through the judge administering the law. God speaks to His people through the pastor preaching the Word of God. Luther's understanding of vocation turned medieval society upside down: if you want to serve God, then serve your neighbor.

Rather than dividing the world into a sacred and secular binary, Luther preferred to use the term *estate*. Luther saw God working in three distinct estates—church, family, and the state. No particular estate was more godly or noble than any of the other estates; serving the family and the state were as spiritual as serving in the church. Preaching the Gospel to a congregation or nursing a newborn child are both godly tasks. Baking bread, burying the dead, and keeping cattle fed are all God-pleasing vocations.

MASKS OF GOD

The doctrine of vocation, like all Lutheran theology, is based on Scripture. Going back to the Word of God, Luther could not find any biblical basis for the medieval teaching that only those living in a monastic order were called by God to serve Him. On the contrary, Luther saw the Bible teaching that God works through all people to accomplish His will and work (Philippians 2:13) and that God calls all Christians through the Gospel (1 Corinthians 7:17).

God works through normal, everyday people doing normal, everyday tasks. God calls normal, everyday Christians to live out their faith as wives, husbands, mothers, fathers, workers, bosses, church members, and citizens. Luther referred to these vocations as the "masks of God." Although it appears that the farmer works to provide grain, it is actually God working through the farmer to provide daily bread. Luther explained it this way:

God could easily give you grain and fruit without your plowing and planting. But He does not want to do so. Neither does He want your plowing and planting alone to give you grain and fruit; but you are to plow and plant and then ask His blessing and pray: "Now let God take over; now grant grain and fruit, dear Lord! Our plowing and planting will not do it. It is Thy gift" . . . These are the masks of God, behind which He wants to remain concealed and do all things.[59]

God continues the work of the sixth day as husband and wife come together to create a child. God comforts little ones through the care and concern of mothers. God shelters children through the strong hands and watchful eyes of fathers. God provides daily bread through soil and seed tilled and sown by the farmer. God protects through the laws and ordinances enforced by police officers. God even refreshes through the work of the brewer and barkeep serving a heady pint of ale. God works through our work.

God works through our work

Doing the Lord's work is not relegated only to professional church workers, highly trained prayer warriors, or the sacred ranks of the altar guild. Instead, Christian living is about God's work through our work. Luther taught that Christian living is as simple as being called by the Gospel and faithfully serving others:

For that reason, every Christian should make sure his actions are in the spirit of God and in the service of his neighbor. A ruler should say to himself, "Christ served me and saw everything through to completion, so I should also want to serve my neighbor, to protect and take him by the hand. That is why God gave me this office, so that I may serve my neighbor." This is an example of a good ruler and his good kingdom. If a ruler sees his neighbor being oppressed, he should

59   LW 14:114.

think, "That is my responsibility. I have to guard and protect my neighbor" . . . This applies in the same way to the shoemaker, tailor, scholar, or teacher. If he is a Christian tailor, he will say, "I will make each garment with the talents that God has given me in order to earn my commission and use it to help and serve my neighbor." Now whoever does not serve others, does not have God living in him and his life is not Christlike.[60]

Purpose in life is not relegated only to Christians taking vows of poverty, celibacy, and monasticism. Prince, servant, farmer, shoemaker, tailor, and parent all live a life of purpose as they faithfully live according to God's calling. God governs, serves, feeds, shoes, clothes, and nourishes His people through the work of others. Vocation is not about what we do to find purpose in our work; instead, vocation is about God accomplishing His purposes in and through the work of His people.

PRIESTHOOD OF ALL BELIEVERS

Not only does God work through the daily efforts of normal people, but He also ministers through the daily ministry of normal people. Scripture talks about the active ministry of all Christians in this way:

But you are a chosen race, a royal priesthood, a holy nation, a people for His own possession, that you may proclaim the excellencies of Him who called you out of darkness into His marvelous light. Once you were not a people, but now you are God's people; once you had not received mercy, but now you have received mercy. (1 Peter 2:9–10)

---

60 Martin Luther, "Sermon in the Castle Church at Weimar," translated by Robert Filter from *Luthers Werke: Kritische Gesamtausgabe* (Weimar: Hermann Böhlau, 1905) 10/3:382.

Jesus does His work through you. He seeks and saves the lost through you. He places His word in your mouth. He forgives the brokenhearted through your proclamation of Christ's forgiveness. He invites rebellious sinners to repent through your invitation to repentance. He delivers the peace of God through your peaceful presence. Jesus lifts the fallen from the floor with your hands. Jesus feeds the famished with your spoon. His work is done through you. Baptism flooded your life with eternal purpose in Christ Jesus: you are part of the priesthood of all believers.

All believers are equal in their relationship to God. All have sinned and fallen short of the glory of God. The Law shows that we are all in desperate need of a Savior. All stand before Christ Jesus as open-handed beggars in need of mercy. And faith receives Christ's righteousness equally in the waters of Baptism and the proclamation of the Gospel. Luther explained the priesthood of all believers, saying, "We all have one baptism, one gospel, one faith, and are all Christians alike; for baptism, gospel, and faith alone make us spiritual and a Christian people."[61]

Rediscovering and applying the scriptural teaching of the priesthood of all believers radically transformed medieval society. Lutheran theology declared that nuns and mothers, monks and fathers, priests and plumbers, popes and paupers were all of equal worth before God. According to the priesthood of all believers, the homeless Christian living on the outskirts of town is of the same standing before God as the corpulent cardinal in red robes of silk. Living for God is not about fleeing the work to which God has called you so that you can live in a monastery praying all day; rather, living for God is about faithfully being used by God to perform the work to which He has called you.

---

61   LW 44:127.

To be certain, the priesthood of all believers does not negate the need for pastors. Lutheran theologians defended the Office of the Ministry in Article V of the Augsburg Confession. Pastors engaging in Word and Sacrament ministry are the means by which the Gospel is delivered to the Church. The Gospel cannot be heard unless it is proclaimed (Romans 10:14). The pastor's purpose is first and foremost Word and Sacrament ministry. Pastors preach the Gospel, administer the Sacraments, and shepherd the flock following Jesus.

Although the pastor speaks the words, God does the verbs; the pastor may speak the words of forgiveness, yet it is God who has done all the work of securing forgiveness in Christ Jesus. It is in the mouth of the pastor that Christ has located the proclamation of the forgiveness of sins. From the mouth of the called and ordained pastor one can and should expect to hear the Gospel. This word of forgiveness is as valid as if Christ Himself spoke the words. The Office of the Ministry is established by Christ and conferred upon the individual pastor through the call of a congregation.

Does this negate the priesthood of all believers? By no means! As mentioned in the previous chapter, Lutherans live and breathe theological tensions. Scripture teaches that God calls all believers to perform work in the kingdom of God. And Scripture teaches that God calls some believers to perform work in the kingdom of God as pastors. God's Word does not teach either one or the other. Both callings are noble, true, and valid. Pastors declare Christ's forgiveness to the congregation. And all believers declare Christ's forgiveness to fellow Christians. Both rely fully on the promise of Christ.

The difference is in vocation. God has called different people to different vocations. God has called some to be part of the universal priesthood and others to be part of the Office of the Ministry. The Church engages the world knowing that God has delivered His forgiveness to us through different means. Individual Christians have been called to deliver Christ's forgiveness to one another. The pastor has been called to deliver Christ's forgiveness to the community of believers in Word and Sacrament ministry. Different vocation. Different calling. Same purpose: God's work through us.

HELLO, MY NAME IS CHILD OF GOD

Vocation is extremely relevant in modern society. Everywhere you look, people are struggling to have a clear sense of identity and purpose in their lives. If you do not believe me, try this: My name is [*insert your name*]. I am a [*fill in the blank*].

My name is Alex. I am a painter.

My name is Carol. I am an accountant.

My name is Tom. I am a fisherman.

My name is Jill. I am a soccer player.

My name is Jeff. I am Jackie's boyfriend.

My name is Jackie. I am Jeff's girlfriend.

People constantly introduce themselves this way. We define ourselves by our jobs, hobbies, relationship status, hometown, or political persuasion. This is a problem. Using these attributes as the source of our identity will inevitably result in an identity crisis.

I speak from experience. I have been there before.

My source of identity was totally disrupted as I began my seminary studies. I left home and drove across the country. I left behind my childhood house, my family, and my friends. I left behind a smart, godly, and beautiful woman named Elizabeth. (Thankfully, she kept taking my phone calls and later became my wife.) I went to a city I had never seen before.

The many sources of my identity—hometown, job, family, and friends—were far, far away. I was filled with doubt and fear and questions: Am I sure that I want to become a pastor? Can I cut it academically? Can I pay the tuition? What if this isn't for me?

My first day on campus was orientation. All the new students were required to attend new-student orientation sessions. I was running a bit late for one of the sessions, and I left my nametag behind. When I arrived, we broke into small groups and had to introduce ourselves. Everyone had a nametag except for me. The first person introduced himself by holding up his nametag, looking at it, and saying, "My name is Jim."

One by one, people followed in the pattern of the first person by holding up their nametags as they introduced themselves. Then it was my turn. Trying to make light of the situation, I said, "I don't have a nametag. I guess that makes me a nameless nobody."

The truth is, I felt like a nameless nobody. I felt like a lost, lonely, nobody.

Someone in the group immediately responded by saying, "You are not a nameless nobody. You are a baptized child of God!"

Wow. That struck me. I was reminded that in my Baptism, God placed His name on me for all eternity. God gave me eternal purpose and identity in Baptism. Through the waters of Baptism, God called me to be His own for all eternity. Even though my hometown may change, my identity in Christ will never change. Even though my job title will constantly change, God's purpose for my life remains the same.

Vocation is a way for you to experience God's eternal purpose for your life

Eternal purpose comes from God. If you try to find lasting purpose in your job, then your purpose in life will change faster than you can clean out your office. If your purpose in life is wrapped up in your house, then you will be facing a purposeless life when it is time to sell. If your purpose in life comes from a sports team, political party, children, or anything else in all of creation, then you had better be prepared for disappointment. Lasting purpose is found only in God's purpose for your life. Vocation is a way for you to experience God's eternal purpose for your life. The work that God does through your daily work has eternal purpose.

Consider how vocation impacts your daily life. Realizing God's eternal purpose for you will forever change your work:

Stress: Where should I go to college? What should I study? Where should I apply for a job? What if I do not get the job? What if I get the job and I do not like it? What if I lose the job? What if I epically fail at this job? Work is stressful. Constant competition, tight deadlines, and impossible goals can make for staggering levels of stress in the workplace.

Vocation offers serious hope for workplace stress. God is at work through your daily work. It is not on you alone to sow the seeds, sell the goods, and bring home the bacon. God goes into the field with you, provides fruit from your labor, and gives you rest according to your needs. Work will give you stress. And God will give you rest: "Come to Me, all who labor and are heavy laden, and I will give you rest" (Matthew 11:28).

Layoffs: Getting a pink slip hurts. Changing careers against your will is a drag. Being asked to clean out your desk is a life-changing moment. Nevertheless, God does not give His people pink slips on vocation. Just because your job changes, that does not mean that God is no longer at work through you. Shifting vocations simply means that God is shifting the work that He plans to do through you.

Losing your vocation as engineer provides greater opportunities to focus on your vocation as mother, wife, neighbor, and church member. Adding the vocation of father requires balancing this new vocational responsibility with your existing vocations as son, brother, employee, and golf partner.

Paychecks: Do not let anyone reduce vocation down to a paycheck. Society claims that the more you make, the more important your vocation is to others. If you do not receive payment for your labor, then you must not be working. This is simply not true. Many of the most important vocational responsibilities do not receive a paycheck. Do not let anyone put a price on caring for children, aging parents, or people in need. Nobody else can replace God's work through a mother or father. Nobody else can take the place of a child caring for his or her elderly parents. There are many vocational responsibilities that only one person in the entire world can fulfill: you.

God is at work through your work regardless of a paycheck. Vocation is not the same thing as a job. Jobs are what you do to earn a living. Vocation is what God does through the work He has called you to perform. God may call you to work for little or no pay. God may call you to work for lots of pay. Either way, God is at work through your daily work.

Work Ethic: Recognizing how God is at work through our work can change our work ethic. Coming in late, sneaking out early, surfing social media, and endless gossiping are more than stealing from your employer. Stealing time on the job is also stealing from the work of God. Failing to meet the responsibilities of parenthood hurts not only the children but also God's ongoing work in their lives. Being an absentee husband or wife hurts not only our spouse, but also hinders God's care for that person. If God blesses others through us, then sinning against our vocations disrupts God's blessing in the lives of others.

Working hard in your various vocations maximizes God's blessings for others. God cares for many children through the diligent social worker tackling a pile of foster-family applications. God feeds many people through the farmer steadfastly tending the field. God gives great comfort through the father knowing when to leave work and spend time with his family.

Retirement: Sleeping in, golfing all day, and generally doing nothing sounds really great . . . until you actually do it. Retirement is distressing for many people because their identity and purpose in life is connected to their occupation. If you are a teacher, then what are you when you retire from teaching? If you are a lawyer, where is your purpose in life when you stop representing clients? Vocation offers purpose even in retirement.

Since God calls people to many different vocations, retiring from a career does not mean purposelessly drifting into the sunset. Retiring from a career frees up time and energy for other vocations: spouse, grandparent, sibling, citizen, church member, and neighbor. God is still working through you in retirement.

CONCLUSION

God gives lasting purpose, usefulness, and identity to His people through vocation. God calls us in many different ways:

- Through the waters of Baptism, God calls us to be His dear children clothed in Christ's righteousness.

- Through the Gospel of Jesus Christ, God calls us to be part of the priesthood of all believers.

- Throughout our lives and daily interactions, God calls us to the many different vocations of spouse, parent, child, sibling, worker, boss, church member, citizen, and neighbor.

These are just some of the many vocations to which God calls us. These are not jobs that we perform. Rather, these vocations are the ways in which God works through our work.

Being Lutheran is finding purpose in God's calling. Rather than finding purpose in a job, we rely on God to give our lives purpose. Jesus gave Onesimus eternal purpose. Jesus gave Andrew eternal purpose. Jesus gave Zacchaeus eternal purpose. And Jesus gives you eternal purpose.

Vignette: Scott

Refresh. Refresh. Refresh. Scott watched as the views on his newly uploaded video increased every time he refreshed the web page. Recording the content for the video took over a year. Editing and uploading the video took less than an hour. Scott had spent the past year recording sermons at the campus chapel. He took all the sermons and selected brief snippets in which the preacher proclaimed the Gospel: "You are forgiven." "Christ Jesus makes all things new." "God gave His life for you." "God raised us up with Christ."

Once he had all the Gospel snippets extracted from the sermons, he mashed them all together and set it to a drum loop. It was far from a revolutionary work of digital editing. Nevertheless, listening to the Gospel proclaimed over and over again was powerful. Scott finalized the video and loaded it on a video-sharing website. And it spread.

Scott was not exactly trying to share the Gospel with the world by making this video. He simply liked the preaching in his campus chapel. He liked tinkering with digital videos. Editing digital videos was his creative outlet; it allowed him to take raw content and mash it up in a new and artistic arrangement. In fact, the main reason he loaded it on the video-sharing website was so that he would have a backup of the finished file.

When the video reached ten thousand views, Scott's pastor called him and asked if they could meet sometime. Scott agreed, and they scheduled a meeting. His pastor was astonished that the video could have so many views. He told Scott that God was at work spreading the Gospel through his ability to create engaging videos. Scott had never considered that God had a purpose for his interest in digital media. Tinkering with videos went from a hobby to God's active work in the world through Scott.

As it is for all people, graduating from college was a pivotal time for Scott. He really wanted to serve God by working for a church or some sort of ministry organization. He prayed that God would open up an opportunity for him to use his talents for the kingdom of God. He sent his résumé out to dozens of congregations and ministry organizations. And every one of them said the same thing: "We would love to have you join us . . . but we simply do not have room in the budget for a digital content specialist."

While he had no success in finding a job within the church, he had multiple job offers from businesses and municipalities. Realizing that he would soon have to begin paying off student loans, Scott took a job within municipal government as a digital content specialist. He told himself that he would do this until God opened up a way for him to serve in the church. He took the job but kept looking for ministry positions.

At the municipal offices, Scott's job responsibilities were expansive: maintain the property tax e-pay website, create safety videos in collaboration with the police and fire departments, and help run the various social media platforms for the community. He enjoyed the diversity of his work. And he was good at what he did.

His first summer on the job, Scott was instrumental in helping the community deal with a heat wave. Hundred-degree weather was forecasted for five days in a row. There had not been any rain for nearly two weeks. Local government officials met to discuss how to respond to this impending heat wave. The mayor, police chief, fire chief, medical director, and city council held an emergency meeting to create a plan. Scott was asked to prepare a content strategy for sharing safety information with community members. His plan was multifaceted and had layers of communication to reach different demographics in the community. He proposed multiple communication streams including social media, a township website, phone blasts, digital videos, email, and even some door-to-door checks on elderly citizens.

The township implemented Scott's plan. The heat wave arrived. It was forecasted for five days. It extended to seven days. Unlike other neighboring areas, not a single person died in the community from the heat wave. Cooling centers were packed. Door-to-door visits saved the lives of nearly a dozen senior citizens. There was even a huge squirt gun fight through the parks and recreation department. Nearly everyone agreed that Scott's content strategy was essential to getting important safety information out to the community.

As the temperature went down, so did Scott's desire to find a new job. He was really pleased with where God had placed him. He realized that God was working through him as he provided the community with digital content. Even though he was not working for a church, God was working through him to care for others.

Scott continued to tinker with digital videos of sermons and other biblical accounts. He made a stop-motion film based on Scripture references of Jesus inviting people to follow Him. Clay and a camera was all he used. It began with a clay sculpture of Jesus approaching some clay sculptures of fishermen. The voiceover read the words of Mark 1:16–18. He showed Simon and Andrew dropping their nets and following Jesus. This continued with person after person until there was a huge crowd of clay figures following Jesus.

This video, like many of the others Scott has made, received upwards of ten thousand views. Scott loves making these videos. Still, he knows that it will be a long time until he can quit his day job and make creative films all day long. He is fine with that. Scott knows that God is working through him whether he is composing a tweet about a heat wave or creating a film about the Gospel. Jesus Christ has given Scott lasting and eternal purpose. God has a plan and purpose for Scott's service to the community as a digital content specialist. And God has a plan and purpose for Scott's creative tinkering with videos and sermons. Scott has eternal purpose in Christ Jesus.

Chapter 9
Discussion Questions

1. Read Philemon 17–19. Paul offered to pay any debts required of Onesimus. What other occurrences in Scripture are there of a debt paid on someone else's behalf?

2. Jesus gave Andrew eternal purpose. How did Andrew's work as a fisherman serve others for a lifetime? How did Andrew's work as a disciple serve others for all eternity?

3. Before Jesus transformed the life of Zacchaeus, how was his work as a tax collector supposed to serve others? How did Zacchaeus distort his work to serve himself instead?

4. Read Ephesians 2:8–10. How has Jesus given you eternal purpose? How has Jesus made you useful to God and others?

5. What comes to mind when you think of a calling? Can a job be a calling? Can a calling be a job? Read Ephesians 6:5–9.

6. Read Philippians 2:12–13. How does it change your perspective on work when you realize that God works in and through your work?

7. People often struggle to find a clear sense of identity and purpose in their lives. Agree or disagree? How have you seen others struggling with identity and purpose? How have you personally struggled with identity and purpose?

8. Read Acts 19:11–12. What work was God doing through Paul's hands? What work does God perform through your hands?

9. Even though Scott was not working for a church, God was working through him to care for others. Is it harder to see how God is at work in some vocations than it is in others? Does this mean that God is less active in these vocations?

Chapter 10

LOCAL

Seek the LORD *and His strength;*
seek His presence continually!
(1 Chronicles 16:11)

Our lives are a mash-up of places. We are born in one place, yet
die in another. We live in one zip code, yet worship in another. We
study in one academy in order to teach elsewhere. Rather than living
in a place, we live in several places.

Many miles separate the many places we frequent: home, work, and
a slew of communal meeting spaces. Daily commutes of forty, sixty,
or eighty miles are normal. Triple-digit daily commutes are hardly
remarkable. We sleep at home, work in an office, and meet friends
at a pub. We eat breakfast on the expressway, send emails across the
continent, and text around the globe. Smartphones transport us
away from actual spaces into digital spaces full of virtual personas,
avatars, and usernames.

An average day involves at least three places engaging three different
communities of people. This makes daily life increasingly nonlocal.
Living in all these nonlocal places is not without consequence. We
have become greatly detached from our local community. We are
a placeless, dislocated, and transient culture. Global positioning
systems tell us where we are located without telling us anything
about the nameless people living within that place. Checking in
on our phones tells others where we are physically located without

revealing anything unique about the place. Authentic human attachment—truly belonging to a community—is rapidly disappearing from our placeless culture.

Many have tried to counteract this trend. Some have proposed a slogan to reverse the placelessness of modern society: "Think Global, Act Local." Many local stores and farmers markets have championed this slogan as a way to return to local living. Small Business Saturday is a response to the shopping frenzy of Black Friday. Purchasing food from a local farm is preferred over buying a vacuum-packed meal from a factory. Kickball leagues, music festivals, and community events are all popular attempts to promote authentic community through local living.

Nevertheless, local living does not always build true community. Sharing a zip code does little to unite people. Neighbors are still thoroughly isolated from one another. Front porches are still empty. People at a farmers market seldom know one another by name. Kickball leagues fall apart before the beer gets warm.

The ties that unite individuals living together in a given community are often weak and easily undone. Far stronger is the bond that comes from being united in Christ Jesus. The unity that comes from gathering around Word and Sacrament as a body of believers offers a far greater opportunity for truly local community. No other common bond can draw diverse people together like the local congregation gathered around Jesus.

THINK GLOBAL, ACT LOCAL

Jesus Christ is God thinking globally while acting locally. Born in a specific time and place, Jesus is the local embodiment of the global Creator. God's global plan for all creation took place on a local scale. The Gospel of John opens with God's global work in Christ Jesus:

In the beginning was the Word, and the Word was with God, and the Word was God. He was in the beginning with God. All things were made through Him, and without Him was not any thing made that was made. . . . And the Word became flesh and dwelt among us, and we have seen His glory, glory as of the only Son from the Father, full of grace and truth. (John 1:1–3, 14)

The whole creation was made through Jesus. The planets commenced their celestial dance at His command. The Mariana Trench was carved with His speaking. Whales, sea turtles, and bioluminescent fish came into being through Him. Everest, Kilimanjaro, and Denali ascended by His authority. He traced a path for the Amazon, Mississippi, and Nile Rivers. All things were made through Christ Jesus.

And the global Creator came to dwell locally. He became flesh and blood, muscle and sinew. God entered creation through a family. It is no mistake that two of the Gospels, Matthew and Luke, include extensive genealogies of Jesus. God did not take on a fake body. He did not have synthetic blood flowing through His veins. The real body and red blood of Jesus came from a family with local roots:

The book of the genealogy of Jesus Christ, the son of David, the son of Abraham. Abraham was the father of Isaac, and Isaac the father of Jacob, and Jacob the father of Judah and his brothers, and Judah the father of Perez and Zerah by Tamar, and Perez the father of Hezron, and Hezron the father of Ram . . . and Eliud the father of Eleazar, and Eleazar the father of Matthan, and Matthan the father of Jacob, and Jacob the father of Joseph the husband of Mary, of whom Jesus was born, who is called Christ. (Matthew 1:1–3, 15–16)

Jesus is the Son of God and the Son of David. Jesus is the Son of God and the Son of Joseph. In Christ Jesus, heaven came to earth, transcendence touched the terrestrial, and the infinite domain of God dwelt in a finite location.

He made a home in Nazareth. He grew up working with locally sourced wood. He ate the olives that grew from the local trees in the neighborhood. He drank the wine that was pressed from grapes grown just down the road. His sandals were covered in Galilean dust. He knew His neighbors by name. He bought food at the city market. He dined with family and friends. Jesus lived locally.

God dwelling locally in Jesus of Nazareth was problematic for many people. He was just a small-town boy born and raised in Nazareth. They knew Jesus as a child. They babysat Him when He was young. They had eaten with Him in their homes. They taught Him how to read Hebrew. And that is why they took offense when Jesus returned home:

> He went away from there and came to His hometown, and His disciples followed Him. And on the Sabbath He began to teach in the synagogue, and many who heard Him were astonished, saying, "Where did this man get these things? What is the wisdom given to Him? How are such mighty works done by His hands? Is not this the carpenter, the son of Mary and brother of James and Joses and Judas and Simon? And are not His sisters here with us?" And they took offense at Him. (Mark 6:1–3)

It was scandalous to think that God would dwell locally in Christ Jesus. It was impossible to think that the Creator of all things would become human flesh and live in the same locale as sinful people. It was absurd to believe that God so loved the world that He would have His only Son live among sinners. Surely God would not work global salvation through the local dwelling of Jesus of Nazareth. Certainly God would not get slivers in His hands from working with wood and allow His feet to get dirty with the Galilean dust as He walked from place to place. God would not stoop that low.

He did.

God worked global salvation through the local living of Jesus Christ. God came to a specific time and place to deliver eternal salvation. No part of Jesus' ministry was nameless or placeless. He was born to Mary and Joseph in Bethlehem. He did not engage an abstract people to be His disciples; He called specific individuals by the names of Peter, James, Thomas, and Judas. He grieved the death of Lazarus because He knew Lazarus and was friends with his family. His betrayer came to Him in a specific garden in Gethsemane. He carried the cross down streets with names, past local markets, and by government offices. Soldiers lifted Him on a cross next to criminals with real names and real faces. A real person, Joseph of Arimathea, took His body and placed it in a local garden tomb.

> **God worked global salvation through the local living of Jesus Christ. God came to a specific time and place to deliver eternal salvation.**

And then the stone was rolled away. Jesus was raised from the dead. He again walked the local streets. He ate the local fish once more. He met the disciples on a specific mountain to send them out with the specific instructions of sharing the Gospel. Global salvation came through the local life, death, and resurrection of Jesus. In Christ Jesus, God performed global work through the very local work of Jesus.

That is why the Gospel is Good News. Something is regarded as news if it is an event that happened in a specific time and place; news is different than an opinion or advice because it relies on events in a specific time and place. News always occurs within the existing context of a place; news of a military victory makes sense only within the preexisting context of political strife. And news always shapes the future of a place; news of a drought ending leads to widespread rejoicing and hope for a better tomorrow. The life, death, and resurrection of Jesus Christ is Good News because it was the action of God within a specific time and place.

CHRIST COMING TO US

Since then, Jesus has ascended into heaven and has remained far, far away. When you die and go to heaven, only then will you be with Jesus, right? Not true. However, Christians throughout history have often held this sentiment. Jesus never dwells far from His people. He is constantly coming to us through Word and Sacrament. God is knocking, seeking, and speaking to you daily through the Word of God. The kingdom of heaven is always at hand.

The kingdom of heaven is always at hand

God comes to us through the external Word. God meets you where you are in Scripture. The Apology of the Augsburg Confession states:

> God cannot be interacted with, God cannot be grasped, except through the Word. So justification happens through the Word, just as Paul says in Romans 1:16, "[The Gospel] is the power of God for salvation to everyone who believes."[62]

Perhaps this does not sound like a radical confession. It is. During the Reformation, Lutherans had to fight hard for this belief.

---

62   Apology of the Augsburg Confession, Article IV (II), paragraph 67.

There was a movement called the Radical Reformation that arose in Germany and Switzerland in the early 1520s. Thomas Müntzer and Andreas Karlstadt, among others, emphasized inner revelation over the external Word of God. An inner feeling or experience of God's active speaking was placed over the authority of Scripture. This direct revelation was known among the Radical Reformers as the "living word of God." They believed that God spoke to His people apart from Scripture. A quiver in the liver, a thump of the heart, or a strong feeling qualified as revelation from God.

A related movement, known as the Anabaptist movement, also arose during this time. Müntzer was among the first to refuse infant Baptism. The Anabaptist movement placed a great emphasis on the inner experience of God's speaking to the individual believer. This group believed that an individual must first be able to articulate his or her faith before Baptism. They viewed Baptism as an external act of obedience in response to an internal experience of belief. Infant Baptism did not fit in this paradigm since a very young child cannot make a promise of obedience or verbal confession of belief.

Prior to and as a response to these movements, Luther emphasized the external Word of God. He believed that God speaks through Scripture. Luther rejected the new teaching of the Radical Reformers that God comes to people apart from the external Word. Nevertheless, this does not mean that God's speaking is distant and far from daily life. Instead, Luther believed that God actively speaks through the preaching and hearing of the Word.

For Luther, Scripture was not merely an account of divine work in a distant time and place. He understood the Bible to be a head-on collision between sinners and the mercy of God. Hearing the Word of God is a local encounter with the active love and work of Jesus Christ. Luther embraced Scripture as God's present and active speaking today:

> When you open the book containing the gospels and read or hear how Christ comes here or there, or how someone is brought to him, you should therein perceive the sermon or the gospel through which he is coming to you, or you are being brought to him. For the preaching of the gospel is nothing else than Christ coming to us, or we being brought to him.[63]

Believers do not listen for an echo of God's speaking in the past. Rather, God's speaking is shifted into the present location. Luther believed that God's speaking shifted from past to present in the hearing of the Word. Preaching was to move that past work of God in Scripture into the present location. Sermons are not a time to idly gaze at the distant work of Christ; sermons are a head-on confrontation with God coming to His people locally by means of the external Word. The presence of Jesus happens in the hearing of God's Word.

Holy Communion, like the public proclamation of God's Word, is an occasion in which Christ comes to us. Luther believed that the words of Christ, though spoken both miles and centuries away from Wittenberg, were relocated in a new place:

> Listen to this: "given for you"; "shed." I go to the sacrament in order to take and use Christ's body and blood, given and shed for me. When the minister intones, "This cup is the New Testament in my blood," to whom is it sung? Not to my dog, but to those who are gathered to take the sacrament. . . . That's why I have said that these words are spoken, not to stones or a pillar, but to Christians. "For you." Who does "for you" mean? The door or the window, perhaps? No, those who today hear the words "for you."[64]

---

63 LW 35:121.
64 LW 51:190.

Luther made it clear that Christ speaks not to the stones, pillars, doors, or windows but to the people. According to Luther, this powerful utterance of Christ is made local every time it is spoken to faithful ears. Luther even went as far as to claim that the ears are the primary Christian organ.

Local preaching, therefore, was about Christ coming to a specific location. Luther masterfully perceived how Christ's speaking was to be shifted into a specific place. Although he rejected God's direct revelation apart from Scripture, Luther was very willing to shift Christ's speaking into a new setting. For example, in his Sermon at the Dedication of the Castle Church in Torgau, Luther preached:

> And here again he [Christ] says the same thing: "Which of you, having an ass or an ox that has fallen into a well, will not immediately pull him out on the sabbath day?" What he really wanted to say to them in our plain German was: You are just plain oxen and asses yourselves and even more stupid than those you untie, and it may well be that the ass can read better than you can, and the ox might lead you to school, for he can well teach you to untie him when he is thirsty and to water him on the sabbath, or to pull him out of the well if he has fallen into it, so that he will not perish.[65]

At the dedication of a local congregation, Luther shifted Christ's speaking into the rather coarse "plain German" of that location. He understood God as speaking to a specific place. Jesus did not just say these words long, long ago; Jesus was speaking to the people in that place that very day.

---

65   LW 51:339.

INVERTED CHURCH HIERARCHY

In the very same sermon, Luther explained how God appointed the congregation to be the location of His work: "God very wisely arranged and appointed things, and instituted the holy sacrament to be administered in the congregation as a place where we can come together, pray, and give thanks to God."[66] Here, and in many other writings, Luther inverted the standard Church hierarchy. Luther, as was his practice, turned the Church of his day upside down.

The Roman Catholic Church in the Middle Ages had a very hierarchical view of authority known as an episcopal polity. This structure allowed authority to flow from the top down to the bottom. The pope, also known as the Bishop of Rome, was at the top of the hierarchy. Authority flowed downward through a diocese down to the local congregation. The individual congregation or parish depended on the authority of the diocese. The diocese depended on the authority of the pope. Describing the power structure of his day, Luther wrote:

> Human words and teaching instituted and decreed that only bishops, scholars, and councils should be allowed to judge doctrine. Whatever they decided should be regarded as correct and as articles of faith by the whole world, as is sufficiently proven by their daily boasting about the pope's spiritual law. One hears almost nothing from them but such boasting that they have the power and right to judge what is Christian or what is heretical. The ordinary Christian is supposed to await their judgment and obey it.[67]

---

66   LW 51:337.
67   LW 39:306.

Christ Jesus, according to Luther, taught that this hierarchy should be turned upside down. Luther believed that Jesus was the Head of the Church. Individual believers depended solely on the authority of Jesus:

> Christ institutes the very opposite. He takes both the right and the power to judge teaching from the bishops, scholars, and councils and gives them to everyone and to all Christians equally when he says, John 10[:4], "My sheep know my voice." Again, "My sheep do not follow strangers, but flee from them, for they do not know the voice of strangers" [John 10:5]. Again, "No matter how many of them have come, they are thieves and murderers. But the sheep did not listen to them" [John 10:8].[68]

The sheep are to judge whether they are hearing the voice of Christ. The local congregation, sheep hearing the voice of the Good Shepherd, is the recipient of Christ's authority. Not only is the local congregation the place where Christ comes to us, but it is also the nexus of church authority.

THE LOCAL CONGREGATION

The congregation—the place where God is present through Word and Sacrament ministry—is where Christ comes to His people. The local congregation is the place where Jesus dwells among us. Not the golf course. Not on social media. Not while drinking your cup of coffee in the stillness of the early morning. Jesus comes to you in the hearing of God's Word and the receiving of the Sacraments.

Are you looking for Jesus? You will find Him in your local congregation.

---

68   LW 39:306.

That may not be where you expected to find Him. Perhaps your first guess was heaven. That answer is correct. Jesus told His disciples, "In My Father's house are many rooms. If it were not so, would I have told you that I go to prepare a place for you? And if I go and prepare a place for you, I will come again and will take you to Myself, that where I am you may be also" (John 14:2–3).

Are you looking for Jesus? You will find Him in your local congregation

Heaven is not the only place in which Jesus is located. He also told His disciples, "For where two or three are gathered in My name, there am I among them" (Matthew 18:20). Jesus is just as present in the worship service as He is in heaven. He comes from heaven to earth in the preaching and hearing of God's Word. Jesus blesses our worship service with His presence. Worship is not merely lifting our praises up to God. Worship is God coming to us in divine service. The Divine Service (*Gottesdienst*) is God's service to us.

God meets us in the worship of the local congregation. God dwells in the presence of sleepy teenagers and blue-haired old ladies. God speaks to us over the din of burping babies and gossiping gadflies. God touches you with mercy in the midst of retro rugs and pinewood pews. The aroma of God rises up over the smell of putrid perfume and pungent potlucks. God comes to us in the Word and Sacrament ministry of the local congregation.

Worship is not the only way in which God works through the local congregation. God works through the local congregation in the following ways:

Diversity: God brings diverse people together in the local congregation. Rich and poor, young and old, white collar and blue collar, black and white are united in Christ. Kneeling at the feet of Jesus and receiving His grace together does far more for racial harmony than any government program. God's grace does not discriminate. The kingdom of God is not segregated. Local congregations are to be the vanguard of the new creation showing the world what it looks like to be children of God: "There is neither Jew nor Greek, there is neither slave nor free, there is no male and female, for you are all one in Christ Jesus" (Galatians 3:28).

Prayer: Brothers and sisters in Christ support one another on a local level through prayer. Christ followers bear one another's burdens by praying for one another. There is often confusion surrounding why the local congregation prays for its members. Prayer is sometimes regarded as a way to control or placate God. If someone is sick, then we will try to get as many people as possible to pray for that person. We do this because we believe that if enough people pray for something, then God has to grant their requests. This is not true. God answers prayer, whether it is the prayer of one person or the prayer of thousands of people together. The local congregation prays for one another as a way to bear others' burdens.

Prayer is a powerful way to carry a burden for someone else. If someone is sick, then the local congregation straps the weight of that sickness on its own back through prayer. If someone is celebrating a great blessing, then the local congregation does a happy dance with that person through prayer. God gave us prayer as a way to support one another locally: "First of all, then, I urge that supplications, prayers, intercessions, and thanksgivings be made for all people" (1 Timothy 2:1).

Spread the Gospel: God builds His kingdom through the local congregation. He pilfers Satan's kingdom through the parish. The local congregation is where Christ is present and active among His people. That means that it is a command post for the kingdom of God. The benediction marks the beginning of a commando raid on Satan's domain. As members of the local congregation make their way out into the community, they carry the Gospel with them. Your local congregation may not resemble the Navy Seals. Nevertheless, God uses these people to share the Gospel of Jesus Christ: "What I tell you in the dark, say in the light, and what you hear whispered, proclaim on the housetops" (Matthew 10:27).

Mutual Consolation: The local congregation is a conduit for God's love and care for His people. Sick people are overwhelmed with cards and casseroles. New parents have their front porch decorated with balloons and are loaded up with diapers. The newly unemployed receive job leads and personal recommendations. The newly retired find opportunities for service. God builds His people up through the local congregation. What may appear to be a tuna casserole is actually a divine token of support and consolation. What others deem a box of diapers is really the Body of Christ swaddling its fellow members in love. God cares for His people through the people of the local congregation: "So we, though many, are one body in Christ, and individually members one of another" (Romans 12:5).

Accountability: God holds His people accountable on a local level through the congregation. Rogue readings of Scripture are hard to maintain in a confessing community of believers. Absence from worship and life together is noticed and addressed by the local congregation. Unrepentant sins are laid bare when a fellow church member sees you out to dinner with someone else's spouse. Challenges to be in Scripture are made by fellow brothers and sisters in Christ. God provides us with accountability through local relationships: "If your brother sins against you, go and tell him his fault, between you and him alone. If he listens to you, you have gained your brother" (Matthew 18:15).

THE DYSFUNCTIONAL LOCAL CONGREGATION

Local congregations do not always function as God intended. Living together as a community of believers can be messy. Instead of being the Body of Christ, local congregations often behave like a body of chaos. Lively and active congregations can quickly disintegrate into lazy, self-serving cesspools of slander and gossip. Rather than actively living life in Christ, many local congregations live as the bickering Bride of Christ.

The bickering usually begins when a local congregation faces a challenge. It can be anything. It may be aging membership, dwindling worship attendance, or disengaged youth. It may be a chronically unbalanced budget or congregational infighting. It may even be a subtle, nagging feeling that the community would not notice if the congregation disappeared.

Squabbling takes over. The original issue morphs into peripheral debates: "The reason people aren't coming is because our parking lot has potholes." "If only we could replace those blue hymnals with the traditional red ones." "Using a guitar in worship would engage the youth." "We should really form a committee to address the problem that we are having with our committees." "The Lenten suppers have too much sodium." "Let's bring this up at the next congregational meeting so we can vote on it."

Meanwhile, the neighborhood lives and dies without the mercy of Jesus Christ. Countless people remain disconnected from God. Death and the devil claim hostages by the millisecond. Lives disintegrate while the committee debates the color of the carpet in the fellowship hall.

Local congregations become dysfunctional when they forget who is in charge of the Church: "And He is the head of the body, the church. He is the beginning, the firstborn from the dead, that in everything He might be preeminent" (Colossians 1:18). Jesus is the Head of the one holy Church (*una sancta*) globally. And Jesus is the Head of the church locally.

Another way the local congregation becomes dysfunctional is by confusing the Gospel. Congregations pervert the Gospel of Jesus Christ by turning it into moral advice, rules for godly living, or a path toward being a good person. Luther said that a local congregation lives or dies by the Gospel:

> The sure mark by which the Christian congregation can be recognized is that the pure gospel is preached there. For just as the banner of an army is the sure sign by which one can know what kind of lord and army have taken to the field, so, too, the gospel is the sure sign by which one knows where Christ and his army are encamped.[69]

Listen to the voice of the Good Shepherd. Openly proclaim the pure Gospel. It's really not that hard. Nevertheless, Satan will do anything in his power to divert the local congregation from doing these two things.

---

69   LW 39:305.

CONCLUSION

Everyone wants authentic community. We want deep and meaningful connections with the people and places in which we live. Life together is far greater than an isolated existence. Seeking to obtain authentic community apart from Jesus Christ is useless. Zip codes do not unite. Farmers markets, kickball leagues, and music festivals come and go offering fleeting glimpses of community. The local congregation centered on Christ Jesus offers authentic community for all eternity.

Christ comes to us through Word and Sacrament ministry. Christ speaks to us today through the Word of God. Christ visits us in the waters of Baptism, the bread and wine of Holy Communion, and the forgiveness of Absolution. All of this happens in the local congregation. Jesus is not hiding. He is located in the local congregation.

Christ has located His gifts in the Church. Forgiveness is not floating out there in a cloud. Christ has told His people where forgiveness can be found: where the Word is proclaimed, where the Sacraments are delivered, and where Absolution is given. In other words, you can find forgiveness in the local congregation.

Knowing where Christ is located allows you to do evangelism. You can speak with certainty about where grace is located. You do not have to go out into the neighborhood and tell people to look for God, hope for God, or search for God. You can seek out the lost and point them to where Christ has promised to be present. In a dislocated and placeless age, you can help them find what they have been looking for by pointing them to Christ's presence located in the local congregation.

Vignette: *[Insert Name Here]* *Lutheran Church*

One Sunday morning, Gerry stood atop the pews. He frantically waved a broom in the air like a madman. Sue walked in, grabbed a broom, and joined him in waving the broom in the air. While those two flailed away like crazy people, Linda stepped in and told them that they were doing it all wrong. She went down to the church kitchen, got two metal pots, walked back to the sanctuary, and began banging them together as loud as she could. Ridiculous hardly describes the scene.

In the midst of the waving brooms and banging pots, the guest preacher walked in the sanctuary. He paused. He watched. He considered looking for the nearest exit. Before he could make a break for it, Gerry saw the guest pastor. He set his broom down and walked over to welcome him to the congregation: "Hi, Pastor! I'm Gerry. I'm one of the elders here. We talked on the phone."

The pastor shook his hand and inquired about what was going on in the sanctuary. Gerry explained that a bird had flown into the church and they were trying to coax it out with brooms and pans. He made a lame joke about how the bird must be the presence of the Holy Spirit. Then he went back to swinging his broom.

Since the congregation was without a pastor at the moment, they relied on guest preachers each week to preach and lead the service. That Sunday, the guest preacher's sermon was based on Philippians 4: "Do not be anxious about anything, but in everything by prayer and supplication with thanksgiving let your requests be made known to God" (v. 6). That is a hard text to preach on when an angry bird is dive-bombing the congregation.

Apart from the occasional bird in the sanctuary, the congregation was thriving. They had a call committee in place looking for a new pastor. This committee took its task very seriously. Every meeting began and ended in prayer. The individual members of the committee made a point of praying that God would provide the right pastor for the congregation.

God finally provided the right pastor for the congregation. The elders worked with the call committee to schedule a voters meeting. The meeting began in prayer. Then the call committee presented the findings from their work. It was evident to all that they had spent a lot of time and effort in this task. Bob made a motion that the assembly of voters should formally thank the call committee for their work. Alice seconded the motion. The entire congregation sang the doxology.

Next, the call committee presented their recommendation for calling a pastor. They had decided to call a young pastor right from the seminary. After some brief discussion, there was a motion to extend a call to the pastor. Half a dozen people seconded the motion and the congregation voted. Unanimous. They prayed and sang the doxology once more.

The pastor accepted the call. He was ordained and installed two months later. The congregation threw a huge potluck to celebrate. The fellowship hall was a cornucopia of ham sandwiches, casseroles, and of course Jell-O. There was Jell-O with fruit, Jell-O with layers, Jell-O with whipped cream, and even a Jell-O tower. The Body of Christ gathered in this local congregation was celebrating God's blessings in the form of a new pastor. And the whole kingdom of God celebrated with them.

While everyone in the congregation had opinions about what their new pastor should do, his first sermon made it clear what he planned to do. His sermon focused on Paul's words to Timothy: "O Timothy, guard the deposit entrusted to you" (1 Timothy 6:20). He said that Timothy was not tasked with guarding the congregation's endowment. Timothy was not instructed to preserve potlucks, pipe organs, or attractive church programs. Timothy was not there to form a praise band or decorate the youth room.

He was there to guard the Gospel.

Paul charged Timothy with proclaiming the message of Jesus Christ. Timothy was to preach the pure Gospel that all things are made new through Christ's death and resurrection. The old life of death and decay is over; the new life of love and restoration has begun.

Potlucks have a purpose in service to the Gospel. Bible classes have a purpose in furthering the Gospel. Vacation Bible School has a purpose because it proclaims the Gospel. Committee meetings have a place in the church because they facilitate the sharing of the Gospel. Nevertheless, this local congregation was only to be concerned with one thing: the Gospel of Jesus Christ.

They lived life together in Christ. They gathered together to hear God's Word. They received Christ's mercy in the Sacraments. They rejoiced when God blessed their community with newborn babies. They cried when dear members were called to Christ's nearer presence in death. They planted a congregational garden and supplied local food pantries with produce. They baptized adults and confirmed teenagers. They sat through boring voters meetings. They perfected their ability to shoo birds out of the sanctuary.

And, above all else, they followed Jesus. Christ came to the people in this local congregation through Word and Sacrament ministry. Jesus came from heaven to earth daily in this local congregation. They gathered together in Christ Jesus' name, and He was present.

They were not flashy. Their carpet was outdated and worn. They had little quirks (like waving brooms and banging pots) that seemed odd to first-time visitors. Nevertheless, this local congregation—and all local congregation proclaiming the pure Gospel of Jesus Christ—is the kingdom of God at work in the world. The local congregation is a place fit for the King. The local congregation is where King Jesus comes to dwell among us.

Chapter 10
Discussion Questions

1. How have you personally experienced the disintegration of local living? Is technology to blame?

2. Read Luke 3:23-38. Luke begins with extensive details about the genealogy of Jesus. Why might modern readers easily dismiss these genealogies? Why were these genealogies vitally important to early Christians?

3. Read Matthew 13:53-58. Why was God dwelling locally in Jesus of Nazareth problematic for so many people? Did it go beyond the fact that they knew Jesus as a child?

4. Luther understood the Bible to be a head-on collision between sinners and the mercy of God. Have you ever experienced God speaking to you through Scripture? Read Hebrews 4:11-13.

5. Read Matthew 13:1-9. Why does Jesus use the expression in verse 9 here and elsewhere throughout the Gospels? How are the ears more important to believers after the ascension of Jesus?

6. Jesus is just as present in the worship service as He is in heaven. Why is the presence of Jesus frequently overlooked in worship? Read Matthew 28:16–20.

7. The kingdom of God is not segregated. How can the Church on earth better resemble the racial harmony in the kingdom of God?

8. Read 1 Thessalonians 5:12–22. Why are believers told to pray without ceasing? What is your practice of praying for others?

9. The local congregation is a place fit for the King. How has God worked in your life through the local congregation? Where do you see authentic community happening in your church?

CONCLUSION

You made it to the end of the book. Congrats. I pray that you have learned something along the way and have found new ways to live in the faith you have received.

We have explored how being Lutheran means challenging a culture that is closed, apathetic, confused, lazy, and pastel. We have discovered how Lutherans cherish the distinct work of God in making us new in Jesus through ordinary means, accept that God leaves certain tensions unresolved, and celebrate how He gives us eternal purpose in Christ and authentic community in the local congregation.

Being Lutheran is ultimately about following Jesus

All of this comes to a singular point: being Lutheran is ultimately about following Jesus. We go where Jesus goes, we listen when Jesus speaks, we trust when Jesus promises, we learn when Jesus teaches. And we live because Jesus lives. This is what it means to be Lutheran.

WHY I AM LUTHERAN

Personally, I am Lutheran because it means faithfully following Jesus. This confession allows me by the grace of God to follow Jesus so closely that I am stepping on the backs of His sandals. Thankfully, He does not mind. Following Jesus is not of my own doing; this is simply and totally the gift of God. I am Lutheran because this is the most faithful articulation of the Gospel of Jesus Christ. I am Lutheran because this is where the Gospel is clearly proclaimed, the Word of God is valued, the Sacraments are rightly administered, and the love of Christ is shared with others. I am Lutheran because of every chapter in this book. This is why I am Lutheran. Consider this my own personal manifesto on being Lutheran.

Let's be certain about a few things: I am not Lutheran because I want to follow Martin Luther. Despite bearing his name as a Lutheran, I do not follow Martin Luther. I don't follow Luther because he is arguably the most influential person in history other than Jesus. I don't follow Luther because he has a ton of books written about him. I don't follow Luther because he was a phenomenal theologian, engaging thinker, or bombastic writer. I don't even follow Luther because he brewed his own beer.

I follow Jesus yet keep bumping into Luther.

And I am not Lutheran because I want to follow Melanchthon, Chemnitz, Walther, Bonhoeffer, or anyone else for that matter. I don't follow these Lutherans because of who they were, what they wrote, or the incredible lives of faith they lived. I don't follow them because of their epic beards.

I follow Jesus yet keep bumping into Melanchthon, Chemnitz, Walther, Bonhoeffer, and scads of other Lutheran theologians.

Luther himself encouraged people to follow Jesus. He detested the fact that people called themselves "Lutheran." He would have preferred believers identify with the name of Christ rather than the name of Luther:

> In the first place, I ask that men make no reference to my name; let them call themselves Christians, not Lutherans. What is Luther? After all, the teaching is not mine [John 7:16].... How then should I—poor stinking maggot-fodder that I am—come to have men call the children of Christ by

my wretched name? Not so, my dear friends; let us abolish all party names and call ourselves Christians.[70]

Follow Jesus. That is what Luther wanted believers to do. That is what Melanchthon, Chemnitz, Walther, Bonhoeffer, and scads of other Lutherans wanted believers to do. Follow Jesus.

WHY AREN'T YOU LUTHERAN?

For those of you who don't belong to the Lutheran Church, let me ask you a question: why aren't you Lutheran? This book has made it clear that being Lutheran is about following Jesus. It is not about being Scandinavian or German. It is not about knowing your way around potlucks. It is not even about Martin Luther. Being Lutheran is about following Jesus. So why aren't you Lutheran?

I pray that this book has introduced you to Jesus. Sure, you might have come to know some other people along the way: Martin Luther, Philip Melanchthon, Dietrich Bonhoeffer, and many others. Nevertheless, this book intentionally proclaims the name of Jesus much more than the name of another. Jesus Christ—not Martin Luther—has the power to save you.

Jesus is Lord. Jesus saves. Jesus invites you to know Him. I sincerely desire that, if you did not know Jesus before this book, the Holy Spirit has created faith in you through the hearing of the Gospel and that you now know Jesus as Lord and Savior. I hope that this book has allowed you to see Jesus clearer than ever before.

Perhaps you already knew Jesus through a different heritage before reading this book. You may be from the Reformed, Roman Catholic, Baptist, or Pentecostal tradition. Certainly you know Jesus in this way. Nevertheless, I pray that you have come to know Jesus better

---

70   LW 45:70.

through this foray into Lutheran theology. Being Lutheran is about having the theological roadblocks cleared away and having nothing standing between you and Jesus. No good works. No Law pretending to be Gospel. No popes or princes. No moralism. Nothing standing between you and the Good News of Jesus Christ.

This is where the Gospel of Jesus Christ is most clearly and fully articulated.

Why aren't you Lutheran?

WHY ARE YOU LUTHERAN?

For those of you who *are* Lutheran: Why are you? Give some serious thought to this question. It will come up at multiple points in your life. Perhaps you considered this question when you were an awkward teenager nervously awaiting the Rite of Confirmation. Maybe you thought about this when you were preparing to be married. However, the complexity of your thinking has undoubtedly continued to grow. Just because you answered this question once in your life does not mean you have answered it forever. Explore your deeply held beliefs. Question your default positions. Examine what you do and why you do it. Reflect on what you believe and how you got there.

Are you Lutheran only because your parents were? Many people treat their faith like a hereditary default. They assume that two sets of Lutheran genes must automatically come together to produce a Lutheran child. It is easy to treat faith as a cultural inheritance. Resist the notion that the box next to "German," "Swede," or "Norwegian" must also be checked "Lutheran." Many people think that being Lutheran is synonymous with Bavarian or Nordic culture. Simply because you have German potato salad or lutefisk coursing through your veins does not mean you have to be Lutheran.

Or are you Lutheran for another reason? People have different reasons for being Lutheran: "This church is close to our home." "We go here because it makes Grandma happy." "We go to the Lutheran church because it has a good children's ministry." "I like the music at this church." "We like how the Lutherans make weak coffee." "The sausage and sauerkraut suppers are the reason we are here."

These are tenuous reasons for being Lutheran. When Grandma dies, the reason to be Lutheran dies. When the music director moves, the rationale for being Lutheran moves as well. Before the baptismal water dries, the thirst for church dries. Worship attendance drops considerably once the doctor says no more sausage and sauerkraut dinners.

Being Lutheran for no reason is dangerous: Children are baptized and never confirmed. Children are confirmed and never connect in a meaningful way. Couples are married and gone while the recessional hymn is still playing. The dead are buried, and the family never returns. Sometimes they join another denomination. Mostly they just drift.

My hope is that after reading this book, you are Lutheran for a different reason. I hope that genetics, Grandma, and great coffee are not your driving reason for being Lutheran. I hope you have found some deliberate reasons for being Lutheran.

Amidst the many confessions of faith, claim this one as your own. This is where the Gospel of Jesus Christ is most clearly and fully articulated.

Soli Deo Gloria: To God alone be the glory!

LEADER GUIDE

Chapter 1

1. What is the appeal to open source?

> **Free access is the most obvious appeal to open source. Who doesn't like free stuff? The lack of an entry fee provides widespread opportunities for collaboration. Instead of limiting access to corporations or wealthy individuals, open source gives diverse people a seat at the table.**

2. How have you witnessed sin close you off to other people in your own life? Read Acts 28:17–31.

> **Daily life is teeming with the closure of sin. Relationships are closed by anger, hate, and distrust. Communities are closed by racial tension, economic disparity, and busy schedules. The reading from Acts shows how Paul faced the closure of sin in religious opposition and civil imprisonment.**

3. Jesus opens our relationship to God. How has Jesus opened your eyes, ears, heart, mind, and hands to God?

Jesus opens our eyes to see hurting people without the Gospel, vulnerable people in need of protection, and neighbors desiring friendship. Jesus opens our ears to hear the cry of widows and orphans, the faith of young children, and the promise of the Gospel. Jesus transforms hearts, minds, and hands. He gives you a new heart of faith, opens your mind to divine truth, and uses your hands to work for your neighbors.

4. This chapter looks at Saul, Lydia, and Peter. Are there other individuals in Scripture who were opened up to God by Jesus Christ? Read Acts 8:9–25 for one example.

Simon the Magician was opened up to God by Jesus Christ. Others include Zacchaeus (Luke 19:1–10), the Philippian jailer (Acts 16:25–40), and the Ethiopian eunuch (Acts 8:26–40).

5. Luther fought to make worship and Scripture accessible to all people. What are some ways that these gifts are neglected today? How might we reverse this practice?

People allow many things to crowd their Sunday morning worship. Soccer games, yard work, and sleep are viewed as more important than worship. Scripture is disregarded as arcane, obsolete, or boring. These practices can be reversed through teaching. Knowing the work of God in worship and learning how Scripture is the Word of God makes these a priority in daily life.

6. Since the Reformation, open access to the Gospel has been threatened. What are some ways that open access to the Gospel is threatened today? Are these new threats or ancient threats? Read 1 Peter 5:8–9.

Open access to the Gospel is threatened in many ways. People deride Christianity as an unintelligent, backwards, even oppressive movement. Our culture tries to close the door to faith by making it subservient to scientific knowledge. The Gospel is closed when people overbook their schedules and overlook Jesus. Behind all of these threats to the open Gospel is the old ancient foe described in 1 Peter 5:8–9.

7. The Good News of Jesus Christ is the only open source of salvation for all people. How does your congregation share the Gospel? How do you personally share the Gospel?

Worship is an obvious way that congregations share the Gospel. However, there are many other ways: Bible study, private confession, mission trips, and evangelism efforts. Personally sharing the Gospel is certainly not disconnected from these efforts; however, you have a different sphere of influence than your congregation. You have a personal relationship with your neighbors in a way that the congregation cannot. Share the Gospel as a congregation and as an individual.

8. The vignette about Seliman discusses how open access to the Gospel is closed throughout many parts of the world. Can persecution benefit the proclamation of the Gospel? How do you see God at work through persecution? Read Daniel 3:8–30 and Acts 12:6–19.

> The Early Church thrived during intense persecution. And long before the Church in Acts, God's power was made manifest through the men in the fiery furnace. Persecution cannot stop the Gospel. God is powerful to take the hardship of His people and turn it into a mighty witness for all.

9. How might you more openly live out your faith in Jesus Christ? What part of your daily life needs to be opened by the Holy Spirit?

> The distance between Sunday and Monday can be massive. Many people have a difficult time connecting their life of faith with Monday morning. God promises to fill you with the fullness of God through prayer (Ephesians 3:14–21). Praying for spiritual strength to openly live out your faith is the best place to start. The Holy Spirit will open what has been closed by sin.

Chapter 2

1. Nothing impresses us anymore. Agree or disagree?

Perhaps it is still possible for us to be impressed. However, it is increasingly difficult. What was deemed impressive by previous generations is now brushed aside as boring. Digital technology has afforded us a wealth of new information and media, yet it has robbed us of our ability to be impressed by ordinary occurrences.

2. Jesus challenged apathy long before His birth. Where do you see the promise of Jesus challenging apathy in the Old Testament? What were the prophets trying to do through their prophetic words? Read Isaiah 53.

These words of Isaiah challenge apathy with their vivid depiction of sacrificial love. The prospect of someone suffering in the place of others is enough to shake people out of their malaise. The prophets in the Old Testament were speaking on behalf of God as they pointed God's people to Jesus.

3. Read Luke 9:23 and verses 57–62. What is the difference between these two invitations from Jesus? Why does it matter that one invitation is given to the crowd while the other is given to a specific person?

In Luke 9:23, Jesus is addressing a group of His followers when He teaches them that a disciple is called to take up his cross and follow Jesus daily, that is, to submit oneself in humility to the Kingdom that now comes in preaching

(and in His day, the miracles) and open oneself to the contempt of the world. In Luke 9:57–62, we get another stark example of the radical nature of the call to discipleship. To take up the cross daily is to proclaim the kingdom of God. But Jesus' word of encouragement in 9:60 is directed to a specific believer worried about burying his father. Jesus extends the invitation "to all" believers in Luke 9:23, but He was speaking to specific individuals in verses 57–62, and this should not be broadly applied to all people. It is important to note such distinctions when applying the words of Jesus to your own life.

4. Read Romans 3:21–26. According to these verses, who performs the work of salvation? What comfort comes from knowing that God alone is the source of salvation?

> These verses make it clear that all are justified by God's grace as a gift through the redemption that is in Christ Jesus. There is comfort in this because salvation does not depend on our own efforts or work.

5. Passive righteousness deals with our standing before God. Active righteousness deals with our standing before others. Why is it so important to rightly distinguish these two kinds of righteousness?

> Confusing the two kinds of righteousness is very easy. And it is very problematic. Actively trying to earn righteousness before God will only leave you disappointed. Likewise, it is wrong to passively hope that God's grace will perform your daily tasks, pay your taxes, and tuck your kids in at night. It is vitally important to distinguish passive

and active righteousness in order to rightly understand the free gift of divine grace and the earthly responsibility of daily life.

6. Luther read the Bible cover-to-cover twice a year. Why would someone so familiar with the Bible reread it each year? What is your practice of daily Bible reading?

Luther continued to read the Bible twice a year because he felt God's Word had something more to say to him. Simply because he had read it all the way through was not a reason to put the Bible on the shelf. Developing a practice of daily Bible reading will fill your mind and your heart with the Word of God.

7. Read Acts 17:10–12. Like the believers in Berea, Lutherans carefully examine the Scriptures. What more do you need to learn in order to better defend your faith in Jesus Christ?

Lutherans are not the first to take Scripture seriously. Many generations of God's people have carefully examined the Scriptures. Knowing the Bible allows you to defend your faith. Perhaps you need to learn more about the formation of the biblical canon, the problems with evolutionary theory, or how the Old Testament relates to the New Testament.

8. Jesus invites you to die to yourself and be made alive in Him. What part of you has died as a result of following Jesus? What part of you has new life as a result of following Jesus? Read Romans 6:4.

Jesus puts death to death. He puts sin—slander, hate, greed, lust—on the cross. Following Jesus will cause these parts of you to die. Likewise, following Jesus brings new life and the fruit of the Spirit (Galatians 5:22–23). New life in Jesus means that you will have new love, joy, peace, patience, kindness, goodness, faithfulness, gentleness, and self-control.

9. Dietrich Bonhoeffer chose to die living out his faith rather than to live with a lukewarm faith. What role did prayer and Bible reading play in his daily life? How might these spiritual disciplines have compelled him to return to Germany and defend innocent lives?

Bonhoeffer pushed against the practices of most theologians in his day. Rather than bending to the common practice, he practiced his own habit of prayer and Bible reading. Bonhoeffer was shaped by his practice of prayer and Bible reading in such a profound way that he was compelled to return to Germany.

Chapter 3

1. Relativism claims that truth is confined to a specific cultural or historical context. How might relativism benefit Christianity? How might relativism hinder Christianity?

A benefit of relativism is that it puts all truth claims on a level field; relativism believes that all truth claims should be respected, even if not all truth claims should be accepted. This allows Christians to speak up and share their beliefs with others. The obvious problem with relativism, however, is that it denies the existence of a durable or transcendent truth. This is clearly contrary to the teaching of Jesus.

2. Read Matthew 21:23–27. Why did Jesus refuse to tell the chief priests and elders the source of His authority?

Jesus refused to tell them something they had already heard and denied. Jesus made it clear throughout His ministry that He was sent by God the Father. The chief priests and elders had already made it clear that they would never believe this to be true.

3. Read Luke 9:1–6. Jesus gave His authority to the disciples. Why were they told to not bring anything (no staff, bag, bread, or money) for the journey? What was Jesus trying to teach the disciples by sending them out with nothing more than His authority?

Going out empty-handed forced the disciples to rely on the authority of Jesus. Had they taken money with them,

the disciples might have thought their efforts were successful due to the power of money. Taking nothing with them made it so there was no confusion about the source of their success.

4. Augustine moved from confusion to confession by the work of the Holy Spirit. Read 1 Corinthians 2:6–16. What is the wisdom of this age in 1 Corinthians 2:6? What is the wisdom of God in 1 Corinthians 2:7? Are these different types of wisdom in opposition to one another?

> The wisdom of this age referenced in 1 Corinthians 2:6 is human reason. This is what people deem right and wrong, good and bad, wise and foolish. On the other hand, the wisdom of God is what God deems right and wrong, good and bad, wise and foolish. These different types of wisdoms are very often in opposition to one another.

5. Luther did more than simply give his barber a quick answer. Why did Luther encourage him to develop his own articulation of prayer? What is the benefit of using the Lord's Prayer, Ten Commandments, and the Apostles' Creed as a guide for prayer?

> Luther's encouragement for his barber to develop his own articulation of prayer shows the deeply personal nature of prayer. Even if you are praying with others, prayer is still a personal and intimate moment with God. The benefit of using the Lord's Prayer, Ten Commandments, and the Apostles' Creed as a guide is that your praying is anchored in long-standing confessions of God's people. Rather than simply going your

own way, these guides allow you to pray in a God-established way.

6. Read Matthew 22:23–33. Theological bloodletting is nothing new; Jesus confronted the Sadducees regarding their skepticism of the resurrection. What did Jesus use to correct their confusion? Why was the crowd astonished at His teaching?

> **Jesus used Scripture to correct their confusion. He pointed them to the Word of God to show them that they had let the blood from their brains. The crowd was astonished at His teaching because He was willing to confront the wisdom of the age with the wisdom of God.**

7. Read Matthew 19:1–9. Why is it important to recognize that Jesus treated the Old Testament as historically and theologically reliable? What does that reveal about how Jesus viewed Scripture?

> **Jesus trusted Scripture and taught that Adam and Eve were real people. Recognizing how Jesus treated the Old Testament as historically and theologically reliable should encourage us to do the same. He viewed Scripture as the authoritative Word of God. We follow Jesus when we believe the same.**

8. What does it mean to intellectually grapple with the Gospel? Does embracing Jesus with your brain replace embracing Jesus with your heart?

> God has given you a brain. Use it to learn and understand what God has done for you in Christ Jesus. The apostle Paul did this when he reasoned and persuaded people about the kingdom of God (Acts 19:8). To be certain, embracing Jesus with your brain does not replace trusting and believing Jesus with your heart; Satan knows a lot about Jesus, yet he does not believe Jesus is Lord.

9. Reread the vignette. Do you know anyone like María? Read 1 Corinthians 3:18–23. What does Paul mean when he tells his readers to become a fool in order to become wise?

> The kingdom of God turns human thinking upside down. María had her thinking turned upside down by Jesus; she went from priding herself on disproving the existence of God to knowing nothing but Christ crucified. Paul encourages readers to trust in God's ways (divine wisdom) as opposed to our own ways (worldly wisdom). This might come at the cost of appearing foolish to others.

Chapter 4

1. Read Genesis 2:1–3. God worked in order to make His creation. What do the six days of creation reveal about God's nature? Is work part of God's plan for creation or a result of sin?

> **A desire to work is clearly a part of God's nature. God spent six days actively working on His creation. And it is important to note that this work was done before sin entered into creation. Work was part of God's plan before sin. However, sin has distorted and destroyed fruitful work.**

2. Jesus Christ is proof that God loves work. What work did Jesus do before the cross? What work did Jesus do after the resurrection? Read John 4:31–38.

> **The work that Jesus did before the cross and after the resurrection is the same: Jesus does the work of God the Father. He works to accomplish the will of God. He works to do the work of God. Jesus worked hard at these tasks.**

3. The wedding in Cana shows Jesus doing the work of viticulturist, vintner, and sommelier immediately. What are some other miracles in which Jesus performs human work immediately? Read John 6:5–14.

> **Jesus feeding the five thousand with bread and fish is another example of Jesus performing human work immediately. He performed the work of baker and fisherman instantaneously. What would have taken others hours of work, Jesus accomplished in seconds. His is fruitful labor indeed.**

4. Read Luke 10:25–37. For what purpose did Jesus tell the parable of the Good Samaritan? Is this parable an encouragement to work for others or a glimpse into God's work for us? Could it be both?

> The parable of the Good Samaritan is often used as an encouragement for people to be better neighbors. However, seeing the love and work of Jesus is the primary purpose of this parable. Jesus binds our wounds, takes care of us, and pays our price for healing. He is the Good Samaritan, and we are the wounded traveler. As imitators of God (Ephesians 5:1), we are sent out to do the same mercy work.

5. Read Matthew 5:17–20. What does it mean that Jesus came to fulfill the Law, not to abolish it? What is the role of God's Law now that Jesus has fulfilled it through His life, death, and resurrection?

> Although the distinction is subtle, Jesus came to fulfill the Law rather than abolish it. This means that Jesus has upheld the Law rather than reject it. He lived it in a way that we could not. The role of God's Law is now to point us to Jesus. Rather than being a path to earning salvation, the Law shows our sin and need for a Savior.

6. Antinomianism means rejecting the role of God's Law in the Christian life. Are Lutherans antinomians? If not, what is the role of the Law in the life of a Christ follower?

> Lutherans are far from antinomians. We believe that the Law should curb, mirror, and guide our lives. The Law

curbs our sinful impulses, reveals our brokenness and need for a Savior, and guides our daily decisions.

7. Sanctification is the lifelong process of becoming holy. Read 1 Corinthians 12:1–11. Who is the primary actor in sanctification? Does the work of the Holy Spirit in sanctification look the same for everybody?

The Holy Spirit drives the work of sanctification. This is not a human work; it is the work of God in and through us. Although the same Holy Spirit performs the work of sanctification, the sanctified life looks different for each person. God takes the unique gifts and blessings He has given us and draws them out in sanctification.

8. Read Matthew 7:15–20. In Christ, the work that you do is holy work. Does it always appear that way? Is the work of a Christian fundamentally different than the work of an unbeliever?

Our work often looks ordinary and boring. Even though our work is holy work, this may not be evident to those around us. The work of a Christian is fundamentally different than the work of an unbeliever; good trees bear good fruit. Jesus has made us good trees capable of bearing good fruit. This may look like ordinary work, yet it is holy work.

9. Dr. Bessie led an incredibly productive and compassionate life. How did her relationship with Jesus shape her daily work for others? How does your relationship with Jesus shape your daily work for others?

> Dr. Bessie trusted that her relationship with God was complete in Christ Jesus. She did not have to work for God's love because Jesus had already performed that work on her behalf. Therefore, Dr. Bessie was driven by a strong desire to work for the needs of others.

Chapter 5

1. Read Matthew 5:1–12. How does Jesus recolor conventional thinking through this teaching? Why might other religious teachers resist this colorful teaching of Jesus?

> **Jesus recolors conventional thinking by lifting up those who are poor in spirit, mourning, meek, hungry, and thirsty. He upholds the merciful, pure in heart, peacemakers, and persecuted. Other religious teachers would resist this teaching because they would have to reflect it in their own lives. Jesus actually did reflect these teachings in His own life.**

2. Read Matthew 17:1–13. What is the meaning behind Jesus becoming radiantly white? Why did Peter, James, and John respond with terror when they saw Jesus transfigured?

> **This occurrence, known as the transfiguration, was a preview of Christ's coming glory. It was a glimpse at the true color of the resurrected Jesus. Witnessing this massive display of God's glory apparently made Peter, James, and John feel completely overwhelmed and overpowered by the Son of God; witnessing the transfiguration of Jesus exposed His glory and their frailties.**

3. Jesus engaged a whole array of colorful people with the mercy of God. Did Jesus discriminate against certain ethnicities? Was racism an issue during that time in history? Read Matthew 15:21–28.

Jesus displayed an incredible openness to other ethnicities. Racism was, as it still is today, a serious issue during the time of Jesus. Although Jesus' response to the Canaanite woman may seem harsh, it is actually a display of His openness to other ethnicities. A Jewish man conversing with a Canaanite woman was scandalous during the time of Jesus. The Jewish people went out of their way to avoid contact with Canaanite people. Nevertheless, Jesus extended the healing power of divine mercy to this woman of a different ethnicity. Although Jesus came to be Israel's Messiah, He gave His life for all people of all races.

4. Christians carry Christ with them wherever they go. How does this change your perspective on daily life? Are menial tasks made holy because of Christ's presence?

The presence of Jesus changes everything. Words of forgiveness have the power of Christ. Acts of service build the kingdom of God. Your presence carries the peace of Christ. Even menial tasks—changing diapers, going to work, befriending someone on the bus—are holy with the presence of Christ.

5. Luther taught that Christians are "Christs one to another and do to our neighbors as Christ does to us" (LW 31:367). What does this look like in your life? How do you bring Christ's love, forgiveness, and peace to the people around you?

We often think that being Christs one to another means doing ministry activities. We assume that we are only bringing Christ's love when we volunteer at church or do religious things. This is not the case. Being a good neighbor, raising children, loving your spouse, paying your taxes, and mowing your lawn are all ways that you can bring Christ's love to the people around you.

6. Read Matthew 10:16–18. Jesus prepared His disciples to stand out from the crowd. How does your faith in Jesus lead you to stand out from the crowd? What are some ways that you blend in with the crowd? Is this necessarily a bad thing?

It is not a bad thing to blend in with the crowd. That is assuming that the crowd is following Jesus. The Church is becoming increasingly distinct from the culture. As God's people, we are called to reflect Him first and foremost. This will cause us to stand in contrast with the world around us.

7. Luther faced public ridicule for opposing the culture of his day. Have you ever faced public ridicule for your faith in Jesus? How can you face persecution in a godly way? Read Matthew 10:19–25.

> In some countries, public ridicule is nothing compared to the persecution of Christians. In other countries, mild discomfort is all that Christians receive by way of public ridicule. You can face persecution in a godly way by trusting in God even in the midst of hardship.

8. How is cultural disobedience different than civil disobedience? Read 1 Peter 2:13–17.

> Cultural disobedience is resisting the accepted way of the culture. Civil disobedience is resisting the rules and laws of the land. Christians are called to follow and uphold the rule of government. We are not, however, called to follow the ways of the culture.

9. Jack vividly reflects the color of Jesus. How much do your actions, lifestyle, or practices reflect the color of the culture?

> This is a personal question. It is very easy to reflect the color of the culture. Our likes, dislikes, fears, hopes, and loves are heavily shaped by the culture in which we live. Explore what barriers are keeping you from reflecting the color of Jesus.

Chapter 6

1. Read 1 Corinthians 15:12–19. There is nothing of lasting worth without the hope of God in Christ Jesus. What is the difference between hope and optimism?

> **Hope is always based in reality.** Gardeners have reason to hope that a seed will turn into a plant because the reality of seeds is that they turn into plants; within a seed is the material needed for a plant. Optimism is simply anticipating good fortune. Christian hope is based in the reality that Jesus is victorious over death. Within Jesus is all the righteousness, holiness, and perfection needed for eternal life. Gardeners have reason to hope in seeds because all that is needed for a plant to grow is contained in a seed; Christians have reason to hope in Jesus because all that is needed for eternal life is found in Him.

2. Many people have ended up in error trying to make sense of the incarnation of Jesus Christ. Read 1 Timothy 3:16. What do many people erroneously believe about the incarnation? Is this erroneous belief intentional or accidental?

> The incarnation is among the most profoundly mysterious occurrences in all creation. It is not at all surprising that this topic would be so prone to error and confusion. Many have accidently fallen into error trying to confess the mystery of God in human flesh. Some have believed that Jesus only appeared to be human (Docetism). Others have believed that Jesus was only human and not truly divine (Arianism). These erroneous beliefs usually occur when somebody overemphasizes one truth at the expense of

other truths (e.g., overemphasizing the humanity of Jesus at the expense of His divinity).

3. All of creation rejoiced at the coming of Jesus. Did all of creation come under the curse of sin? What happened to the ground and animals as a result of human sin? Read Genesis 3:17–21.

All creation was brought into ruin by the sin of Adam and Eve. The ground produced thorns and thistles. Animals were killed to make clothing for humans. Human sin was powerful enough to take all of creation down with it. But new life in Christ Jesus was powerful enough to repair all of creation.

4. Scripture is teeming with examples of new life coming to individuals through faith in Jesus. Besides those mentioned in the chapter, are there other individuals in Scripture who have been made new through faith in Christ? Read 1 Timothy 1:12–17.

The apostle Paul was made new through faith in Christ. He makes it clear that before new life in Christ, he had no good in him: "though formerly I was a blasphemer, persecutor, and insolent opponent" (1 Timothy 1:13). Jesus destroys the death of sin and brings new life.

5. Read Ephesians 2:8–9. What is grace? What does it mean to be saved? Why are accurate definitions for these words so important?

Grace is undeserved goodwill and favor shown by God to sinners. To be saved is to receive God's salvation from condemnation. It is very important to have accurate definitions for these words because many of our beliefs are built upon these words. These words can be distorted in many ways and result in confused beliefs.

6. Why might Luther teach that if the article concerning justification falls, then everything falls? Why is salvation by grace through faith such a vital confession for Lutherans?

Misunderstanding justification jeopardizes all other Christian beliefs. If justification is confused, then the person of Jesus is confused. If justification is misunderstood, then salvation is misunderstood. If justification is lost, then grace is lost. This confession—salvation by grace through faith in Christ—is the solid ground upon which Lutheran theology is built.

7. Even your own salvation is to the glory of God. How is your salvation to God's glory? What are some ways that people diminish God's glory in salvation? Read 1 Corinthians 10:31–33.

Your salvation is to God's glory because it is God's gift to you. Salvation is earned not by our works but by Christ Jesus. People try to diminish God's glory in salvation by turning it into a work that is accomplished by us.

8. Brokenness abounds. What sort of brokenness abounds around you? How does new life in Christ change this brokenness? Read Isaiah 25:6–9.

Look around, and you will see divorce, disease, racism, violence, greed, corruption, depression, and scads of sin's shrapnel. New life in Christ swallows up this brokenness forever and replaces it with the newness of Jesus.

9. Ben received new life from Christ Jesus. Do you know anyone like Ben? Is new life in Christ always a dramatic conversion?

New life in Christ is not always a dramatic conversion like what happened to Ben. Many people receive new life in Christ at Baptism. The conversion of an infant through the waters of Baptism is just as legitimate and profound as the conversion of a wayward adult.

Chapter 7

1. God created man out of a clump of dirt. How was the creation of humans different than the rest of creation? How did God utilize ordinary material in the creation of woman? Read Genesis 1:24–25 and 2:7, 21–22.

> Rather than speaking man into being as He did with the rest of creation, God formed man out of a clump of dirt. In the same way, God used bone to form woman. Instead of keeping His distance, God used the ordinary material of creation to make His human creatures.

2. Read John 9:1–7. What are some other ways that Jesus could have performed this miracle? Why do you think He performed it the way He did?

> Jesus could have simply spoken a word and healed this man. Jesus could have also written the man a prescription for expensive ointment from an apothecary. Instead, Jesus used simple mud and water to heal this man's blindness. These ordinary materials let the extraordinary power of Jesus shine through even brighter.

3. Read Mark 6:30–44. What are some other ways that Jesus used the ordinary to perform the extraordinary?

> Jesus used the material that was on hand—five loaves and two fish—to perform this miracle. This miracle drew from the ordinary material that was already present in the community in order to work an extraordinary miracle. Like the healing of the blind man with mud, the ordinary material used for the miracle magnifies the power of Jesus.

4. The Crusades were a hunt for extravagant and expensive, glitzy and glamorous objects. Crusaders were seeking a once-in-a-lifetime experience that would solidify their salvation. How do Christians today chase after these sorts of once-in-a-lifetime experiences?

> Many people try to buy experiences rather than stuff. Nevertheless, experiences can be just as expensive, glitzy, and glamorous as material objects. Chasing after memorable experiences in order to solidify salvation can take the shape of mission trips, tours of the Holy Land, or spiritual pilgrimages. Trusting in these experiences to solidify your salvation is dangerous. Believers must be cautious to not trust in anything or anyone other than Jesus. Trusting that a trip overseas will rejuvenate your faith is just as dangerous as trusting in a relic to deliver salvation.

5. Read Philippians 3:17–21. Luther found no peace in relics. Where do people look for peace today? How are these modern objects of comfort different than religious relics? How are they similar?

Many people today try to find peace in traveling, technology, binge-watching television, social media, and a whole slew of other objects. These are unlike relics in that they are not explicitly religious items. However, they are similar to relics in that anything we fear, love, or trust in is an idol.

6. Lutherans believe that it does not belong to human authority to promise grace. What does this say about the Lutheran understanding of Sacraments? What do they deliver?

Lutherans believe that Sacraments are divinely instituted with the promise of grace. Central to the Sacraments is the certain promise and delivery of God's grace.

7. Jesus gave the Church the authority to forgive sins. Are there other places in Scripture in which God has given His people great responsibility? Read Genesis 1:28 and 2:15.

God has given His creatures the great responsibility of dominion and guardianship over creation. Just as being caretaker over creation is a significant responsibility, so is the forgiveness of sins.

8. Baptism is never distant in the life of the believer. How does your Baptism impact your daily life? What can you do to remember the present impact of your Baptism? Read Galatians 3:23–29.

> Living in your baptismal identity is a daily reality. Greater than your name, job, or zip code is your identity in the Father, Son, and Holy Spirit. Making the sign of the cross is a great daily reminder of your Baptism. Reminding yourself that you are a child of God is another way to live in your baptismal identity.

9. Sharon had to receive Holy Communion at home as a result of her illness. How is this different than the Private Mass of the Middle Ages?

> Private Mass in the Middle Ages claimed to be an extraordinary work of forgiveness; it was over and above the ordinary Mass that other people took part in. Receiving Holy Communion at home does not promise some sort of special forgiveness; rather, it is an extension of the ordinary Word and Sacrament ministry of the local congregation.

Chapter 8

1. Read Genesis 2:7. What comes to mind when you think of a creature? What is necessary for a creature to exist?

> Some people may find *creature* to be a strange word for humans. *Creature* can connote creepy, crawly animals. However, the word *creature* simply indicates a created being. Creatures are dependent upon a creator for existence.

2. Hardship led Job to question the hidden mind of God. Does God not approve of creatures asking questions? Read Matthew 7:7–11.

> On the contrary, God encourages His creatures to ask many things of Him. It is important to keep the Creator and creature distinction in place. Prayerfully asking God for a blessing is different than trying to assume the role of Creator and demanding to know the hidden mind of God.

3. Jesus referred to His disciples as friends. How are friendships formed? What does it tell you about God that He befriends human creatures?

> Friendships are often formed as a result of close proximity. The fact that Jesus calls His disciples friends shows that He dwelt closely with His disciples. God befriending human creatures is proof that God does not dwell far from His people.

4. Read John 1:14–18. How did so many people overlook God dwelling among them?

> Many people overlooked God dwelling among them because He dwelt in human flesh. Jesus performed many miracles, taught with authority, and conquered death. Nevertheless, there were still many who refused to admit that God was dwelling among them.

5. Read John 15:26–27. What are the two different names Jesus uses for the Holy Spirit here? What do these names tell us about the work of the Holy Spirit?

> Jesus calls Him the Helper and the Spirit of truth. These names reveal that the Holy Spirit helps believers in truth. These names reveal the nature of the Holy Spirit.

6. Erasmus concluded that people had the freedom to choose salvation or damnation. How does Scripture depict the human will? Read Ephesians 2:1–10.

> Scripture, unlike Erasmus, depicts the human will as bound by sin. Ephesians tells us that we are dead in sin and without the freedom to choose salvation, but God has chosen salvation for us.

7. God has revealed everything necessary for salvation in Jesus. What questions do you still have for God? Why might God have left these questions unanswered for you?

> **Many people have questions for God: Why did I have a miscarriage? Why did I get cancer? Why did my mother die when I was young? These questions, though troubling, are not essential to our salvation in Jesus.**

8. You cannot answer life's difficult questions without knowing Scripture. What is your practice of Bible reading? Do you read the Bible daily? How might a habit of Bible reading help you answer life's questions according to Scripture?

> **It is important to have a habit of Bible reading. This lets God's Word norm our thinking, acting, and living. Without a practice of reading the Bible, it is impossible to answer life's questions according to God's revealed truth.**

9. Tim and Hannah lived in the tension of trusting in God despite multiple miscarriages. Why should you pray even if God answers your prayers according to His will? Read Luke 18:1–8.

> **God is good. He is not an unjust judge. His will is better than we could ever imagine. He encourages us to come to Him with our prayer, and He promises to listen. Even though God answers prayers according to His will, He desires for us to come to Him in prayer.**

Chapter 9

1. Read Philemon 17–19. Paul offered to pay any debts required of Onesimus. What other occurrences in Scripture are there of a debt paid on someone else's behalf?

> Jesus on the cross proclaims, "It is finished" (John 19:30). This expression was also used in the ancient world to declare that a debt had been paid in full. Jesus paid the full price of our sin.

2. Jesus gave Andrew eternal purpose. How did Andrew's work as a fisherman serve others for a lifetime? How did Andrew's work as a disciple serve others for all eternity?

> Andrew served others as a fisherman by providing food for people to eat and participating in the local economy. As a disciple, Jesus used Andrew to proclaim the Gospel, build the kingdom of God, and deliver Christ's forgiveness to others. This work extends into all eternity.

3. Before Jesus transformed the life of Zacchaeus, how was his work as a tax collector supposed to serve others? How did Zacchaeus distort his work to serve himself instead?

> Zacchaeus was supposed to collect the honest amount of taxes and then faithfully deliver those to the government. However, he distorted his work and used it as an opportunity to serve himself by skimming money off the top and taking more than he was supposed to take. This was a common practice among tax collectors.

4. Read Ephesians 2:8–10. How has Jesus given you eternal purpose? How has Jesus made you useful to God and others?

In Christ Jesus, we are the workmanship of God capable of doing good works. He has taken us from a purposeless life of sin and given us the purposeful life of faith. Through faith in Christ, our life is a good work for God and neighbor.

5. What comes to mind when you think of a calling? Can a job be a calling? Can a calling be a job? Read Ephesians 6:5–9.

A calling often brings to mind a profound and special task; someone has a calling to work with orphans in a third world country. However, a calling is not limited to special or extraordinary tasks. A job is a calling. God calls us to work as accountants, mothers, fathers, cashiers, pastors, nurses, and countless other tasks.

6. Read Philippians 2:12–13. How does it change your perspective on work when you realize that God works in and through your work?

God's work in and through our work transforms our perspective on daily tasks. Changing diapers is God at work caring for a little one. Attending a town council meeting is God fostering order in the community. God is at work through us. This has a profound impact on our work ethic. We do holy work because God is working through us; cutting corners, laziness, lying, and cheating stand in the way of God's work through us.

7. People often struggle to find a clear sense of identity and purpose in their lives. Agree or disagree? How have you seen others struggling with identity and purpose? How have you personally struggled with identity and purpose?

Many people struggle with a lack of identity. It is very easy to attach our identity to something transient like a job, relationship, or political party. People pour themselves into these things, hoping to feel a sense of identity.

8. Read Acts 19:11–12. What work was God doing through Paul's hands? What work does God perform through your hands?

God was performing miracles through Paul's hands. It is important to note that God did not have to work in this way. And even today, God works through our hands to provide for the needs of others, heal their brokenness, and protect their vulnerabilities.

9. Even though Scott was not working for a church, God was working through him to care for others. Is it harder to see how God is at work in some vocations than it is in others? Does this mean that God is less active in these vocations?

There are some vocations where it is obvious how God is at work. Doctors are the healing hands of God. Pastors are the voice of God proclaiming the Gospel. Mothers are the caretakers of God's children. However, other vocations are subtle with how God is at work. Landscapers are the caretakers of creation. Bakers provide food for people to eat. God is at work in all vocations.

Chapter 10

1. How have you personally experienced the disintegration of local living? Is technology to blame?

A simple litmus test for this question is to ask how many neighbors you know by name. Can you name a dozen by name? five? two? Technological advances do make it easier to avoid community; garage-door openers make it so that you never have to get out of your car to talk to a neighbor.

2. Read Luke 3:23–38. Luke begins with extensive details about the genealogy of Jesus. Why might modern readers easily dismiss these genealogies? Why were these genealogies vitally important to early Christians?

Modern readers may fail to see the importance of these genealogies. However, early Christians would have a much better knowledge of the individuals listed in the genealogies. This list locates Jesus in an actual, local community.

3. Read Matthew 13:53–58. Why was God dwelling locally in Jesus of Nazareth problematic for so many people? Did it go beyond the fact that they knew Jesus as a child?

Proximity made it hard for people to accept Jesus as the Messiah. Nevertheless, it was not only because they knew Him as a child. It was scandalous to think that God would lower Himself to dwell in a local community.

4. Luther understood the Bible to be a head-on collision between sinners and the mercy of God. Have you ever experienced God speaking to you through Scripture? Read Hebrews 4:11–13.

> God speaks to us through Scripture. He kills and makes alive through the living Word of God. Perhaps you have been convicted or encouraged by a Scripture reading. God comes to us through His Word.

5. Read Matthew 13:1–9. Why does Jesus use the expression in verse 9 here and elsewhere throughout the Gospels? How are the ears more important to believers after the ascension of Jesus?

> Jesus encourages people to use their ears and hear His message. The kingdom of God has always relied on proclamation to grow and extend. Following the ascension of Jesus, hearing is more important than seeing.

6. Jesus is just as present in the worship service as He is in heaven. Why is the presence of Jesus frequently overlooked in worship? Read Matthew 28:16–20.

> Just as people overlooked Jesus when He was dwelling among them in human flesh, it is very easy to overlook Jesus dwelling among us in worship. It is hard to imagine that God would lower Himself to dwell in the worship of the local congregation.

7. The kingdom of God is not segregated. How can the Church on earth better resemble the racial harmony in the kingdom of God?

Valuing the equality and dignity of all races is the first step in promoting racial harmony. Engaging the neighborhood with the Gospel regardless of race or socioeconomic standing is vital to diversity. Open hospitality is another powerful factor in breaking down segregation.

8. Read 1 Thessalonians 5:12–22. Why are believers told to pray without ceasing? What is your practice of praying for others?

Prayer is not merely an opportunity to get something from God. Rather, prayer is a powerful relationship between God and His people. Developing a practice of prayer is essential to a vibrant life in Christ. Consider scheduling a time in your week that you will commit to an extended period of prayer.

9. The local congregation is a place fit for the King. How has God worked in your life through the local congregation? Where do you see authentic community happening in your church?

God floods the life of His people with blessings through the local congregation. Friendships are made in local congregations. Strength is given through the encouraging words of brothers and sisters in Christ. Powerful words of Christ's forgiveness transform the brokenness of sin. This is the authentic community of the local congregation